Cooking for a Crowd

Cooking for a Crowd

SUSAN WYLER

PHOTOGRAPHS BY
JERRY SIMPSON

HARMONY BOOKS
NEW YORK

Text copyright © 1988 by Susan Wyler
Photographs copyright © 1988 by Jerry Simpson

Published by Harmony Books, a division of Crown Publishers, Inc.,
225 Park Avenue South, New York, New York 10003, and
represented in Canada by the Canadian MANDA Group

HARMONY and colophon are trademarks of Crown Publishers, Inc.
Manufactured in the United States of America
Design by Ken Sansone

Library of Congress Cataloging-in-Publication Data

Wyler, Susan.
    Cooking for a crowd.

    1. Quantity cookery. 2. Menus. I. Title.
TX820.W95   1988   641.5′7   87-27534
ISBN 0-517-56833-0

10 9 8 7 6 5 4 3 2

Contents

Acknowledgments • 7

Introduction • 8

Flavorful Dinner for Good Friends for 10 to 12 • 11

Goose for Thanksgiving for 10 • 21

An Old-Fashioned Sunday Supper for 12 • 29

An Elegant Dinner with Fine Wines for 10 to 12 • 33

Dinner for a Summer Evening for 12 • 40

Do-Ahead Sit-Down Dinner for 12 • 43

Backyard Barbecue for 16 • 47

A Hearty Winter Meal for 16 • 54

Couscous Party for 16 • 60

Noonday Brunch for 16 • 64

Christmas Dinner for 16 to 20 • 78

Southwestern Buffet for 16 to 20 • 86

Thanksgiving for a Large Gathering of 16 to 20 • 94

Easy Southern Shrimp Boil for 20 to 24 • 102

Elegant Evening Buffet for 20 to 24 • 108

The Ultimate Tailgate Party for 24 • 115

Texas-Style Barbecue for 24 to 30 • 120

Dessert and Champagne Party for 36 • 126

A Halloween Party for 36 to 48 • 132

Afternoon Open House for 50 or More • 137

Wedding Supper for 50 • 149

Cocktail and Hors d'Oeuvres Party for 15 to 50 • 155

Index • 157

Acknowledgments

No one writes a book alone. My heartfelt thanks:

To Betty Rice and Blair Brown Hoyt, whose friendship and encouragement made this book possible.

To Harriet Bell, my excellent editor and friend, whose fine taste is, I hope, reflected here.

To Ken Sansone, the designer, and Jerry Simpson, the photographer, who made this book so beautiful.

To Bob Chambers, the food stylist, who produced daunting amounts of food under sometimes lugubrious conditions without losing his quiet wit or his cool.

To Charles Pierce, who helped.

To Linda Cheverton, the prop stylist, who set all the scenes.

To Kathy Belden, who fielded telephone calls, questions and messengers with never-failing good humor and grace.

To literary agent Ginger Barber, who gave me my start as a writer.

To all who so generously contributed recipes: Harriet Bell, Rose Levy Beranbaum, Jean-Marc Burllier of Lafayette, Craig Conlee, John Dougherty of the Waldorf, Giovanna Folinari Ruffino, Lenore Gordon, Grandma Leata Grandbouche, Ray Hertz, Margaret Hess, Convito Italiano, Karen Lee, Lola Restaurant, Lydie Marshall, Danny Meyer of Union Square Cafe, Rick Rodgers, Rosa Ross of Wok on Wheels, San Simeon, Ila Stanger, Jerrie Strom, Irene Thomas, Robert Willson of Parties Plus, Hoke Wilson of the Inn at Thorn Hill and Paula Wolfert.

To Chateau Rouge and St. Florent and to Rory Callahan and the California Wine Institute, who taught me all I know about wine and generously contributed some extraordinary bottles for photography and for drinking.

To all my colleagues at *Food & Wine*, with whom I've shared many good times and who have set such high standards of quality and taste, and to American Express Publishing, for allowing me to do this book.

To Catherine Bigwood, who taught me how to write.

To my neighbors, especially Dwight and Fran Yellen, who sacrificed their diets on many a Sunday night to help taste those big desserts.

To Julia Child, who first showed me and many others of my generation how to cook, and to Paula Wolfert, a most generous mentor and food writer extraordinaire.

Especially to my dearest friends, who shared many a happy evening and much cooking for a crowd, rated the recipes, applauded my cooking and kept me going when the going got tough—Sara and Philippe Caron, Rose and Elliott Beranbaum, Richard and Emily Buckingham, Marilyn and David Jacobs, and Jay Jacobs.

To my grandmother, Molly Schaffman, who sees poetry everywhere.

And most of all, to Rollie.

Introduction

If you enjoy cooking as I do, nothing can equal the satisfaction of large pots of food bubbling away on the stove, filling the house with their tempting aromas; nothing makes you feel better prepared than a freezer full of hors d'oeuvres, ready to be popped into the oven at a moment's notice. A tremendous sense of pride accompanies an oversize roast, a spectacular buffet, a dozen desserts. Though I throw umpteen dinner parties a year, the only time I take pictures is at the big, grandstand affairs. Part of it is the beauty of bounty, and more, I think, the pride of accomplishment and real pleasure at feeding all those friends.

My personal style of entertaining is casual and relaxed. I dine out when I want to eat restaurant food, mull over rare, hard-to-find ingredients and marvel at the work of art constructed on the plate. That is, after all, what I'm paying for—something that's too much trouble to do in my own kitchen. At home I want to enjoy myself. Because I love to cook, I frequently entertain by having dinner parties. I adore long evenings of tasty food with good talk and close friends. But good food doesn't have to be fussy food, and even important occasions can be celebrated in a warm, comfortable way.

I think I remember just about every big barbecue I've ever been to—raucous, casual, easy on the cook. I fondly recall my own second wedding, which I catered in my home. And, of course, there was Thanksgiving each year, with Mother and Grandmother and the aunts huddled in the kitchen for days, putting together unbelievable amounts of food in a dazzling variety of shapes, sizes and colors.

Entertaining and good food are more a part of our lives than ever, but times have changed. Extended families are rare. If you're having sixteen for the holidays, friends may well outnumber relatives, and though no doubt someone will offer to bring dessert, responsibility for the dinner will fall upon your shoulders.

Cooking for a crowd requires special skills. Talented, even professional, cooks I know think twice about recipes when the guest list balloons. Their tried-and-true favorites don't work the same when amounts are doubled or tripled. Cooking times are off, and the effects of seasonings just aren't the same.

I'm astounded by my dear friend Barbara, who can whip up dinner for a couple of dozen as easily over a campfire ten thousand feet up in the Rockies as over the stove in her cozy kitchen without letting her good-natured smile slip for a moment. I am not as competent. Nor as good-natured. I grew up in a generation of adults who cooked for two to four on a good day.

But because I love being surrounded by large groups of family and friends, practice has made me, if not perfect, certainly more comfortable with bigger numbers. I've developed recipes I know I can rely on and realistic strategies that work. These pages are filled with tasty but doable recipes for real people who love to eat and party. I wrote this book to share my experience with other busy cooks who want to entertain confidently with style.

It's been said before and I'll say it again: the key to successful entertaining is allowing yourself to feel like a guest at your own party. If you're relaxed and having a good time, your guests will, too. Easier said than done, of course. There's no question about it, cooking for a crowd is a lot of work, and it's not inexpensive. But you can make it easier on yourself and if it's in your nature, downright enjoyable if you learn what's important and what's not, what's possible and what's not worth attempting.

I'll never forget one Christmas open house I attended several years ago. The hostess passed huge silver platters of individual canapés, miniature quiches and artful little tidbits. Dessert, too, was all Lilliputian, tiny cherry cheesecakes and double-decker brownies in itty-bitty foil cups. The effect was cute, if time-consuming to eat. When I asked the hostess how she could possibly have constructed all that food, her husband proudly confessed he'd taken the last three days off from work to help. Enough said. If you're not hiring a caterer, *think big*.

Turkey, ham, roast beef, brisket and whole salmon, which naturally serve many, make great centerpieces around which you can plan appropriate menus. Whether you give them a special preparation or present them straightforwardly, dressed up with interesting condiments and accompaniments, they are tailor-made for large groups. With a big security blanket like this, you can go on to cook as much or as little as you like and, in a pinch, fill in with prepared foods purchased from a good specialty food shop.

Party food should be colorful and brightly flavored. It should be easy to serve and easy to eat. Most, if not all, of the cooking should be done in advance. Big bowls of salads, casseroles and gratins work wonderfully in quantity, especially when they can be prepared ahead and refrigerated or served at room temperature.

When you're cooking for a crowd it is not the time to decorate plates with three different sauces or to assembly-line a half-dozen kinds of hors d'oeuvres. One or two individual appetizers are manageable if they can be prepared ahead and, if to be served hot, reheated quickly at the last moment. Garnishes should be colorful but simple, preferably arranged around the edges of bowls and platters so they don't disappear as soon as the first guests help themselves. Avoid too much labor-intensive work. Even on a budget, try to weigh your time against the effort. Sometimes it pays to opt for cleaned shrimp or skinned and boned chicken breasts. But unless you're Malcolm Forbes, a big party is definitely not the time to pull out Beluga caviar and foie gras.

Memories feast on large gatherings. Recollections of childhood are crowded with long, loud dinners: festive formal tables, heaping platters of food, favorite relatives elbow-to-elbow, fork in hand, all talking together, the security of being completely surrounded by family. Later on there are dances and cookouts, pool parties, graduation parties, cocktail parties, dinner parties and just plain *parties* crowded with friends. It is the holidays, after all, with their regular return, and the unpredictable celebrations in between—weddings, graduations, reunions, birthday parties and simply social gatherings—that punctuate the years and mark off special occasions in our lives. They give us pleasure and the primal comfort of strength in numbers. Whenever you plan to cook for a crowd, I hope you will turn to this book to help you add to the list of those fond memories.

EQUIPMENT AND SERVING PIECES

Most of us don't own a lot of large commercial equipment; even if we consider investing in it, storage space is limited. That's why I developed these recipes to work with the pots and pans most people do own. There are, however, several pieces of equipment and a few serving pieces that are generally useful and will make life a lot easier if you plan to entertain on a large scale, even if only a couple of times a year.

Do invest in a 9-quart flameproof casserole. Enameled cast iron is my first choice because of its even heating and heavy bottom. A big stockpot is invaluable for soups and for boiling large batches of corn or shrimp. At least one or two large platters and a couple of oversize bowls will make entertaining a crowd much easier. A 15-inch paella pan, one oversize oval gratin, an 18 x 13-inch half-sheet or jelly-roll pan and a couple of 9 x 14-inch baking dishes—glass, ceramic or enameled cast iron—are very handy. In a pinch, you can improvise with heavy-duty aluminum foil pans. They've saved the day for me many times, though they are not attractive for serving. The large roasting pans make excellent water baths for baking dishes.

As for dishes and utensils, I've collected many items over the years. One year I gave a bridal brunch for a friend and, rather than use paper, which is not all that cheap, I bought a stack of attractive but inexpensive glass plates. Both glass and plain white can be mixed and matched easily. Inexpensive flatware can also be set aside for these large parties. Real silverware does add a touch of grace.

For a really big crowd on a formal occasion, you may consider renting. If you do, check the total price for everything you need. Remember details like extra teaspoons and ask how the dishes will be picked up after the event. Some companies provide cartons in which to stack the *dirty* rentals—a real boon if you have no outside help. Look in the Yellow Pages under party supplies for china, glass, silverware and linen rentals. The same firms can usually supply coatracks, wine coolers, coffee urns and large silver platters as well.

If the party is more casual, I don't hesitate to use good paper plates and napkins and heavy-duty, reusable plastic forks. These days, manufacturers offer lovely patterns in many different styles and colors. Also consider colorful, durable plastic plates, often displayed in the picnic section of household departments. If you're not renting, stock up on plastic cups for cold drinks and coated heatproof paper for hot coffee. I usually allow at least half as many more cups and napkins than the number of guests.

I hope you will use this book as a guide and for inspiration. There are times when it's a pleasure to call the family to your home for a big holiday dinner or to invite all your friends over for a festive outdoor barbecue, all-day open house or spectacular, elegant sit-down dinner. Some of us are known for one or two really huge parties we throw regularly every year. Everyone looks forward to them, there are a core of repeat guests and the events become something of a reunion over the years. That's when I hope you'll follow the step-by-step scheduling instructions and recipes that follow, to throw the party of your dreams. Enjoy the planning and the cooking. Play the role of grand host or hostess to the hilt. Garner all the praise you can. Delicious food and confidence are all you need.

On other occasions, cooking for a crowd may be spontaneous or a necessity at a moment that is inconvenient for you. At those times, please use this book as inspiration and my suggestions as an outline, and take advantage of the modern way to entertain: fill in with takeout. Choose a menu that appeals to you and substitute purchased foods or prepared dishes from specialty food shops or the deli section of your supermarket for any recipe that is too time-consuming. For example, at a sit-down dinner, serve prosciutto and melon, garnished with cracked black pepper and wedges of lime, instead of spending precious time cooking a first course. Rather than making dessert, buy it or offer a good-quality commercial ice cream with a quick homemade sauce. Remember, it's always better to entertain easily than not to entertain at all.

Three-Mushroom Lasagna with Gorgonzola
Sauce

•

Mediterranean Seafood Casserole
Garlic Croutons

•

Composed Salad of Carrots, Beets,
Cucumber and Watercress

•

Hazelnut Dacquoise with Chocolate Cream

Flavorful Dinner for Good Friends

FOR 10 TO 12

This is quite simply delicious food to share with favorite people. I love all the flavors that make up these recipes—wild mushrooms, mild blue cheese, tomatoes, garlic, fennel, seafood and, last but not least, chocolate and hazelnuts. Maybe it's the vibrant Mediterranean flavors of these dishes and maybe it's the close friends I've shared them with, but I'm convinced this menu guarantees an extraordinarily pleasant evening, especially for the cook, since much of the dinner can be accomplished in advance. To me, this blending of modern trends with traditional tastes reflects the best of informal entertaining.

While the lasagna can be made with dried noodles, the variety of mushrooms produces a subtle and complex flavor that deserves the delicacy of fresh pasta. If you don't feel like making your own, many stores sell fresh sheets for lasagna. Though the entire dish can be assembled up to a day in advance, bake it shortly before serving to preserve its subtle flavor and light texture.

I love the taste of bouillabaisse, but I'm not comfortable with soup as a main course at a company dinner, and I don't like the fishy smell that permeates the house. That's why I developed this casserole, which has all the vibrant, Mediterranean flavors of the original—olive oil, garlic, saffron, leeks—and all the delectable seafood, but requires no fish stock. Only the cooking liquid from the mussels and clams is used. Garlic croutons help to sop up the delicious juices.

Though the dishes are savory and rich, this is a relatively light meal, so I offer a more substantial salad than usual before dessert. Colorful and different, it makes a striking presentation on the plate.

Dark chocolate and toasted hazelnuts are an unbeatable combination, and here they are combined in an elegant presentation that is guaranteed to draw moans and groans from the most sophisticated of guests. It can be completely assembled up to twenty-four hours before serving. Although the nut meringue layers soften slightly, the hazelnuts remain crunchy, and as with most chocolate desserts, it improves overnight.

Do-Ahead Planning

Up to 2 days in advance: Make the tomato sauce base for the seafood casserole.

Up to 1 day in advance: Make the pasta and assemble the lasagna. Cover and refrigerate. Cook the mussels and clams and complete the sauce for the seafood casserole. Refrigerate separately; remove about 30 minutes before you plan to cook the seafood casserole. Cook the beets and shred them; shred the carrots. Toss both with dressing. Wash and trim the watercress. Prepare the Hazelnut Dacquoise with Chocolate Cream.

Up to 6 hours before serving: Make the Garlic Croutons. Follow instructions in Step 2 of Roquefort Caesar Salad on page 51, but use 2 loaves of French bread and ½ cup olive oil and do not cut the slices into cubes.

About 1½ hours in advance: Shred the cucumbers, toss them with dressing and assemble the composed salads. Refrigerate.

About 30 minutes before serving: Bake the Three-Mushroom Lasagna. Assemble the Mediterranean Seafood Casserole. Finish the casserole either before you sit down to eat the lasagna or after you clear the table from the first course.

Homemade Lasagna Noodles
MAKES ABOUT ¾ POUND, ENOUGH FOR 2 PANS OF LASAGNA

Though you can roll out pasta dough by hand with a heavy rolling pin (I did it for years), it takes muscle. A food processor and an inexpensive hand-cranked pasta machine turn this process into a breeze.

3 eggs
2¼ cups all-purpose flour

1. In a food processor fitted with the metal blade, in two batches, combine the eggs and flour. Process until well blended and the mixture resembles coarse sand. Turn out the dough and knead into a ball. Cover with a sheet of plastic wrap and a kitchen towel to keep it moist.

2. Tear off lemon-size pieces of dough to work with. Keep the remaining dough covered until you are ready for it. Pass the piece of dough through the widest setting on the pasta machine. Fold the dough in thirds like an envelope and pass through the same setting. Repeat two more times to complete the kneading of the dough. Then pass the dough through consecutively smaller settings until it is rolled through the thinnest setting. Drape the dough over a rack (or the back of a chair) to dry for at least 20 minutes. Trim into manageable 6- to 8-inch lengths before cooking. (The noodles can be sealed in plastic bags and refrigerated for up to 2 days before using.)

THREE-MUSHROOM LASAGNA WITH GORGONZOLA SAUCE

12 TO 16 SERVINGS

2 ounces dried porcini mushrooms
½ pound (2 sticks) plus 1 tablespoon unsalted
    butter
3½ tablespoons olive oil
4 large shallots, minced
2 pounds fresh mushrooms, minced
1½ teaspoons salt
½ teaspoon freshly ground black pepper
½ teaspoon tarragon
Cayenne pepper
¼ cup fresh lemon juice
2 small garlic cloves, minced
¾ pound fresh shiitake mushrooms, stemmed,
    caps sliced ¼ inch thick
½ cup all-purpose flour
2 cups milk
1 cup heavy cream
¼ pound Gorgonzola dolcelatte cheese
¾ cup freshly grated Parmesan cheese (about 3
    ounces)
Homemade Lasagna Noodles or 1 package (16
    ounces) lasagna noodles

1. In a small bowl, cover the porcini with 3 cups boiling water. Let stand until softened, 20 to 30 minutes. Lift out the mushrooms; reserve the liquid. Coarsely chop the porcini. Strain the liquid through a double layer of cheesecloth and reserve 2 cups.

2. Meanwhile, in a large heavy skillet, melt 2 tablespoons of the butter in 1 tablespoon of the oil over moderately high heat. Add 2 tablespoons of the minced shallots and half the fresh mushrooms. Sauté, stirring frequently, until the mushrooms give up their liquid, it evaporates and they become lightly browned, 5 to 7 minutes. Season these mushroom *duxelles* with ¼ teaspoon each salt, black pepper and tarragon, a dash or two of cayenne pepper and 1 tablespoon of the lemon juice. Scrape into a bowl. Wipe out the skillet with a paper towel. Repeat with 2 more tablespoons of the butter and 1 tablespoon oil, adding 2 more tablespoons of the shallots and the remaining minced fresh mushrooms. Season as above. Add to the bowl. Wipe out the skillet.

3. In the same large skillet, melt 3 tablespoons of the butter in the remaining 1½ tablespoons oil over moderately high heat. Add the remaining minced shallots and the garlic and sauté for 30 seconds. Add the shiitake and porcini mushrooms and sauté, stirring frequently, for 3 minutes. Reduce the heat to moderately low and cook, stirring frequently, for 5 minutes. Add 1 cup of the reserved porcini liquid and simmer, partially covered, for 5 to 10 minutes, until the mushrooms are tender but still slightly chewy. Uncover and cook, stirring frequently, until the remaining liquid evaporates. Season with the remaining 2 tablespoons lemon juice and salt and pepper to taste. Add to the mushroom *duxelles* and set aside.

4. In a large heavy saucepan, melt 1 stick of butter over moderate heat. Add the flour and cook, stirring, for 2 to 3 minutes without letting the flour color. Whisk in the remaining 1 cup mushroom liquid, the milk and the cream. Bring to a boil, whisking constantly, until thickened and smooth. Reduce the heat and simmer, whisking frequently, for 5 minutes. Whisk in the Gorgonzola and ½ cup of the Parmesan cheese until melted. Season with 1 teaspoon salt and several dashes of cayenne pepper.

5. In a large pot of boiling salted water, cook the lasagna noodles until just tender, about 1 minute after the water returns to a boil for fresh noodles, about 12 minutes for the dried variety. Drain and rinse under cold running water. Place in a bowl of cold water and, one by one, lay the noodles out in a single layer on kitchen towels to dry.

6. To assemble the lasagna, generously butter 2 large baking pans, 14 x 9 x 2 inches. If the sauce has cooled, reheat it slightly over low heat. Arrange a layer of noodles in the bottom of each dish, trimming to fit, if necessary, and overlapping the edges only slightly. Spread a thin layer of mushrooms over the noodles (using one-quarter of the total amount in each pan) and drizzle about 1 cup of sauce over the mushrooms in each pan. Repeat with another layer of noodles, mushrooms and sauce. Top with a final layer of noodles. Spread the remaining sauce over the noodles, dividing evenly, and sprinkle ¼ cup grated Parmesan cheese over the top of each. Dot each with 1 tablespoon butter. (The lasagnas can be assembled completely and refrigerated, covered, overnight, or frozen for up to 2 weeks.)

7. Preheat the oven to 375° F. Bake the lasagna (thawed if frozen) uncovered for 20 to 30 minutes, until heated through and lightly browned on top.

MEDITERRANEAN SEAFOOD CASSEROLE

12 SERVINGS

The do-ahead trick in this recipe is to steam the clams and mussels in Step 2 until they just open. When they are reheated, they will finish cooking and taste fresh. If you cook them completely in advance, they will toughen when reheated.

⅓ cup plus 2 tablespoons extra-virgin olive oil
4 medium leeks (white and tender green) or 2 large onions, chopped
6 large garlic cloves, chopped
2 cans (28 ounces each) Italian peeled tomatoes, drained and coarsely cut up
1½ teaspoons fennel seeds, crushed in a mortar
Pinch of saffron threads
½ teaspoon salt
2 shallots, minced
1½ cups dry white wine
½ teaspoon crushed hot red pepper
¾ cup coarsely chopped flat-leaf parsley
4 pounds mussels, preferably cultivated (such as Great Eastern), debearded
2 dozen cherrystone clams, scrubbed
3 pounds firm-textured white fish fillets, such as scrod, red snapper, halibut, cut into 3 x 2-inch pieces
12 jumbo shrimp or langostinos, rinsed in their shell
1 pound bay scallops or quartered sea scallops
2 tablespoons Pernod

1. In a large nonaluminum flameproof casserole, heat ⅓ cup of the oil. Add the leeks and cook over moderate heat, stirring occasionally, until they are very soft and just begin to color, about 10 minutes. Add two-thirds of the chopped garlic and cook until fragrant, about 1 minute. Add the tomatoes, fennel seeds, saffron and salt; simmer until the sauce thickens, about 20 minutes. Set aside. (The tomato sauce can be made up to 2 days ahead and refrigerated, covered. Reheat before Step 3.)

2. In a large nonaluminum saucepan, heat the remaining 2 tablespoons oil. Add the shallots and remaining garlic and sauté for 30 seconds. Add the wine, hot pepper and ¼ cup of the parsley and bring to a boil. Dump in the mussels and clams, cover tightly and steam, stirring up the shellfish from the bottom once or twice, until they just open, about 3 minutes. Immediately remove the mussels and clams from the broth and set aside in their shells; discard any that do not open. Strain the broth through a double thickness of cheesecloth and add to the tomato sauce. (The recipe can be prepared to this point up to 1 day in advance. Cover and refrigerate the shellfish and sauce separately. Let stand at room temperature for about 30 minutes before you plan to cook the casserole.)

3. Shortly before you are ready to serve the first course, assemble the casserole. Arrange the fish and shrimp in a large paella pan or flameproof casserole. Sprinkle the scallops around the pan. Quickly bring the tomato sauce to a boil. Stir in the Pernod and pour over the seafood. Cover, bring to a simmer and cook without stirring for 5 minutes. Uncover and tuck the mussels and clams around the other seafood. Cover and simmer until the shellfish are hot and the shrimp are cooked through, about 5 minutes longer. Sprinkle the remaining parsley over the top. Serve in shallow soup plates.

Composed Salad of Carrots, Beets, Cucumber and Watercress

10 TO 12 SERVINGS

Finely julienne the vegetables for this colorful salad if you have a julienne blade on your food processor or a mandoline. If not, use the shredding disk to grate them.

> 2 bunches of beets
> 3 long, narrow European seedless cucumbers
> ¾ teaspoon coarse (kosher) salt
> 8 large carrots
> 1½ tablespoons fresh lemon juice
> 2 tablespoons balsamic vinegar
> ¼ cup olive oil
> 1 teaspoon grated orange zest
> 3 tablespoons fresh orange juice
> 2 teaspoons sugar
> 2 tablespoons rice wine vinegar
> 1½ teaspoons Oriental sesame oil
> 1 tablespoon toasted sesame seeds
> 2 tablespoons minced chives or scallion green
> Watercress, for garnish

1. Preheat the oven to 350° F. Trim the stems off the beets, leaving about 3 inches attached. Wash the beets and wrap in heavy-duty aluminum foil. Bake in the oven for 1 hour, or until just tender but still firm. Let cool; then trim and peel.

2. Julienne the cucumbers in a food processor or on a mandoline. Put in a bowl and toss with the salt. Let stand for at least 15 minutes while you prepare the other vegetables.

3. Peel the carrots and julienne them. Place in a bowl and toss with the lemon juice, 1 tablespoon of the balsamic vinegar and 2 tablespoons of the olive oil.

4. Julienne the beets. Put them in a separate bowl and toss with the orange zest, orange juice, 1 teaspoon of the sugar and remaining 1 tablespoon balsamic vinegar and 2 tablespoons olive oil.

5. Drain the cucumbers; pat dry on paper towels. Put the cucumbers in another bowl and toss with the rice vinegar, sesame oil, toasted sesame seeds, chives and remaining 1 teaspoon sugar.

6. To assemble, arrange mounds of carrots, beets and cucumbers on a large platter or on individual plates. Set a few sprigs of watercress in the center for garnish.

Hazelnut Dacquoise with Chocolate Cream

12 SERVINGS

An elegant but surprisingly light dessert, this is, in a word—fabulous!

1½ cups hazelnuts (6 ounces)
1¼ cups granulated sugar
¼ cup confectioners' sugar
6 egg whites
¹/₁₆ teaspoon cream of tartar
Pinch of salt
8 ounces semisweet chocolate
½ cup brewed coffee
1 tablespoon Frangelico (hazelnut liqueur),
   optional
1 teaspoon vanilla extract
2 cups heavy cream
Toasted hazelnuts or shaved chocolate, for garnish

1. Preheat the oven to 250° F. Butter and flour 3 baking sheets. Make sure they can all fit in your oven, even if the edges of 2 overlap slightly. Trace a 10-inch circle onto each sheet.

2. In two batches in a food processor, grind the hazelnuts with ½ cup of the granulated sugar until finely ground. Transfer to a bowl.

3. Sift the confectioners' sugar over the ground hazelnuts and toss to mix.

4. In a large bowl, beat the egg whites until foamy. Add the cream of tartar and salt and beat until the whites begin to peak. Gradually beat in the remaining ¾ cup sugar, about 1 tablespoon at a time. The meringue will be very stiff.

5. Fold the ground hazelnuts, one-third at a time, into the meringue. Scoop one-third of the nut meringue onto each circle on the baking sheets and smooth to even 10-inch rounds with a spatula. (Or if you're handy with a pastry bag, pipe into rounds.)

6. Bake for 45 minutes. Turn off the oven, but leave the nut meringue layers in the warm oven for 30 additional minutes, until completely dry and crisp. Gently scrape around the edges of the rounds with a spatula to loosen them and transfer to racks to cool.

7. In a very heavy saucepan or double boiler, melt the chocolate in the coffee over low heat, stirring until smooth. Remove from the heat and let cool, whisking occasionally, until almost room temperature and slightly thickened. Whisk in the Frangelico and vanilla.

8. In a large bowl, beat the cream until fairly stiff. Fold one-third of the cream into the chocolate to lighten it. Pour the chocolate down the side of the bowl into the remaining cream and fold until no streaks remain.

9. To assemble the dacquoise, gently place one of the meringue layers on a cake stand or large round serving platter. Scoop a heaping cupful of the chocolate cream on top and spread over the meringue, leaving a ½-inch border all around. Put another meringue on top and repeat. Place the last meringue, with the smooth, flat side up, on top and frost the top and sides with the remaining chocolate cream. If the sides look a little messy, refrigerate the dacquoise for about half an hour, or until the cream begins to set up, then smooth out the sides with a long narrow spatula, packing the cream into any gaps that show. Clean off the edge of the cake stand or platter. Garnish the top with the toasted hazelnuts or shaved chocolate and refrigerate until serving time.

FLAVORFUL DINNER FOR GOOD FRIENDS for 10 TO 12 includes a Mediterranean Seafood Casserole laden with shrimp, clams, mussels, scallops and snapper.

AN ELEGANT DINNER WITH FINE WINES starts with Seafood Medallions with Herbed Lemon-Walnut Mayonnaise and ends with Almond Custard Torte with Peaches and Raspberries.

AN OLD-FASHIONED SUNDAY SUPPER for 12: Deviled Chicken; broccoli; beets and cauliflower with lemon butter; mashed potatoes.

BACKYARD BARBECUE for 16 (clockwise from bottom): on the grill are Barbecued Carnitas; Grilled Pepper-Lime Chicken and Grilled Corn San Miguel Style; on the bench find Chipotle Chile Mayonnaise; Stuffed Grape Leaves; Black Bean Salad.

Oysters with Ginger Beurre Blanc

▪

Roast Stuffed Goose with Port Sauce
Prune and Pork Dressing
Creamed Brussels Sprouts and Chestnuts
Rutabaga and Potato Puree
Cranberry Chutney

▪

Lemon Mousse Meringues with Raspberry
Sauce
Chocolate Truffles

Goose for Thanksgiving

FOR 10

This holiday menu happens to be one of my favorites. The juxtaposition of flavors is perfect, and almost all the dishes can be prepared in advance. Goose is a wonderful bird—all dark meat and flavorful without tasting gamy. Roasted to a rich mahogany brown, it makes a glorious centerpiece to the holiday table, and every part can be put to good use. The fat can be rendered to make the world's best fried potatoes, the neck and giblets can be browned for an easy stock, and the liver—rich and mild—makes an excellent addition to almost any stuffing. I love goose so much that, when we're all through, I hack up the carcass, throw it into a pot with some aromatic vegetables and herbs and make goose soup.

Go for goose if you are planning a relatively small Thanksgiving. A 12- to 14-pound bird will serve only ten people. That's assuming there are a lot of trimmings and you don't plan on leftovers. If you're expecting a larger crowd, you could cook two geese, but it becomes such a chore to drain off all the fat, you're better off with a big turkey.

This oyster recipe, also, is geared to a small crowd. Lightly poaching the oysters a day ahead keeps them fresh tasting and minimizes last-minute work. They stay moist and plump, and after being gratinéed with the sauce, are indistinguishable from fresh. If you prefer a different sort of starter, or if you want to include a soup as well, either the Curried Carrot-Ginger Soup (page 96), whose humble vegetable base belies its extraordinary character, or the Maple-Butternut Bisque (page 81) would be lovely.

The goose's Prune and Pork Dressing is a meaty and substantial stuffing. About half of it will fit inside the goose; the remainder is baked in a separate dish during the last half hour the goose roasts.

The sauce is really a simple pan gravy, enlivened with some chopped shallots and port.

Both the Creamed Brussels Sprouts and Chestnuts and the Rutabaga and Potato Puree have a mild, subtle sweetness that complements the rich goose beautifully. If your family can't imagine Thanksgiving without sweet potatoes, substitute the Gratin of Sweet Potatoes Flambéed with Bourbon (page 99) for the pureed potatoes. For a real groaning board, add the Braised Fennel au Gratin (page 100). The tangy, spiced Cranberry Chutney can be prepared weeks in advance.

After so much food I like a light, refreshing dessert with just enough sweetness to satisfy. These stunning meringue shells, filled with tart lemon mousse and topped with intense raspberry sauce, qualify perfectly. My dinners usually include only one dessert because I try to match it to the entire menu, but I know that many people enjoy presenting a dazzling variety, especially during the holidays. Chocolate truffles, available both in local chocolate shops and by mail (Manon, from Belgium, are my favorites), are my concession to the multiple dessert table here, but, if you like, include your family's favorite pumpkin pie, chocolate cake or fruit tart.

Do-Ahead Planning

Up to 3 weeks in advance: Make the Cranberry Chutney; store in the refrigerator.

Up to 5 days in advance: Make the meringue shells; store them in an airtight container at room temperature.

Up to 3 days in advance: Make the lemon mousse and the Raspberry Sauce.

The day before Thanksgiving (the busiest day): Poach the oysters; reduce and reserve the cooking liquid. Boil the shells. Make the goose stock. Prepare the bread cubes and prune and pork mixture for the dressing. Make the Creamed Brussels Sprouts and Chestnuts. Make the Rutabaga and Potato Puree.

Thanksgiving day—about 4 hours before serving: Finish the dressing. Stuff and truss the goose and put it in to roast.

About 30 minutes before the goose is ready: Put the extra dressing in the oven to bake. Reheat the Creamed Brussels Sprouts and Chestnuts in the oven (or reheat at the last minute in a microwave oven). Make the Ginger Beurre Blanc; set over warm water.

As soon as the goose comes out of the oven: Make the Port Sauce; keep warm. Broil and serve the oysters. Reheat the Rutabaga and Potato Puree.

Shortly before dessert: Assemble the Lemon Mousse Meringues.

Oysters with Ginger Beurre Blanc

12 SERVINGS

Poaching the oysters a day ahead gives you a triple boon: the shellfish remain as fresh tasting as if they were just opened, there is no mess before serving and the poaching liquid gives you a delicious base for your sauce.

As part of a multicourse meal, I feel that 4 large oysters are a perfect serving to start. If you must offer 6 oysters to each guest, increase the proportions accordingly. By the way, beurre blanc is a tricky sauce, and if yours ever breaks, simply retitle the dish "Oysters with Ginger Butter." No one will be any wiser, and the dish will be just as delicious—I speak from experience.

*4 dozen large oysters on the half-shell, 1 cup
    liquor reserved
½ pound (2 sticks) plus 2 tablespoons unsalted
    butter
2 medium shallots, minced
¼ cup dry white wine
3 tablespoons champagne vinegar or white wine
    vinegar
½ cup chopped fresh ginger
Dash of cayenne pepper*

1. Unless you are very handy with an oyster knife, ask the fish market to open the oysters for you. Have them pack them on the half-shell on ice and reserve the oyster liquor separately. (Preopened oysters that come in containers are mushy and unpleasant.) Just before you cook the oysters, take them out of their shells. Rinse them briefly under cold running water only if there is grit or pieces of shell on them. Reserve the shells.

2. In a large skillet, melt 2 tablespoons of the butter. Add the shallots and cook over moderate heat until softened and translucent but not browned, 1 to 2 minutes. Add the wine, vinegar and reserved oyster liquor. Bring just to a simmer. Add the oysters and poach, turning once, until the edges just begin to curl, about 1 minute. If in doubt, remove the oysters earlier rather than later (they will be cooked again). Put them in a covered container and refrigerate at once.

3. Add the ginger to the poaching liquid in the skillet and boil until the liquid is reduced to 3 tablespoons. Strain into a small bowl, pressing on the ginger to extract as much flavor as possible. Cover and refrigerate.

4. Boil the oyster shells in a large pot of water for at least 15 minutes; drain. When they are cool enough to handle, rinse them well under running water, rubbing off any pieces of meat that cling to the shell. Drain well; then refrigerate in a plastic bag. (The recipe can be prepared to this point up to a day ahead.)

5. Before cooking the oysters, arrange the shells in a single layer in several roasting pans. I use disposable ridged aluminum foil broiling pans; each pan will hold 16 oysters.

6. Shortly before you plan to serve the oysters, remove them from the refrigerator, drain, reserving the liquid, and set 1 in each shell. Pour any accumulated liquid into a small heavy saucepan. Add the 3 tablespoons reserved poaching liquid, bring to a boil and cook until reduced to 2 tablespoons. Whisk in the cayenne pepper and 2 tablespoons of the butter. Remove from the heat and beat in 2 more tablespoons butter until just blended. Return to low heat as necessary and continue whisking in the butter, 2 to 3 tablespoons at a time, making each addition after the previous one is almost incorporated, until all the butter is added and the sauce is thick and emulsified. Set over a pan of warm water (it will hold for about 20 minutes).

7. Preheat the broiler. Spoon a little dab of the beurre blanc over each oyster, to coat. In batches as necessary, broil the oysters just until they are heated through, 1 to 2 minutes; do not overcook. Spoon a heaping teaspoon of the remaining sauce over each oyster and serve at once.

Roast Stuffed Goose with Port Sauce

10 TO 12 SERVINGS

The only trick to this recipe is to order a fine fresh goose from a good butcher.

> 1 fresh goose, 12 to 14 pounds
> Coarse (kosher) salt and freshly ground pepper
> Prune and Pork Dressing (recipe follows) or your favorite stuffing
> 2 shallots, chopped
> ½ cup port or Madeira
> 3 cups Brown Goose Stock or chicken stock
> 2 tablespoons cornstarch
> 1 tablespoon fresh lemon juice
> 2 tablespoons unsalted butter

1. Preheat the oven to 425° F. Remove any loose fat from the goose. Rinse inside and out with cold running water and pat dry. Season liberally inside and out with coarse salt and pepper. Prick all over (I use a couple of hat pins), especially in the fatty parts. Stuff loosely. The bird will hold 6 to 7 cups of stuffing; bake the remainder separately as directed. Sew up the cavity and tie the legs together.

2. Put the goose in a large roasting pan and roast for 30 minutes. Remove any accumulated fat with a bulb baster, prick the goose again and baste with hot water. Reduce the oven temperature to 350° F. and roast for about 3 hours longer, or until the skin is crisp and the meat is tender. Baste every 20 minutes or so with enough hot water to keep the fat in the roasting pan from burning and remove the accumulated fat from the roasting pan with a bulb baster as necessary to avoid smoking.

3. Transfer the goose to a carving board and cover loosely with foil to keep warm. Pour out all but 1 tablespoon fat from the roasting pan. Add the shallots and set over moderate heat. Sauté for 1 minute, or until softened. Pour in the port and bring to a boil, scraping up all the flavorful brown bits from the bottom and sides of the pan. Boil for 1 minute. Add 2½ cups of the stock and return to a boil. Pour the sauce into a saucepan.

4. Dissolve the cornstarch in the remaining ½ cup stock; stir into the sauce. Bring to a boil, stirring, until thickened and smooth. Add the lemon juice and whisk in the butter. Season with salt and pepper to taste.

BROWN GOOSE STOCK: Render about 2 tablespoons of the goose fat in a heavy medium saucepan. Add the cut-up goose neck, giblets and wing tips, and a sliced onion and carrot. Sauté over moderately high heat until deeply browned. Add 6 cups water, 2 bruised garlic cloves, and a bay leaf, several sprigs of parsley, ¼ teaspoon thyme, 8 peppercorns and 8 to 12 mushroom stems if you have them. Reduce the heat to low and simmer, skimming occasionally, for 1½ to 2 hours; strain. Measure the stock and, if necessary, boil down to 3 cups.

Prune and Pork Dressing

MAKES ABOUT 12 CUPS

> 1 pound good-quality pitted prunes, quartered
> ¾ cup port, such as Croft Distinction
> 4 tablespoons unsalted butter
> 2 large onions, chopped
> 2 celery ribs with leaves, finely diced
> ¼ pound Black Forest or other flavorful ham, finely diced
> 1 pound lean ground pork
> 1½ teaspoons minced fresh thyme, or ¾ teaspoon dried
> ⅛ teaspoon nutmeg, preferably freshly grated
> 1½ teaspoons salt
> ½ teaspoon freshly ground pepper
> Goose or turkey liver (reserved from bird you are stuffing), diced
> 1 loaf (1 pound) firm-textured white bread
> 1 cup unsalted goose, turkey or chicken stock
> ½ cup chopped parsley
> 1 egg, lightly beaten

1. Put the prunes in a bowl. Pour in the port and ½ cup hot water and let soak while you prepare the rest of the stuffing.

2. In a large flameproof casserole, melt the butter over moderate heat. Add the onions and celery, cover and cook, stirring once or twice, until the vegetables are softened and translucent, about 10 minutes. Uncover, add the ham and cook until the onions are just beginning to turn golden, about 10 minutes longer. Add the pork and season with ½ teaspoon of the thyme, the nutmeg, ½ teaspoon of the salt and ⅛ teaspoon of the pepper. Cook, stirring occasionally, until the pork is no longer pink, about 5 minutes. Add the liver and cook, stirring frequently, for 2 minutes. Pour the port from the prunes into the pan and let cook, stirring occasionally, for 2 minutes longer to boil off the raw alcohol smell. Add the prunes, blend well and remove from the heat.

3. Dry out the bread slices in a very low oven (200° F. or less) or let stand until stale. Cut into ½-inch cubes. (The recipe can be prepared to this point up to a day ahead. Set the bread aside in a plastic bag. Transfer the prune mixture to a large bowl, cover and refrigerate.)

4. Shortly before you stuff the bird, add the bread cubes to the prune mixture and toss to blend. Drizzle on the stock, mixing to moisten. Season with the remaining salt, pepper and thyme. Add the parsley and egg and toss to blend well. (Pack any stuffing that does not fit into the bird into a greased baking dish, cover with foil and bake during the last ½ hour.)

GOOSE

Goose is an incredible bird, so flavorful that every part of it can be used for something. I make goose only once a year, but with the renderings from that single bird, I have a jar of delicious fat that can be used year-round—for special fried potatoes, soups, sauces, stews. Often just a single tablespoon can make all the difference in a dish that needs a boost of flavor.

To render goose fat, pull out all the loose firm white fat. I usually add the extra skin as well. Cut into 1½-inch pieces and put it in a saucepan with enough water to cover. Bring to a simmer over moderately low heat and cook, uncovered, stirring occasionally, until all the water is evaporated, the clear fat is bubbling away and the solids have browned.

With a skimmer or slotted spoon, transfer the large brown pieces, or cracklings, to paper towels to drain. Sprinkled lightly with coarse salt, these make wonderful crunchy nibbles with drinks, and they can be frozen until you need them, then reheated. They are also fabulous tossed in a wilted salad of bitter greens or in an omelet with chopped garlic and parsley. Let the fat in the saucepan cool; then strain it through a fine mesh sieve of several layers of cheesecloth into a clean jar. Cover and store in the refrigerator for up to a year. As a final bonus, I always make a delicious soup out of the roasted goose carcass and lightly browned cabbage, with an enrichment of Roquefort cheese.

CREAMED BRUSSELS SPROUTS AND CHESTNUTS

12 TO 16 SERVINGS

2 pounds Brussels sprouts
1 pound chestnuts
4 tablespoons unsalted butter
1 cup heavy cream
½ teaspoon salt
¼ teaspoon pepper

1. Trim the Brussels sprouts. Cut a tiny X in the stem ends of each with the tip of a small knife. Bring a large saucepan of salted water to a boil. Add the sprouts and cook for 7 minutes, until they are about three-quarters cooked. Drain, rinse under cold water to cool and drain well. Chop very coarsely.

2. Preheat the oven to 375° F. Cut an X into the flat side of each chestnut. Put in a shallow baking pan and roast for 15 to 20 minutes, until the ends of the cut shells curl back and the chestnuts are softened. As soon as they are cool enough to handle, peel and chop the chestnuts very coarsely.

3. In a large saucepan, melt the butter in the cream. Add the Brussels sprouts and chestnuts; season with the salt and pepper. Cook over moderate heat, stirring occasionally, until most of the liquid is absorbed, 5 to 10 minutes. Season with additional salt and pepper to taste, cover and set aside for up to 3 hours, or refrigerate overnight. Reheat in a saucepan over moderate heat or in a gratin dish in the oven with your roast before serving.

RUTABAGA AND POTATO PUREE

12 SERVINGS

5 pounds rutabagas (yellow turnips)
2 pounds baking potatoes
½ pound (2 sticks) unsalted butter, at room temperature
Salt and freshly ground pepper

1. Cut the peel off the rutabagas with a paring knife, removing any traces of green underneath. Cut them into large chunks. In a large pot of boiling salted water, cook the rutabagas until very tender, 15 to 20 minutes; drain.

2. Peel the potatoes and cut them into chunks. In a large saucepan of boiling salted water, cook the potatoes until tender, 15 to 20 minutes; drain.

3. Pass the vegetables through the medium disk of a food mill or a ricer to mash. Beat in the butter until blended and smooth. Season with salt and pepper to taste. (The puree can be prepared a day ahead and reheated in a microwave oven or over moderate heat, stirring frequently.)

CRANBERRY CHUTNEY

MAKES 2 QUARTS

A pleasant relief from the standard, cloyingly sweet cranberry sauce usually served at Thanksgiving, this condiment is tangy, enhanced with apples and pears and complexly flavored with spices and seasonings.

1 large onion, chopped
3 tablespoons minced fresh ginger
¾ cup cider vinegar
¾ cup sugar
Juice and grated zest from 1 large navel orange
2 garlic cloves, crushed through a press
½ teaspoon ground cinnamon
½ teaspoon coarsely cracked black pepper
½ teaspoon ground coriander
¼ teaspoon mace or nutmeg
¼ teaspoon ground cloves
¼ teaspoon salt
Several dashes of cayenne pepper, to taste
2 large tart apples, such as Greening or Granny Smith, peeled and cut into ½-inch dice
2 large firm pears, peeled and cut into ½-inch dice
2 bags (12 ounces each) fresh cranberries
2 cinnamon sticks, optional

1. In a large nonaluminum saucepan or flameproof casserole, combine the onion, ginger, vinegar, sugar, orange juice and orange zest, garlic, ground cinnamon, black pepper, coriander, mace, cloves, salt and cayenne. Bring to a boil and cook over moderate heat for 5 minutes.

2. Add the apples and cook for 5 minutes. Add the pears and cook, stirring occasionally, for about 5 minutes, or until the apples and pears are tender but still hold their shape. Add the cranberries, bring to a boil and cook, stirring once or twice, until they just pop their skins, about 5 minutes. Stir in ¼ cup water and remove from the heat.

3. If you have the cinnamon sticks, put 1 in each of two 1-quart mason jars. Divide the cranberry chutney between the jars and let cool; then cover and refrigerate at least overnight and for up to 3 weeks before serving.

LEMON MOUSSE MERINGUES WITH RASPBERRY SAUCE

12 SERVINGS

A tart lemon mousse, set off with an intense raspberry sauce, contrasts pleasantly with sugary meringues in this elegant dessert.

6 egg yolks
3 tablespoons sugar
⅓ cup fruity, off-dry wine, such as Vouvray (if you only have dry white wine, increase the sugar to ¼ cup)
1½ teaspoons grated lemon zest
½ cup fresh lemon juice
1 teaspoon gelatin, dissolved in 2 tablespoons water
½ cup heavy cream, whipped
12 Meringue Shells (recipe follows)
Whipped cream, optional
Raspberry Sauce (page 28)

1. Set a bowl of cold water on your counter. In a heavy medium saucepan, preferably enameled cast iron, or in a double boiler, beat the egg yolks to break them up. Gradually whisk in the sugar and then the wine, lemon zest and lemon juice. Set over moderate heat and cook, whisking constantly, until the mixture is hot, foamy and thickened, 5 to 10 minutes. Beat in the dissolved gelatin and whisk over heat for about 30 seconds longer.

2. Remove from the heat. Set the bottom of your pan in the bowl of cold water and whisk for about a minute to stop the cooking. Remove from the water and whisk for 1 to 2 minutes longer, until the mixture is thick and cool. Fold in the whipped cream. Cover and refrigerate. (The mousse mixture can be made up to 3 days in advance.)

3. To assemble the dessert, shortly before serving, use a large spoon or ice cream scoop to mound the lemon mousse neatly in the meringue shells. Top with a dollop of whipped cream and drizzle on a little Raspberry Sauce. Pass the remaining sauce separately.

INDIVIDUAL MERINGUE SHELLS
MAKES 12

Since these can be made up to a week in advance, they do make dessert easy on the cook. Just be sure to store in a tightly closed container and do not attempt to make them on a very humid day. Instead of the lemon mousse suggested above, the shells can be filled with ice cream before being topped with a chocolate or fruit sauce for a delightful *meringue glacée.*

6 egg whites
⅛ teaspoon cream of tartar
½ teaspoon vanilla extract
¾ cup superfine sugar
¾ cup confectioners' sugar

1. Preheat the oven to 225° F. Butter and flour 2 large baking sheets or line them with parchment.

2. In a large bowl, beat the egg whites with an electric mixer until frothy. Add the cream of tartar and vanilla and beat on high speed, gradually adding the superfine sugar, 1 tablespoon at a time. Gradually beat in ¼ cup of the confectioners' sugar. The egg whites should be very stiff and stand up in spiky peaks when the beaters are lifted. If they are not that firm, continue beating a little longer.

3. Put the remaining confectioners' sugar in a sifter. In two batches, sift the sugar over the meringue and fold in with a rubber spatula.

4. Either put the meringue in a pastry bag with a ½-inch plain tube and pipe out a dozen 4-inch rounds with low rims on the baking sheets, or scoop the meringue into 12 mounds and shape them into nests with the back of a spoon, trying to make the bottoms relatively flat, about ½ inch thick, and the sides higher all around.

5. Bake the meringues for 1 hour 15 minutes. Turn off the oven and let the meringues sit in the closed oven for at least 3 hours, or until crisp and dry throughout. Peel off the parchment, if used, or carefully remove from the baking sheet with a wide spatula. Store in an airtight container for up to 1 week.

RASPBERRY SAUCE
MAKES ABOUT 3 CUPS

2 packages (12 ounces each) individually quick-frozen raspberries without added sugar, thawed
⅓ cup red currant jelly or seedless raspberry jam
2 tablespoons framboise or kirsch
2 teaspoons fresh lemon juice
Sugar

1. In a food processor, combine the raspberries with their juice, the jelly, framboise and lemon juice; puree until smooth. Taste and add a little sugar only if you really feel it's necessary; the sauce should be intense.

2. Strain, if desired, to remove the seeds. Pour into a jar, cover and refrigerate for up to 5 days before serving.

Grandma Grandbouche's Curly Endive Salad

■

Oven-Baked Deviled Chicken

Family-Style Vegetable Platter with Lemon Butter

Mashed Potatoes

■

Apricot-Apple Crisp

An Old-Fashioned Sunday Supper

FOR 12

Home-style family food with a regional American flavor is enjoying a renaissance. We want real food and plenty of it. Presentation is still important, but it needn't be elaborate. I always take food fashion with a grain of salt, but this back-to-basics movement has made me much more comfortable in the kitchen.

This simple, homey food lends itself well to family-style service—that is, big bowls and platters from which everyone can help themselves. I serve this meal whenever there will be a large group of family or friends around the table on short notice.

Grandma Grandbouche's Curly Endive Salad comes all the way from Grand Junction, Colorado. She learned the recipe from her mother some eighty years ago. Made from curly endive (chicory) and bacon, it is an American classic, much like Grandma herself. In her teens, Leata Grandbouche worked in her aunt's restaurant in Wyoming, which was the heart of the wild West in those days. She served this very same salad to her customers, real cowboys, who, she insists, were the most gallant of gentlemen.

Deviled Chicken, tasty and crisp, is another easy old-time dish, which can be prepared up to a day ahead and baked just before serving, or, if you prefer, cooked ahead and reheated. It really doesn't matter which chicken parts you use for this dish; just allow ¾ to 1 pound per person.

For the vegetable platter, consider color and texture. One of my favorite combinations is beets, cauliflower and broccoli. I bake beets wrapped in foil to concentrate their sweetness and flavor. Though some people prefer steaming, I like to boil the cauliflower and broccoli separately in large pots of salted water. They cook quickly and it's easy to keep an eye on them and test them repeatedly to achieve just the right texture. Personally, I don't like my vegetables crunchy; I like them cooked until tender with just a pleasant resistance to the bite. After blanching the vegetables, rinse them under cold running water to stop the cooking and set the color; then drain well. Allow ⅓ pound of these vegetables per person and about 1 tablespoon butter per pound. Arrange the vegetables in separate mounds on a large platter. Melt the butter, adding fresh lemon juice to taste. Season with salt and freshly ground pepper and drizzle over the vegetables.

Everyone loves mashed potatoes. Boil baking potatoes (⅓ pound per person), peel and mash with butter and milk or cream to taste. For lighter potatoes, mix in some of the cooking water in place of some of the cream. Season with salt, pepper and a pinch of nutmeg.

Apple crisp is one of those irresistible desserts we too often take for granted. This version incorporates dried apricots for a greater intensity of flavor and more natural sweetness with less sugar. Whole wheat flour is added to the topping for extra crispness. This dessert can be made ahead and served cold or at room temperature, or baked just a few hours ahead and served warm, which is how I love it, with a big scoop of vanilla ice cream.

By the way, these recipes can be doubled; but if you do so, bake the crisp in two baking pans the same size indicated in the recipe.

Do-Ahead Planning

Up to 2 days ahead: Bake the beets for the vegetable platter.

The day before: Rinse and dry the endive. Make the Apricot-Apple Crisp (if you plan to serve it chilled or at room temperature).

Up to 3 hours before serving: Cook the bacon and make the dressing for the salad. Cook the chicken through Step 3. Blanch the cauliflower and broccoli for the Vegetable Platter.

About 2 hours before serving: Make the Apricot-Apple Crisp (if you want to serve it warm). Peel and slice the beets. Make the mashed potatoes.

Shortly before serving: Reheat the dressing and toss with the endive and bacon. Finish the chicken. Reheat the vegetables and toss with the lemon butter. Reheat the mashed potatoes in a microwave or uncovered over moderate heat, stirring frequently.

GRANDMA GRANDBOUCHE'S CURLY ENDIVE SALAD

12 SERVINGS

Grandma tames the bitterness of the curly endive, called chicory in some parts of the country, with a boiled sweet-sour dressing. It should be served at once, while the dressing is still warm.

> *2 large heads of curly endive (chicory), about 2½ pounds*
> *10 strips of bacon (about ½ pound)*
> *¼ cup all-purpose flour*
> *1 cup distilled white vinegar*
> *¼ cup sugar*
> *½ teaspoon salt*
> *¼ teaspoon freshly ground pepper*
> *2 garlic cloves, minced*

1. Wash the endive well. Cut off about 2 inches of the tough stem ends and cut the remainder into 1-inch pieces. Drain well and set aside in a large glass or ceramic serving bowl.

2. In a large skillet, fry the bacon until crisp. Remove the bacon and drain on paper towels. Chop or crumble into small bits.

3. Add the flour to the bacon fat in the skillet and cook over moderate heat, stirring, for 2 minutes. Add the vinegar and 1½ cups water. Bring to a boil, whisking until smooth. Add the sugar, salt and pepper. Simmer, stirring frequently, for 2 minutes, or until the sugar dissolves and the raw flour taste disappears.

4. Just before serving, bring the dressing to a boil in the skillet. Add the garlic and immediately pour over the endive. Add the bacon, toss and serve.

OVEN-BAKED DEVILED CHICKEN

12 SERVINGS

*9 pounds chicken drumsticks, thighs and/or
    breasts
Salt and freshly ground pepper
¼ pound (1 stick) plus 2 tablespoons unsalted
    butter, at room temperature
1½ tablespoons Dijon mustard
1½ tablespoons red wine vinegar
1 tablespoon hot pepper sauce
1½ teaspoons paprika
1 teaspoon thyme
3 cups fresh bread crumbs (made from about 8
    slices of firm-textured white bread)*

1. Season the chicken liberally with salt and pepper. Arrange as many pieces as will fit on a broiling pan in a single layer without crowding and broil about 6 inches from the heat, turning once, until the skin is browned, 5 to 7 minutes per side. Remove to a platter and repeat with the remaining chicken.

2. Reduce the oven temperature to 350° F. In a small bowl, blend together the butter, mustard, vinegar, hot sauce, paprika, thyme and 1½ teaspoons salt.

3. Arrange the chicken, skin side up, in a single layer in 2 or 3 shallow baking dishes or roasting pans. Brush with the seasoned butter. Sprinkle the bread crumbs over the chicken; pat gently to help them adhere. (The chicken can be prepared ahead to this point and refrigerated for up to 3 hours before cooking. Let stand at room temperature for at least 30 minutes before cooking.)

4. Bake the chicken at 350° F. for 15 to 20 minutes, until the coating is browned and crisp and the chicken is tender.

APRICOT-APPLE CRISP

12 SERVINGS

In some circles, of which my husband is a charter member, creamy vanilla ice cream is considered a must with a warm fruit dessert like this. I prefer a minimum of sugar in my sweets; if your apples are very tart, you may wish to toss them with one extra tablespoon.

*½ pound dried apricots
2 tablespoons dark rum, such as Myers's, optional
¼ pound (1 stick) plus 2 tablespoons unsalted
    butter
8 large cooking apples, such as Granny Smith
    and/or Cortland (I like to use a mix for more
    complex flavor)
⅓ cup plus 3 tablespoons sugar
½ cup all-purpose flour
⅓ cup whole wheat flour
¼ teaspoon salt
⅔ cup chopped toasted almonds*

1. Cut the apricots into halves or quarters, depending on their size. Put them in a small heatproof bowl and add just enough boiling water to barely cover them. Add the rum if you're using it and let stand for at least 20 minutes, or until softened.

2. Preheat the oven to 375° F. Use 1 tablespoon of the butter to grease a large (9 x 14-inch) shallow baking dish. Melt 3 tablespoons of the butter and set aside.

3. Peel and core the apples and cut them into slices about 1 inch long and ⅜ inch thick. Put them in the buttered baking dish. Drain the apricots and add them to the apples. Drizzle the melted butter over the fruit. Sprinkle on 3 tablespoons of the sugar and toss to mix. Spread the fruit evenly in the dish.

4. In a medium bowl, combine the all-purpose flour, whole wheat flour, salt and remaining ⅓ cup sugar. Cut the remaining 6 tablespoons butter into small dice, add it to the flour mixture and pinch with your fingertips until it is blended into coarse crumbs. Add the almonds and toss to mix.

5. Squeeze the nut-crumb mixture into nuggets and sprinkle evenly over the top of the fruit. Bake for 45 minutes, or until the apples are tender and the crust is browned. Serve warm or at room temperature.

APPLES

I learned something interesting about apples—
they have an unexpectedly complicated genetic
code, and they don't breed true. What this
means is that if you take the seeds from a
McIntosh apple and plant them, you won't
necessarily get McIntosh apples. You would
probably produce some apple you'd never seen
before. Apples' genes mix, just like human
beings', so that no two apple trees have to be
alike. In order to propagate a particular variety
of apple, farmers graft the branches of one tree
onto the root of another. There are hundreds of
varieties of apple; how sad that we see only two
or three in our supermarkets. And often these
are chosen for durability and longevity on the
shelf rather than for flavor.

Happily, there seems to be something of an
apple renaissance going on. Along with the
general movement toward better, fresher produce and specialty ingredients, some farmers
are growing apple varieties known for their
flavor. Imported apples from New Zealand ensure that now we'll be able to get juicy, firm
apples year-round.

Basically, there are two kinds of apples—
cooking apples, which hold their shape under
heat but tend to be on the dry side, and eating
apples, like Macs, which are juicy and flavorful
but often turn to mush when cooked. Golden
Delicious and Granny Smiths, available in most
supermarkets, are fine cooking apples, but they
are stingy on flavor. Rome Beauties and Cort-
lands have much more taste, and they are relatively common in season. Try lobbying at your
supermarket to encourage the produce buyer
to bring in a greater variety of apples. If you
have a farmer's market near you, look for Wine-
saps, Macouns and Northern Spy. When in
doubt, try to use two kinds of apples to develop
a more complex flavor.

An Elegant Dinner with Fine Wines

FOR 10 TO 12

Seafood Medallions with Herbed
Lemon-Walnut Mayonnaise

Full-bodied white wine, such as California
Chardonnay or French white Burgundy

·

Roast Fillet of Beef

Puree of Peas and Watercress

Creamed Potatoes with Garlic and Thyme

Elegant, herbaceous red wine, such as red
Bordeaux or California Cabernet Sauvignon

·

Green Salad

·

Assorted Cheeses, such as Camembert,
Roquefort and Cantal

French Walnut Bread

Red wine, preferably an older Bordeaux or a
fine Burgundy

·

Almond Custard Torte with Peaches and
Raspberries

Lush dessert wine, such as a Muscat
Beaumes-de-Venise served chilled

·

Espresso

People often make a fuss about pairing food and wine. That's because on those rare occasions when the match is perfect, the effect is stunning—the whole becomes much more than the sum of the parts. On those special occasions when a really fine vintage makes its appearance or when a friend announces he or she is bringing a great bottle to dinner, it is exciting to enjoy a truly exceptional experience by planning the food to complement the wine.

When the wine is the star, the food should be kept simple. Strong flavors and piquant spices should be avoided. The traditional sequence of a wine-oriented meal is white wine, good red wine, best red wine (often but not always the oldest), dessert wine. For that reason, I begin this menu with rich Seafood Medallions, made with lobster, scallops and sole, which will pair perfectly with an equally lush California Chardonnay or French white Burgundy.

33

Beef is the classic match for a good Bordeaux (or its California counterpart, Cabernet Sauvignon), so I serve a simple roast fillet here. As accompaniments, I've chosen a pretty green Puree of Peas and Watercress and Creamed Potatoes, with just a hint of mellow garlic and thyme. The pepperiness of the watercress and the herbal overtones of the thyme will match the character of the Bordeaux or Cabernet Sauvignon.

This is the point in the meal when the French serve their salad to refresh the palate and give new vigor to the appetite. I recommend it highly. Use a simple assortment of greens—perhaps Bibb and red oak leaf lettuce with a few leaves of arugula—and a dressing either based on lemon or with proportions of oil and vinegar no less than 4 to 1.

The cheese course is a French touch that is highly complementary to wine. Offer a variety of cheeses, and be sure they are at room temperature. The walnut bread goes well with both the cheese and the wine.

Though some people prefer their sweet wine after dessert and coffee, peaches and almonds pair beautifully with dessert wine, especially this apricoty Muscat Beaumes-de-Venise, which should be served well chilled.

Though I confess this menu does look intimidating, it was carefully designed with the home cook in mind. Notice that both the first course and the dessert are cold and are prepared in advance. Except for reheating the vegetables, the only last-minute work is roasting the fillet of beef. Since perfect doneness is critical here, I always use an electric timer as a reminder. The hardest part of this dinner is having enough plates to go around. Double up on the salad and cheese courses, if necessary. I often do.

Do-Ahead Planning

Up to 2 months in advance: Bake the Walnut Bread and freeze it.

Up to 3 days in advance: Make the mayonnaise.

Up to 2 days in advance: Bake the cake base. Make the custard. Poach the seafood rolls for the medallions.

Up to a day in advance: Prepare the Puree of Peas and Watercress. Prepare the Creamed Potatoes with Garlic and Thyme. Rinse and dry the salad greens.

Up to 4 hours before serving: Cut the seafood medallions and arrange them on a platter; cover and refrigerate. Marinate the fillet. Slice the peaches and assemble the torte; cover and refrigerate. Remove the cheeses from the refrigerator.

Shortly before serving: Bake the potatoes until heated through. Roast the fillet. Finish off the puree as you reheat it. Dress and toss the salad.

SEAFOOD MEDALLIONS

12 TO 16 SERVINGS

A delectable first course or buffet offering, this impressive dish is really just a fancy fish mousse formed into a fat sausage and then sliced when cold. I like to accompany the medallions with a green-flecked herb mayonnaise.

1 small live lobster, 1 to 1¼ pounds (ask your fish
market to split the lobster just before you pick
it up), or ½ pound medium shrimp, shelled
and deveined
¾ pound sea scallops
¾ pound fillet of sole or flounder
1 egg white
1½ teaspoons fresh lemon juice
1¼ teaspoons salt
1/16 teaspoon cayenne pepper
1½ cups heavy cream
1 tablespoon minced fresh chives
1 tablespoon minced fresh parsley
1½ teaspoons minced fresh tarragon, or ½
teaspoon dried
Butter
Herbed Lemon-Walnut Mayonnaise (recipe
follows)

1. In a medium pot of boiling water, blanch the lobster for 2 to 3 minutes; you want it cooked just enough to pull the meat out of the shell easily. As soon as the lobster is cool enough to handle, remove the meat from the shell and cut it into ⅜-inch dice. Put in a small bowl, cover and refrigerate. If you are using shrimp, just dice them. (This can be done a day ahead.)

2. Cut half of the scallops into ⅜-inch dice, put in a small bowl, cover and refrigerate.

3. Rinse the sole and pat dry. Pull or cut each sole fillet lengthwise in half where it is naturally divided and pull off the little "zipper" of tiny bones that runs down the middle.

4. In a food processor, puree the sole with the remaining whole scallops, the egg white, lemon juice, salt and cayenne. Scrape down the side of the bowl and puree for another 30 seconds. Scrape down the side of the bowl again. With the machine on, slowly add ¾ cup of the cream through the feed tube. Puree for 30 seconds after adding. Scrape the fish mousse into a metal bowl, cover and put in the freezer.

5. Whip the remaining ¾ cup cream until soft peaks form. Gradually whisk the whipped cream into the cold fish puree. Fold in the diced lobster and scallops, the chives, parsley and tarragon.

6. Lightly butter 4 lengths of aluminum foil, about 16 inches long. Spoon one-quarter of the fish mousse in a fat sausage shape about 2 inches in diameter lengthwise along the bottom third of each piece of foil to within 2 inches of the edges. Roll neatly, but allow a little room for expansion. Twist the ends to secure each roll.

7. Put the fish rolls in a large flameproof casserole of cold water. Weight them down with a heavy pot lid that fits inside the casserole, so that they remain covered with water. Bring just to a simmer (180 degrees) over moderately high heat. Reduce the heat to low and simmer for 10 minutes; the water should barely bubble. Turn off the heat, cover the pot and let stand for 10 minutes. Remove the rolls, open the foil slightly to drain off excess liquid, seal again and refrigerate. (The fish mousse can be cooked up to 2 days before serving.)

8. To serve, unwrap the fish rolls and cut each one into medallions ½ to ¾ inch thick. Serve with Herbed Lemon-Walnut Mayonnaise.

HERBED LEMON-WALNUT MAYONNAISE

MAKES ABOUT 1¾ CUPS

This is a rich, delicate mayonnaise, delicious with or without the fresh herbs. Though it can be made in a food processor, I enjoy the pleasure of whisking it by hand, which produces a silkier texture. For guaranteed success, be sure that your egg yolks are at room temperature when you begin.

> 2 egg yolks, at room temperature
> ½ teaspoon Dijon mustard
> ¼ teaspoon salt
> 2 to 3 tablespoons fresh lemon juice
> 1 tablespoon champagne vinegar or white wine
>   vinegar
> ½ cup extra-virgin olive oil
> ¼ cup walnut oil
> ¼ cup corn oil
> Dash of cayenne pepper
> ⅓ cup minced watercress
> 3 tablespoons minced fresh parsley
> 2 tablespoons minced fresh chives
> 2 teaspoons minced fresh tarragon or ¾ teaspoon
>   dried

1. In a medium bowl, whisk together the egg yolks, mustard, salt, 1 tablespoon of the lemon juice and ½ tablespoon of the vinegar. Very gradually, drop by drop at first, whisk in the olive oil. As soon as the mixture begins to stiffen, you can beat in a little more oil at a time.

2. When you have a good emulsion going, whisk in the remaining olive oil, the walnut oil and the corn oil in a thin stream. Beat in the cayenne, the remaining ½ tablespoon vinegar and 1 tablespoon lemon juice. Taste and add up to 1 more tablespoon lemon juice to produce the tartness desired.

3. Whisk in the minced watercress, parsley, chives and tarragon.

ROAST FILLET OF BEEF

10 TO 12 SERVINGS

Though fillet of beef is an expensive cut, there is absolutely no waste, it cooks in 20 minutes or less and carves beautifully. You can increase the cooking time for more well done meat, but fillet is absolutely best when cooked to a rosy rare, as suggested here. This recipe can be multiplied exactly to accommodate as many roasts as you need.

> 1 whole fillet of beef (about 5 pounds), trimmed
>   and tied
> 2 tablespoons Cognac
> 2 tablespoons minced shallots
> ½ teaspoon salt
> 1 teaspoon coarsely cracked black peppercorns,
>   preferably Tellicherry
> ¼ cup extra-virgin olive oil
> 4 strips of bacon, optional

1. About 2 hours before you plan to serve the meat, remove it from the refrigerator, unwrap it and set it in a large glass dish or baking pan. Rub the meat all over with the Cognac, shallots, salt, pepper and 2 tablespoons of the olive oil. Set aside at room temperature, turning once or twice.

2. Preheat the oven to 450° F. About 40 minutes before you plan to serve the meat, heat the remaining 2 tablespoons oil in a large, heavy flameproof gratin dish or roasting pan over moderately high heat. Add the fillet and cook, turning, until browned all over, about 5 minutes. If you are using the bacon, lay it on top of the roast. Transfer the pan to the oven and roast the fillet for 15 to 20 minutes, or until an instant-reading thermometer registers 125° to 130° F. for rare. (Remember, the meat will keep cooking after you remove it from the oven.)

3. Remove the bacon and transfer the roast to a carving board. Cover loosely with foil and let stand for about 15 minutes before carving.

PUREE OF PEAS AND WATERCRESS

12 SERVINGS

3 packages (10 ounces each) small, frozen peas
3 cups (packed) watercress with tough stems
*   removed, about 1½ large bunches*
5 large shallots or white scallion bulbs, sliced
6 tablespoons unsalted butter
1 teaspoon sugar
Salt and freshly ground pepper to taste

1. Bring a large saucepan of salted water to a boil over high heat. Add the peas and shallots; cook for 4 minutes, or until tender. Add the watercress, pushing it beneath the water. Cook for 1 minute longer; drain.

2. Puree the vegetables with the butter in a food processor, in batches if necessary, or pass through the fine blade of a food mill. Season with the sugar and salt and pepper to taste. (The puree can be made to this point up to a day in advance. Refrigerate in a covered container.)

3. Shortly before serving, reheat in a heavy medium saucepan over moderately high heat or in a microwave oven.

CREAMED POTATOES WITH GARLIC AND THYME

10 TO 12 SERVINGS

Whenever I see more than two pounds of potatoes, I try to avoid peeling them. Cooking them first so that the skins slip off easily makes things much easier.

4½ pounds baking potatoes
3 garlic cloves
4 tablespoons unsalted butter
Salt and freshly ground pepper
1 teaspoon minced fresh thyme, or ½ teaspoon
*   dried*
4 cups half-and-half or light cream

1. Cook the potatoes with their skins on in a large pot of boiling salted water for 15 minutes. Drain and rinse under cold running water. (The potatoes can be prepared to this point up to a day ahead; refrigerate.)

2. Peel the potatoes and cut them crosswise into very thin slices. Use a mandoline, if you have one, or the slicing blade on a rectangular grater.

3. Cut 1 of the garlic cloves in half; finely mince the other 2 garlic cloves. Rub the cut garlic all over the inside of a large gratin or baking dish (or two smaller dishes). Grease the dish with 1 tablespoon of the butter.

4. Arrange one-third of the potatoes in a layer in the bottom of the dish, overlapping the slices as necessary. Season liberally with salt and pepper. Sprinkle on one-half of the minced garlic and thyme; dot with 1 tablespoon of the butter. Repeat with half the remaining potatoes and the rest of the garlic and thyme; dot with another tablespoon of the butter. End with a top layer of the remaining potatoes. Season with salt and pepper and dot with the remaining 1 tablespoon butter. Pour the half-and-half over the potatoes. (The recipe can be prepared to this point up to 3 hours ahead. Set aside at room temperature.)

5. Preheat the oven to 375° F. Bring the gratin to a boil on top of the stove or in a microwave. Transfer to the oven and bake for 20 minutes. Increase the oven temperature to 450° F. and bake for 10 minutes, or until most of the cream is absorbed and the gratin is browned on top.

FRENCH WALNUT BREAD

MAKES 2 LOAVES

I've never understood why the cheese course didn't catch on in America on a large scale. I serve it frequently, either to embellish what would otherwise be a very simple meal, or to extend a grand meal and finish off our fine wines. With an assortment of two or three cheeses, I usually pass a salad, to be eaten off the same plate, before or after or at the same time, as the diner wishes. Whenever I can, this is the bread I serve. The walnuts go beautifully with most cheeses—and with wine—and the deep chewy texture is immensely satisfying. Like most breads, it freezes well.

1½ cups (about 6 ounces) walnut pieces
1 tablespoon honey
1 tablespoon dark brown sugar
2 cups warm water (105° to 115° F.)
1 package (¼ ounce) active dry yeast
4 cups whole wheat flour
1 cup all-purpose flour
2 teaspoons salt
3 tablespoons walnut oil

1. Preheat the oven to 325° F. Spread the walnuts out on a baking sheet and bake, shaking the pan once or twice, until they are lightly toasted, 8 to 10 minutes.

2. In a small bowl, dissolve the honey and brown sugar in ½ cup of the warm water. Add the yeast and let stand until foamy, about 10 minutes.

3. In a large bowl, combine the whole wheat flour, all-purpose flour and salt. Make a well in the center and add the yeast mixture and all but 1½ teaspoons of the walnut oil. Blend the flour into the well. Gradually add the remaining 1½ cups warm water, blending to make a stiff but moist dough. Turn out onto a lightly floured surface and knead until smooth and elastic, about 10 minutes.

4. Grease a bowl with the reserved 1½ teaspoons walnut oil. Form the dough into a ball, place in the bowl and turn to coat with oil. Cover with a slightly dampened kitchen towel and set aside to rise in a warm draft-free spot until the dough is doubled in size, about 1½ hours.

5. Punch the dough down and knead in the walnuts. Divide the dough in half and shape into 2 loaves, long or round as you wish. Place on 2 lightly buttered baking sheets, cover lightly with a cloth and let rise until doubled again, about 45 minutes. Meanwhile, preheat the oven to 425° F.

6. Bake the loaves for 15 minutes. Rotate the baking sheets, reversing shelves, reduce the oven temperature to 350° F. and bake for 30 to 35 minutes, or until the bread sounds hollow when the bottom is thumped. Let cool for at least 15 minutes before slicing.

ALMOND CUSTARD TORTE WITH PEACHES AND RASPBERRIES

10 TO 12 SERVINGS

No one will believe you made this yourself. If time is a problem, make the cake base ahead and freeze it, well wrapped; defrost completely before assembling the torte.

¾ cup slivered blanched almonds
⅓ plus ¼ cup sugar
½ cup sifted cake flour
½ teaspoon baking powder
⅛ teaspoon salt
¼ pound (1 stick) unsalted butter, softened
3 eggs, at room temperature
1½ teaspoons vanilla extract
½ teaspoon almond extract
3 ripe but firm peaches
Pastry Cream (recipe follows)
½ to ¾ cup chopped roasted almonds
½ pint raspberries

1. Preheat the oven to 350° F. In a food processor, grind the blanched almonds with ⅓ cup of the sugar. Sift together the flour, baking powder and salt.

2. In a mixing bowl, blend the butter with the remaining ¼ cup sugar with an electric mixer until light and fluffy. Beat in the almond-sugar mixture until blended. Beat in the eggs, 1 at a time, beating well after adding each, and then the vanilla and almond extracts. Finally beat in the dry ingredients in two batches.

3. Turn the batter into a buttered 9-inch round cake pan and bake for 22 to 25 minutes, or until a cake tester comes out clean and the cake has just begun to pull away from the sides of the pan. Unmold onto a rack and let cool completely. (If made ahead, wrap well in plastic wrap and refrigerate overnight or freeze for up to 2 months; defrost before proceeding.)

4. Blanch the peaches in a large saucepan of boiling water for 2 to 3 minutes, until the skins just begin to feel puckery. Drain and rinse under cold running water. Peel the peaches and cut them into ½-inch slices.

5. Up to several hours before serving, set the cake on a cake plate and cover the top and sides completely with the Pastry Cream. Press the chopped almonds into the side of the cake. Arrange the peach slices, overlapping slightly, in a circle around the edge of the cake. Mound the raspberries in the center. Cover the cake and refrigerate until serving time.

PASTRY CREAM

MAKES ABOUT 2½ CUPS

This is an easy, surefire pastry cream that cooks in less than a minute. Because of the gelatin and butter, it is a firm cream that holds up well for filling and frosting.

1 teaspoon unflavored gelatin
2 cups milk
⅔ cup sugar
6 egg yolks
½ cup flour
3 tablespoons unsalted butter
2 teaspoons vanilla extract

1. Sprinkle the gelatin over the milk in a medium saucepan and let stand for 5 minutes to soften.

2. Meanwhile, in a medium bowl, whisk the sugar into the egg yolks. Beat until pale and thick. Whisk in the flour.

3. Bring the milk to a boil. Slowly whisk the hot milk into the egg-flour mixture (the flour will prevent the egg yolks from curdling). Return to the saucepan and bring to a boil over moderate heat, stirring constantly. Whisk vigorously over the heat as the custard boils for 20 seconds, making sure to scrape up the mixture from all over the bottom so it does not scorch. Taste the pastry cream; there should be no uncooked floury taste. If there is, return to the heat and whisk for 10 seconds longer.

4. Beat the cold butter into the pastry cream until melted and smooth. Beat in the vanilla. Place a sheet of plastic wrap directly onto the cream to cover and refrigerate for up to 3 days before using.

Dinner for a Summer Evening

FOR 12

Shrimp, Avocado and Papaya Salad with Coconut-Lime Dressing

■

Mesquite-Grilled Chicken
Grilled Sweet Sausages
Ruth's Spanish Rice
Minted Yogurt Salad

■

Mango Sorbet with Strawberries, Kiwi and Passion Fruit Liqueur
Nut Cookies
Iced Coffee

I love entertaining on those warm evenings when the red sun looks like a painting as it sets slowly in the hazy sky. As the last rays slip through the gold- and mauve-edged clouds, chances are you will find us on the terrace with friends, sipping long cool drinks and talking softly, dragging out the pleasures of summer as long as we can. It's not a time to fuss. I serve easy food, tasty enough to tempt tired appetites, light enough to be refreshing. Usually the main course is prepared on the grill while guests watch; they can even help if they want to—an iced gin and tonic in one hand, barbecue fork in the other. An artful vase of fresh-from-the-garden flowers and a crisp pastel cloth set the perfect table, with small white candles mimicking the fireflies outside the screen.

The first course is cool, waiting in the fridge— buttery ripe avocado and tropical papaya combined with tender pink shrimp in a refreshing coconut-lime dressing. The smooth flavors whet the appetite for the spicy food that follows.

Mesquite-Grilled Chicken uses a dry marinade blended with onions, garlic and a little oil and citrus juice to produce the best barbecued chicken you've ever tasted. Experiment, if you like, with other types of woods, use regular charcoal or gas, or, in a pinch, even the broiler. Grilled sausages add variety and complement the Spanish-style rice, while a mélange of diced garden vegetables in a thick yogurt dressing loaded with fresh mint provides cooling contrast. I recommend ice-cold beer to quench summer thirst and wash down this zesty food.

For a delightful no-work dessert, buy a good mango or raspberry sorbet. Scoop into small dessert bowls and garnish each with a few bright berries and slices of kiwi and a splash of Grand Passion, passion fruit liqueur. Nut cookies—your own, your favorite bakery's or a good commercial brand—provide a crisp accompaniment to tall glasses of iced coffee (brewed extra-strong to stand up to the melting ice), sipped late into the long, warm night.

Do-Ahead Planning

Up to 1 day ahead: Cook the shrimp. Marinate the chicken. Make the yogurt dressing for the salad.

Up to 3 hours before serving: Complete the Shrimp, Avocado and Papaya Salad with Coconut-Lime Dressing. Precook the sausages. Make the Minted Yogurt Salad.

Up to 1½ hours before serving: Make Ruth's Spanish Rice; it will hold for 30 to 45 minutes.

About 1 hour before serving: Grill the chicken and sausages.

SHRIMP, AVOCADO AND PAPAYA SALAD WITH COCONUT-LIME DRESSING

12 SERVINGS

1½ pounds medium shrimp, shelled and deveined
3 large ripe avocados, preferably the California
    kind with pebbly skin, called Hass
Juice of 2 limes
2 medium-large papayas
⅓ pound baked ham, cut into ½-inch dice
1 cup (4 ounces) pecans, lightly toasted
½ cup unsweetened coconut milk
2 tablespoons raspberry or blueberry vinegar
1 teaspoon coarsely cracked pepper
Salt
Lime wedges, for garnish

1. Drop the shrimp into a saucepan of boiling salted water. Let return to a simmer, then cook 1 to 2 minutes, until the shrimp are loosely curled, pink and just opaque throughout; drain.

2. Peel the avocados and cut into ¾-inch dice. Put in a medium bowl and toss with the juice of 1 lime to coat.

3. Peel the papayas, cut in half and remove the seeds. Cut the papaya into ¾-inch dice. Add the papaya, ham and pecans to the avocado.

4. In a small bowl, whisk together the coconut milk, vinegar, pepper and juice of the remaining lime. Season with salt to taste. Toss the shrimp with 3 tablespoons of the dressing. Pour the remaining dressing over the avocado mixture and toss gently to coat.

5. To serve, mound the avocado mixture in the center of a large platter. Arrange the shrimp around the edges. Garnish with lime wedges and serve at room temperature or slightly chilled.

MESQUITE-GRILLED CHICKEN AND SAUSAGES

12 SERVINGS

I like to grill some sweet Italian sausages along with the chicken. If you do that, adjust the number of people it will feed, allowing about ⅔ pound chicken on the bone plus ¼ pound sausage per person. Prick the sausages all over and simmer in a saucepan of water for 10 minutes before grilling to be sure the pork is thoroughly cooked.

8 to 9 pounds chicken—either 3 quartered
    chickens or an equal amount of your favorite
    chicken parts
2 medium onions, quartered
5 large garlic cloves, crushed
1 tablespoon sweet imported paprika
1 tablespoon fresh oregano, or 1 teaspoon dried
1½ teaspoons ground cumin
1 to 1½ teaspoons cayenne pepper (1½ is better,
    but hotter)
2 tablespoons coarse (kosher) salt
1½ teaspoons freshly ground pepper
⅓ cup fresh lime or lemon juice
3 tablespoons corn oil

1. Rinse the chicken and pat dry. Put in a large bowl.

2. In a food processor, combine all the remaining ingredients. Puree until smooth. Pour over the chicken and toss to coat. Let marinate at room temperature for up to 2 hours, or cover and refrigerate for up to 24 hours.

3. Light a covered charcoal or gas grill or preheat the broiler. If you are using mesquite or other wood, soak the chunks for at least 30 minutes. Let the charcoal or gas fire get very hot, then add the wood and splash with water if it flares up.

4. Remove the chicken from the marinade, letting any excess drip back into the bowl. Put the chicken on the grill with the heat on high or the vents wide open and sear for about 5 minutes on each side to brown the outside. Close the vents or turn the heat to low, splash the fire with water, if necessary, cover the grill and smoke the chicken, turning once, for 35 minutes, or until it is still juicy but no longer pink. (The chicken can be smoked earlier in the day. Reheat, wrapped in foil, in a 300° F. oven. Unwrap during the last 5 minutes.)

RUTH'S SPANISH RICE

12 SERVINGS

Less than 12 hours after her mother, Emily, polished off three helpings of this spicy rice, Ruth Buckingham entered the world, so I couldn't resist naming this dish in her honor. I use converted rice here so the recipe can be made a day ahead and reheated in a heavy covered casserole in the oven or, preferably, in a glass container in a microwave. It is also good at room temperature.

 3 tablespoons extra-virgin olive oil
 2 medium onions, chopped
 ⅓ cup slivered almonds
 3 garlic cloves, minced
 ⅓ pound baked ham, diced
 ½ green bell pepper, diced
 ½ red bell pepper, diced
 1 can (14 ounces) Italian peeled tomatoes with
     their juices, chopped
 1½ teaspoons oregano, preferably Mexican
 ½ teaspoon crushed hot red pepper
 ¼ teaspoon (not packed) saffron threads,
     crumbled
 1 can (12 ounces) lager beer, such as Budweiser
 1 teaspoon fresh lemon juice
 1 imported bay leaf
 1¾ teaspoons salt
 ¾ teaspoon coarsely cracked black pepper
 3 cups converted rice
 ½ jar (about 4 ounces) small Spanish pimiento-
     stuffed olives, well drained

1. In a large saucepan or flameproof casserole, heat the oil. Add the onions and almonds and sauté over moderately high heat until the onions are softened and golden and the almonds are lightly browned, 5 to 7 minutes. Add the garlic, ham and bell peppers and sauté until the peppers are crisp-tender, about 3 minutes.

2. Add the tomatoes and their juices, the oregano, hot pepper, saffron, beer, lemon juice, bay leaf, salt, black pepper and 3 cups of water. Bring to a boil, then add the rice. Stir once. Cover and simmer over low heat for 20 to 25 minutes, until the liquid is absorbed and the rice tender. Stir in the olives (I like them whole, but if yours are large, you can slice them thick).

MINTED YOGURT SALAD

12 TO 16 SERVINGS

 1 quart (32 ounces) plain yogurt
 1 pint (16 ounces) sour cream
 1½ teaspoons sugar
 ½ teaspoon salt
 ⅛ teaspoon cayenne pepper
 4 Kirby cucumbers, diced
 1 large bunch of radishes, diced
 2 large tomatoes, seeded and diced
 1 cup chopped scallion green
 ¾ cup chopped parsley
 ⅓ cup chopped fresh mint

1. Line a sieve with cheesecloth, set it over a bowl and let the yogurt drain in it for 3 hours. Transfer the thickened yogurt to a large bowl. Add the sour cream, sugar, salt and cayenne and mix well. (This dressing can be made up to a day ahead and refrigerated, covered. The vegetables can be diced up to 3 hours ahead and refrigerated separately, but the herbs should be chopped shortly before serving.)

2. Add the diced cucumbers, radishes, tomatoes, scallion green and the chopped herbs to the yogurt dressing. Stir to blend well. Cover and refrigerate, if desired, for up to 2 hours before serving. Serve slightly chilled.

Leek and Potato Soup with Port and Gorgonzola

·

Mustard-Pecan Chicken Cutlets
Microwave Emerald Spinach
Wild or Pecan Rice

·

Profiteroles

Do-Ahead Sit-Down Dinner

FOR 12

If all of us have one complaint when it comes to entertaining, it's a lack of time. I know that as much as I love to cook, there are moments after a long day at the office when the idea of company seems absolutely daunting, let alone the prospect of cooking for a crowd. To allow the freedom of a large dinner party on your terms, here is an appealing menu that can be prepared entirely in advance and finished off in roughly half an hour before serving. It takes advantage of all the conveniences we have at our fingertips: a food processor to puree the soup; skinned, boned and pounded chicken breast halves, or cutlets; and the microwave oven, which does such a good job on vegetables in particular.

This delectable Leek and Potato Soup is very different from any other version I've tasted. The leek base is cooked to a golden brown before the potatoes and stock are added, and the soup is enriched with port and creamy Gorgonzola dolcelatte, a milder, sweeter variety of the Italian blue-veined cheese. The overall effect is so subtle, it's hard to guess exactly what's in it, and the flavor is so good, I could eat gallons of it. If you have a very large freezer, you could make the soup weeks ahead and freeze it in a number of containers, but for most people, the refrigerator is probably more practical, in which case you can make the recipe up to two days before serving.

The main course of this meal is southern in feel and simple in terms of preparation. Coat the chicken cutlets with the pecan breading the night before; they actually are better if prepared in advance. Partially cook the spinach and make the wild rice or pecan rice according to package directions or your favorite recipe. Both wild rice, with its wonderful chewy texture, and pecan rice, with its subtle nutty flavor, are fine complements to the chicken. Then, about half an hour before you're ready to sit down and eat, the chicken is baked. Shortly before serving, the spinach is finished and the rice reheated in the microwave. If you don't own a microwave, simply blanch the spinach in a large pot of boiling water for about a minute and reheat the rice in the oven along with the chicken.

Profiteroles are tiny cream puffs. Their size makes them cute or elegant, depending on how you look at it. They're the perfect do-ahead dessert, since they can be baked completely ahead and frozen. Just be sure you purchase a good vanilla ice cream and hot fudge sauce, or make the easy one on page 46. Serve three profiteroles per person.

Do-Ahead Planning

Up to 2 months in advance: Bake the profiteroles. When cool, freeze in plastic bags or an airtight container.

Up to 5 days ahead: Make the Hot Fudge Sauce and store in the refrigerator.

Up to 2 days before the dinner: Make the Leek and Potato Soup with Port and Gorgonzola and refrigerate in a covered container.

The night before the dinner: Coat the chicken cutlets with the pecan breading. Make the Microwave Emerald Spinach through Step 3. Make the wild or pecan rice.

About 30 minutes before serving: Bake the Mustard-Pecan Chicken Cutlets.

Shortly before serving: Reheat the soup. Finish the spinach. Reheat the rice. Warm up the hot fudge sauce and fill the profiteroles with vanilla ice cream.

LEEK AND POTATO SOUP WITH PORT AND GORGONZOLA

12 SERVINGS

I first tasted this soup at one of my favorite New York restaurants, Union Square Café. Leeks are cooked to a melting golden brown before the port, stock and potatoes are added. After being pureed, the soup is bound with cream and Gorgonzola for a rich yet subtle effect that is immensely appealing.

2 large bunches of leeks (1½ to 2 pounds)
1 to 2 onions, coarsely chopped (optional)
¼ pound (1 stick) unsalted butter, quartered
½ cup port, such as Croft Distinction
1 large can (46 ounces) chicken broth
4 cups water
4 large baking potatoes (2¼ pounds), peeled and cut into large dice
⅛ teaspoon cayenne pepper
¾ cup heavy cream
¼ pound Gorgonzola dolcelatte cheese
Salt and freshly ground black pepper

1. Trim off the tough dark green parts of the leeks. Quarter the white part and tender green lengthwise and rinse well in a bowl of cold water; leeks can be very sandy. Slice the leeks into large dice, put in a bowl and add fresh cold water to cover. With your hands, transfer the leeks to a colander. Measure the leeks. If there are less than 6 cups, add coarsely chopped onions to make up the difference.

2. In a very large flameproof casserole, combine the butter and leeks. Cover and cook over low heat for 10 minutes, stirring once. Uncover and cook, stirring occasionally at first and then more frequently, until the leeks are golden brown, 25 to 30 minutes.

3. Add the port to the casserole and scrape up the browned residue on the bottom of the pan. Add the chicken broth and the water. Bring to a boil. Add the potatoes and cayenne, reduce the heat to moderate and cook, partially covered, for 20 minutes.

4. In a blender or food processor, puree the soup in batches until smooth. Return to the casserole. (The soup can be prepared ahead to this point up to 2 days in advance. Reheat before proceeding.)

5. In the blender or food processor, combine the cream and Gorgonzola cheese. Return the soup to a boil. Stir in the Gorgonzola cream and season with salt and black pepper to taste. Serve hot.

MUSTARD-PECAN CHICKEN CUTLETS

12 SERVINGS

After being prepared and coated, these tasty cutlets actually improve if set in the refrigerator for several hours, or even overnight, before baking.

12 skinned, boned and pounded chicken cutlets (4 to 5 ounces each)
1 egg yolk
2 teaspoons champagne vinegar or white wine vinegar
½ teaspoon salt
¼ cup walnut oil (if you don't have walnut oil, increase the olive oil to ¾ cup)
½ cup olive oil
¼ cup Dijon mustard
2 tablespoons fresh lemon juice
2 medium shallots, coarsely chopped
½ teaspoon freshly ground pepper
¼ teaspoon hot pepper sauce
¾ pound pecans, finely chopped
1½ cups fresh bread crumbs

1. In a food processor, blend the egg yolk with the vinegar and salt. With the machine on, gradually add the walnut and olive oils through the feed tube to form a mayonnaise. Add the mustard, lemon juice, shallots, pepper and hot sauce. Blend, scraping down the bowl once or twice, until the mixture is smooth.

2. Combine the pecans and bread crumbs and toss to mix. Pile them up on a sheet of wax paper or on a large plate. Smear a heaping ½ tablespoon of the mustard sauce over the top of one chicken breast. Lift up and place mustard-side down on the crumbs. Smear another ½ tablespoon over the top and turn to coat the second side with crumbs and nuts. Pat gently to help them adhere; set aside in a large buttered baking dish or on a buttered baking sheet (you will need 2 dishes or sheets for all the chicken). Repeat with the remaining chicken, mustard sauce and crumbs. When all the chicken cutlets are coated, cover and refrigerate for at least 2 hours, or overnight.

3. Preheat the oven to 425° F. Put the chicken, uncovered, in the oven and immediately reduce the temperature to 350° F. Bake, rotating the pans once for even browning, for 25 to 30 minutes, or until the coating is lightly browned and the chicken is white throughout but still moist and juicy.

MICROWAVE EMERALD SPINACH

10 TO 12 SERVINGS

There are not a lot of microwave recipes in this book, because though it is a great tool for many steps in these recipes—melting chocolate and butter, heating liquids, crisping bacon—it does not cook large quantities of food very well. This recipe is an exception, because the microwave cooks it so quickly (even though it's done in batches) and in such superior fashion to any other cooking technique I know. As the recipe title implies, the microwave produces spinach that is bright emerald green, maintains the distinct leaves, all its fresh flavor and just enough tenderness—in short, it makes perfect spinach.

4 pounds fresh leaf spinach
4 tablespoons unsalted butter
Salt and freshly ground pepper to taste
8 pinches of nutmeg, preferably freshly grated

1. Wash the spinach well in several changes of water to remove any grit. Lift out into a colander. Pull off the large stems and set the spinach leaves aside. Do not dry them. (This is tedious work. Recruit help if you can.)

2. Cook ½ pound of the spinach at a time (it won't take you more than 20 minutes): Put about an eighth of the spinach leaves in a glass bowl; don't worry if it mounds over the top. Add 1½ teaspoons of the butter and cover with a glass top or pie plate. Microwave on high for 2 minutes. The spinach will sink down at the end, but it will not be completely tender. Do not cook further at this point. Toss gently to blend the top leaves into the hot liquid at the bottom of the bowl without tearing the leaves. Season with salt, pepper and a pinch of nutmeg and turn into another bowl. Repeat in seven more batches with the remaining spinach and butter, salt, pepper and nutmeg.

3. Return all the spinach with accumulated liquid to the glass bowl. Cover and set aside for up to 3 hours, or refrigerate for longer storage.

4. Just before serving, microwave the spinach at 80 percent power for 1 to 2 minutes, until heated through and just tender. Use a slotted spoon to serve.

PROFITEROLES

12 SERVINGS

1 cup water
6 tablespoons unsalted butter, cut into
    tablespoons
1 teaspoon sugar
⅛ teaspoon salt
1 cup all-purpose flour
4 eggs
Egg glaze, made by beating 1 egg with 1 teaspoon
    water
2 pints rich vanilla ice cream
Hot fudge sauce, preferably homemade (recipe
    follows)

1. Preheat the oven to 425° F. In a large saucepan, bring the water, butter, sugar and salt to a rolling boil over moderately high heat.

2. Add the flour all at once. Beat with a wooden spoon over the heat until the flour masses together in a ball, about 2 minutes. Remove from the heat.

3. Turn the flour paste into a food processor with the metal blade. One at a time, add the 4 eggs and process until smooth and shiny. (Or beat them in with a wooden spoon.)

4. Butter 2 large baking sheets. Using a pastry bag and a plain ½-inch tip, pipe the dough onto the baking sheets to form 18 to 20 mounds about 1 inch in diameter and ½ inch high on each sheet; leave about 2 inches in between the mounds. If you're not handy with a pastry bag, use 2 teaspoons. Brush the tops of the mounds with the egg glaze.

5. Bake for 20 minutes, or until puffed and browned. Remove from the oven and cut off the top third of each puff. Reserve the tops. Return the shells to the hot turned-off oven for 5 minutes, or until dry. Let cool, then set aside in a tightly covered container for up to 2 days, or freeze for up to 2 months.

6. To assemble the profiteroles, fill each small shell with vanilla ice cream and put the tops back in place. Arrange 3 on each plate and drizzle a little hot fudge sauce over each serving.

HOT FUDGE SAUCE

MAKES ABOUT 2 CUPS

This is the best hot chocolate sauce I've ever tasted. It can transform the simplest dessert into a grand finale.

1 cup heavy cream
1 cup sugar
¼ pound (1 stick) unsalted butter, cut into
    tablespoons
1 cup unsweetened Dutch-process cocoa powder,
    such as Droste or Poulain

1. In a medium-size heavy saucepan, preferably enameled cast iron, combine the cream, sugar and butter. Bring to a boil over moderate heat, stirring to dissolve the sugar.

2. Reduce the heat to low and boil without stirring (unless the mixture bubbles up too high) for 3 minutes, until thickened but not yet browned. Remove from the heat and whisk in the cocoa powder until smooth. Use hot or let cool, then cover and refrigerate for up to a week before serving. Reheat gently, preferably over a double boiler or in a microwave oven, stirring until smooth and warm.

Grilled Stuffed Grape Leaves

Barbecued Carnitas with Chipotle Chile Mayonnaise

Grilled Clams

•

Grilled Pepper-Lime Chicken

Grilled Corn San Miguel Style

Grilled Sweet Onion Salad

Black Bean Salad with Toasted Cumin and Jalapeño Peppers

Garden Tomatoes, Cucumbers and Radishes

•

Strawberry–Chocolate Chip Bread Pudding

Backyard Barbecue

FOR 16

Outdoor grilling is the favorite form of entertaining for many Americans. Count me in! I love those glowing coals and the rich, smoky flavor they impart to food. I'm especially comfortable with the casual, more informal style of entertaining grilling allows.

Most of the dishes in this menu are prepared over a charcoal fire, and for a crowd, you'll need one or two very large grills. I recommend cooking the chicken and the onions for the salad before everyone arrives. The chicken can be reheated in the oven or on the grill just before serving, or it can be put out at room temperature, as the other food is.

All three appetizers are done on the barbecue, but they cook very quickly. Since the grape leaves are stuffed in advance, you need only brush them with oil before setting them on the grill. The pork is marinated and skewered—ready to cook when you are. The clams need only a light scrubbing beforehand. Then store them in the refrigerator in a loosely covered bowl; don't leave them in a bowl of water or wrap them airtight or they will suffocate. They cook in just a minute or two, and they're delicious.

While the hors d'oeuvres are eclectic, the flavors of Mexico are apparent in the tart lime of the chicken, in the toasted cumin seeds that are the secret of this fabulous black bean salad and in the grilled corn. Since the corn works well with the new sweet hybrids we see in the supermarket almost year-round, you don't have to wait until August to enjoy it, and it's guaranteed to be a big hit.

With so much grilling, I prefer a completely done-in-advance ending to this fabulous barbecue, so I can relax. This Strawberry–Chocolate Chip Bread Pudding can be eaten warm or at room temperature, but for a crowd, I usually make it a day ahead and serve it chilled, cut into squares. It is an amazingly good dessert, just as good as it sounds… maybe even better.

Do-Ahead Planning

Up to 5 days before the barbecue: Make the Chipotle Mayonnaise.

Up to 2 days in advance: Cut up and marinate the pork for the Barbecued Carnitas. Soak the black beans.

The day before the barbecue: Stuff the grape leaves. Scrub the clams. Marinate the chicken. Blanch the corn on the cob. Make the Black Bean Salad. Make the Strawberry–Chocolate Chip Bread Pudding.

About 4 hours before guests arrive: Skewer the pork.

About 2 hours before guests arrive: Grill the chicken. Grill the onions and finish the Sweet Onion Salad. Remove the bean salad from the refrigerator. Prepare the platters of tomatoes, cucumbers and radishes; cover with a damp cloth and set aside.

Shortly before serving: Brush the grape leaves with oil and grill. Grill the Carnitas. Grill the clams. Reheat the chicken. Grill the corn.

GRILLED STUFFED GRAPE LEAVES

MAKES 64

These irresistible appetizers were first served to me by noted cookbook author Rose Levy Beranbaum at her country home. I made them for a video demonstration and couldn't keep the crew from eating every last one. I originally wrote the recipe for a smaller amount, but found we never managed to eat less than four per person, so halve this only if you dare.

> 64 grape leaves in brine (about two-thirds an 8-ounce jar)
> 2 logs (9 ounces each) mild goat cheese, such as Montrachet
> 32 sun-dried tomato halves packed in olive oil, drained and cut lengthwise in half
> Extra-virgin olive oil

1. Rinse the grape leaves and soak them in cold water for at least 1 hour to remove some of the brine. Drain and pat dry. If they have stems, remove them.

2. For each hors d'oeuvre, cut a thin slice of goat cheese and squeeze into a small cylinder. Set in the middle of the bottom edge of a grape leaf. Top with a piece of sun-dried tomato. Fold in the edges and roll up. Set aside, seam side down. (The grape leaves can be stuffed up to a day ahead. Wrap and refrigerate.)

3. Light a charcoal or gas grill to produce a hot fire. Brush the stuffed grape leaves with olive oil and grill over hot coals, turning once, until the leaves are lightly toasted and the cheese is heated through, 3 to 4 minutes. Serve hot.

BARBECUED CARNITAS

MAKES ABOUT 50

Tasty little morsels of grilled marinated pork served with toothpicks and a spicy smoked chile mayonnaise for dipping make a perfect summer appetizer. If cooking indoors, bake the pork cubes in a 325° F. oven for 1 to 1½ hours, until browned and crisp.

2½ pounds boneless pork loin
3 garlic cloves, crushed through a press
2 tablespoons fresh lemon juice
2 tablespoons extra-virgin olive oil
2 teaspoons coarse (kosher) salt
2 teaspoons ground cumin
1 teaspoon thyme
½ teaspoon freshly ground pepper
2 bay leaves, broken in half
Fresh coriander or parsley, for garnish
Chipotle Chile Mayonnaise (recipe follows)

1. Trim any excess fat off the pork and cut the meat into ¾-inch cubes.

2. Put the cubes of pork in a bowl and add the garlic, lemon juice, olive oil, salt, cumin, thyme, pepper and bay leaves. Toss to mix well. Cover and marinate for at least 2 hours at room temperature, or overnight in the refrigerator. (The pork can marinate for up to 2 days before grilling.)

3. Up to 6 hours before cooking, spear the pork on long metal skewers, leaving a little space between each piece of meat. Wrap and refrigerate; let stand at room temperature for at least 1 hour before cooking.

4. Light a charcoal or gas grill to produce a hot fire, or preheat the broiler. Grill the carnitas, turning, until well browned outside and no longer pink in the center, 12 to 15 minutes.

5. Slide the meat off the skewers onto a platter and garnish with sprigs of coriander. Serve with toothpicks and a bowl of Chipotle Chile Mayonnaise for dipping.

CHIPOTLE CHILE MAYONNAISE

MAKES ABOUT 2½ CUPS

Chipotle chiles are smoked jalapeños. In dried form, they are wrinkled and brownish beige; canned, they are usually packed with red adobo sauce. Either will do in this recipe. Along with the ancho chiles also used, they impart a rich, smoky flavor to this zesty mayonnaise.

5 ancho chiles
2 chipotle chiles, dried or canned
1½ cups mayonnaise
3 tablespoons fresh lemon juice
1 teaspoon cumin
½ teaspoon salt
⅓ cup heavy cream

1. On a hot griddle, lightly toast the ancho chiles over moderate heat, turning, until softened but not charred, about 1 minute. Stem and seed the ancho chiles and the chipotles, if you are using dried.

2. Put the ancho and dried chipotle chiles in a heatproof bowl and cover with 2½ cups boiling water. Let stand for 30 minutes. Remove the chiles and pat dry; reserve the soaking liquid.

3. In a food processor, combine the mayonnaise, lemon juice, cumin, salt, and softened chiles. (If you're using canned chipotles, rinse off the sauce and add them here.) Puree until smooth. With the machine on, slowly add the cream through the feed tube. Add ⅓ to ½ cup of the reserved chile soaking liquid, or enough to thin the mayonnaise to a coating consistency for dipping. Cover and refrigerate for up to 5 days before serving.

GRILLED CLAMS

MAKES 48

Clams on the grill are absolutely no work, and they're something of a conversation piece. They cook in just a minute or two over hot coals, and guests can watch as they pop open, their juices bubbling and sputtering over the fire.

4 dozen littleneck or cherrystone (hard-shell)
  clams
Lemon wedges

1. Choose tightly closed clams with unbroken shells. Scrub the clam shells to remove any loose grit. Refrigerate the clams, loosely wrapped, for up to 24 hours before cooking.

2. Light a charcoal or gas grill and get a hot fire going. Set the clams, right side up, on the grill rack. The long black hinges should be on the left; otherwise the clams will open upside-down and the juices will spill out. Not a tragedy if it happens—you can still eat them, and they'll still be delicious. Grill the clams over hot coals until they just open and the juices come bubbling up, 1 to 2 minutes. Serve with lemon wedges.

GRILLED PEPPER-LIME CHICKEN

16 SERVINGS

4 chickens (about 3 pounds each), quartered
1 cup fresh lime juice (from about 8 limes)
¾ cup extra-virgin olive oil
1 tablespoon coarse (kosher) salt
1½ tablespoons coarsely cracked black pepper
2 teaspoons hot pepper sauce
2 medium onions, sliced
Wedges of lime, for garnish

1. Trim off any excess fat from the chickens. Rinse and pat dry. With a small knife, stab the pieces of chicken in 2 or 3 of the meatiest spots.

2. In a large bowl, whisk together the lime juice, olive oil, salt, pepper and hot sauce. Add the chicken and onions and toss to coat with the marinade. Let stand, turning occasionally, for at least 1 hour at room temperature, or cover and refrigerate for up to 24 hours.

3. Preheat the grill or broiler. Over medium-hot coals or about 6 inches from the broiler, cook the chicken, skin toward the heat, for 5 minutes. Baste, turn and baste again. Cook for 10 minutes with the skin away from the heat. Baste, turn and baste. Finish with the skin toward the heat for 5 to 10 minutes, until done, still juicy but no longer pink. Serve with wedges of lime to squeeze over the chicken.

GRILLED CORN SAN MIGUEL STYLE

San Miguel d'Allende is a picturesque village in the lush Guanajuato region of Mexico. Behind its cathedral, the colorful food market bustles with shoppers every day of the week. The smell of fresh tortillas mixes with sweet tropical fruit, pungent fresh herbs and grilled meats. Snacks are sold along the street, including this savory grilled corn, sprinkled with lime juice and cheese.

Exact measurements don't make sense for this recipe. Make as many ears as you like—I usually allow 2 per person.

For 16 ears of corn:

½ cup mayonnaise
1¼ teaspoons hot pepper sauce
1 cup grated aged Sonoma Jack cheese (or
    substitute Cheddar)
3 to 4 limes, cut into wedges

1. As soon as you get the corn home, shuck the ears and blanch the corn in a large pot of boiling salted water for 2 to 3 minutes, just to soften it slightly. Drain and rinse under cold water to stop the cooking. (The corn can be blanched up to a day ahead. Hold at room temperature for up to 4 hours or in the refrigerator for longer. Be sure it is returned to room temperature before grilling.)

2. Light the grill. Mix the mayonnaise with the hot sauce. Put the corn over hot coals and cook, basting with the mayonnaise and turning, until lightly browned all over, 5 to 10 minutes. Remove from the heat and immediately sprinkle the grated cheese over the hot corn. Serve at once with lime wedges.

GRILLING

Grilling is a delightful, low-fat way to cook, whether you're barbecuing over charcoal or gas, whether you have a covered kettle grill or a small hibachi. To avoid a chemical taste on the food, I use an electric starter. When that's not possible, I use ordinary vegetable cooking oil instead of a petroleum starter. It works remarkably well.

Almost all foods derive extra flavor from grilling. If I'm going to the trouble of lighting the barbecue, I follow one of two strategies. I either grill as much of the meal as possible, parboiling vegetables if necessary so they don't take forever, or I grill the main course and make sure that everything else is done ahead and served either chilled or at room temperature. I almost never run back and forth between the barbecue and the stove. For a crowd, I'll frequently grill ahead and reheat the food in the oven or on the grill for convenience.

All kinds of wood chips and chunks are making their appearance these days—mesquite, hickory, pinion, applewood, cherry. They provide extra flavor; some burn longer than charcoal and some provide an extra-hot fire when you need it.

I prefer the chunks because they don't disappear as fast and can be used for smoking as well as grilling. All wood must be soaked for at least 30 minutes before putting it on the grill, or it will flare up and burn off. This is particularly important for smoking.

GRILLED SWEET ONION SALAD

16 SERVINGS

Though this dish can be made with either red or yellow sweet onions, the combination of the two is pretty.

> 4 large red (Bermuda) onions (about ½ pound each)
> 4 large sweet yellow (Spanish) onions (about ¾ pound each)
> About ½ cup extra-virgin olive oil
> Coarse (kosher) salt

1. Peel the onions and cut them into ⅜-inch-thick slices (do not separate the rings at this point). Light a charcoal or gas grill and adjust the fire or temperature setting so that the coals are hot.

2. Brush the onion slices on one side with oil. Set them on a grilling rack over the coals, oiled side down. Press down with a wide, flat spatula to help the heat penetrate the slices. Grill until the bottoms are lightly browned but not charred, 3 to 5 minutes. Brush the tops with oil, turn the slices and cook, again pressing with the spatula, until the second side is browned and the onions are softened but still slightly crunchy, 3 to 5 minutes longer.

3. Transfer the grilled onion slices to a serving bowl and separate into rings. Season lightly with coarse salt and drizzle on the remaining olive oil. Toss to mix. Serve warm or at room temperature.

BLACK BEAN SALAD WITH TOASTED CUMIN AND JALAPEÑO PEPPERS

16 TO 20 SERVINGS

Although there is a quick method for softening dried beans, I suggest soaking them overnight for more uniform texture.

> 2 pounds black turtle beans (frijoles negros)
> 1 large bay leaf
> 1½ tablespoons cumin seeds
> ½ cup sherry wine vinegar
> ⅔ cup extra-virgin olive oil
> 1 large sweet onion, finely diced (about 1½ cups)
> 2 medium green bell peppers, finely diced (about ¾ cup)
> 2 medium red bell peppers, finely diced (about ¾ cup)
> 1 large yellow bell pepper, diced
> 1 to 2 jalapeño peppers, seeded and minced
> 2 garlic cloves, crushed through a press
> 1½ teaspoons salt
> Freshly ground black pepper

1. Rinse the beans well and pick them over to remove any grit. Put them in a large, heavy pot with enough cold water to cover by at least 2 inches. Let stand overnight.

2. Drain the beans into a colander. Return them to the pot with the bay leaf and fresh water to cover by 2 inches. Bring to a boil, reduce the heat and simmer until the beans are tender but still firm enough to hold their shape, 1½ to 2 hours. Drain the beans; discard the bay leaf.

3. Meanwhile, in a small dry skillet, toast the cumin seeds over moderately high heat, shaking the pan frequently to toss them, until they are toasted and fragrant, about 2 minutes. Pour into a small bowl and set aside.

4. In a large bowl, combine the warm beans with the vinegar and oil. Toss to coat. Add the onion, bell peppers, jalapeños, garlic, toasted cumin and salt. Toss to mix. Let stand, tossing occasionally as the salad cools. Season with additional salt and black pepper to taste. Serve at room temperature. (The salad keeps well overnight. Cover and refrigerate; let return to room temperature before serving.)

STRAWBERRY–CHOCOLATE CHIP BREAD PUDDING

16 TO 20 SERVINGS

This incredibly appealing dessert, from Lola, a restaurant in New York City, is quite simply the best bread pudding I've ever eaten. It is good warm, at room temperature or cold. To serve it warm, you'll need a couple of attractive 2½-quart baking dishes 1½ inches deep. To serve it cold, as I frequently do for a crowd, I prepare it in two disposable aluminum ravioli pans 11¾ x 9⅜ inches. When the pudding is chilled and set, I cut it into squares and arrange it on a platter.

> 2 loaves (1 pound each) firm-textured white bread, preferably "sandwich" cut
> ¼ pound (1 stick) plus 2 tablespoons unsalted butter, at room temperature
> 1 pint strawberries
> 2 cups plus 1 to 2 tablespoons sugar
> ½ cup slivered blanched almonds
> ½ cup chocolate chips, preferably "mini"
> 2 quarts half-and-half or light cream
> 4 whole eggs
> 14 egg yolks
> 2 tablespoons vanilla extract

1. Preheat the oven to 350° F. with the racks spaced well apart. Lightly butter one side of all the bread slices with 1 stick of the butter. Set the bread, buttered side up, on 2 large baking sheets and bake for 15 minutes, or until lightly toasted.

2. Meanwhile, hull and thickly slice the strawberries. Put them in a bowl and, depending on their sweetness, sprinkle them with 1 to 2 tablespoons sugar. Toss and set aside.

3. When the bread is toasted, reduce the oven temperature to 325° F. and set a large roasting pan half-filled with water on each rack to act as a water bath. Trim the crusts off the bread and cut each slice of bread diagonally in half into triangles.

4. Use the remaining 2 tablespoons butter to grease 2 baking dishes, 2½ quarts each and 1½ inches deep. Line the sides of the baking dishes with the pieces of bread, points up. Line the bottom of the dishes (don't worry if there are some spaces in between the slices or if the pieces standing up lean over a bit). Stand the remaining bread points up, wedged between the bottom slices.

5. Scatter the almonds and chocolate chips over the bread and between the slices. Lift the strawberries with a slotted spoon, leaving any juices behind, and scatter them around the 2 baking dishes.

6. In a large saucepan, heat the half-and-half and the remaining 2 cups sugar over moderate heat, stirring to dissolve the sugar, until the mixture is hot but not boiling.

7. In a medium bowl, beat the whole eggs and egg yolks to blend. Whisk in the vanilla. Remove the hot half-and-half from the heat and immediately whisk in the eggs. Pour the custard into the 2 baking dishes.

8. Set the baking dishes into the roasting pans and bake for 35 to 40 minutes, or until the custard is just set. Remove from the water baths and serve warm, at room temperature or chilled.

Roquefort Caesar Salad

▪

Herbed Roast Pork Loin
Mustard Sauce
Oven-Roasted Garlic Potatoes
Green Beans with Lemon Butter

▪

Hazelnut Roulade with Banana Cream and
Hot Fudge Sauce

A Hearty Winter Meal

FOR 16

I'm not quite certain why a big chill and a big appetite go together, but there's no question they do. What I like about this food is that while the meal is warming and substantial, it is unquestionably sophisticated and welcome on the grandest table. Notice that both the first course and the dessert are served cold or at room temperature and the beans are cooked ahead, so you only have a couple of dishes to finish cooking once guests arrive.

If ever a recipe deserved its title, Caesar salad is it. Fresh lemon, fruity olive oil, pungent garlic, a hint of anchovy and the tang of fine aged Parmesan cheese make this truly the king of salads. I've added rich Roquefort cheese to increase the body and creaminess and add yet another dimension of flavor. While it's served as a first course here, the two cheeses make this substantial enough to serve as a main-course salad at lunch, which you'll appreciate if you love Caesar salad as much as I do.

The pork recipe is my version of a traditional Tuscan dish called *arista*, the most flavorful, succulent pork you've ever tasted. An easy Mustard Sauce, made from the drippings of the roast, is optional, but tasty.

Crisp garlicky potatoes, "fried" in the oven, and simple green beans dressed with lemon butter complete this savory meal.

After such a substantial dinner, I've chosen a dessert that is delectable but on the light side. In fact, this Hazelnut Roulade with Banana Cream and Hot Fudge Sauce was voted "best dessert sampled" by my neighbors, Dwight and Fran Yellen, who valiantly deserted their diets many a Sunday night to help me taste. It is one of my favorites as well. Besides being absolutely scrumptious, it can be completely assembled up to a day ahead.

Do-Ahead Planning

Up to 1 week in advance: Make the Hot Fudge Sauce.

Up to 2 days before the dinner: Prepare the lettuce. Grate the Parmesan cheese for the salad; refrigerate in a covered container.

Up to 1 day ahead: Make the garlic croutons for the salad. Marinate the pork roast. Boil the potatoes. Make the Hazelnut Roulade with Banana Cream.

Up to 3 hours before serving: Blanch the green beans. Set aside, covered, at room temperature.

About 1½ hours before you plan to begin serving: Roast the pork. Chop the anchovies and make the dressing for the salad.

Half an hour later: Put the potatoes in the oven to roast.

After the pork comes out of the oven and while it rests: Complete the Oven-Roasted Garlic Potatoes. Make the Mustard Sauce. Complete and serve the Roquefort Caesar Salad.

While the roast is being carved: Reheat and complete the Green Beans with Lemon Butter.

Shortly before serving dessert: Reheat the Hot Fudge Sauce.

ROQUEFORT CAESAR SALAD
16 SERVINGS

Two cheeses—Roquefort and Parmesan—make this salad quite substantial.

> 4 heads of romaine lettuce (about 1 pound each)
> 3 loaves of Italian bread (8 to 12 ounces each), cut into ½-inch-thick slices
> 1⅔ cups extra-virgin olive oil
> 6 garlic cloves—3 cut in half, 3 crushed through a press
> 3 cans (2 ounces each) flat anchovy fillets, drained and rinsed
> ⅔ pound Roquefort cheese
> 1¼ teaspoons coarse (kosher) salt
> 1¼ teaspoons coarsely cracked black pepper
> ½ cup fresh lemon juice
> ¾ teaspoon Worcestershire sauce
> ½ teaspoon hot pepper sauce
> 3 eggs
> ⅔ cup freshly grated Parmesan cheese

1. Cut off the tough bottom inch or two from each head of romaine. Separate the leaves, rinse well and soak in a large bowl of ice water for at least 30 minutes. Tear the leaves into large bite-size pieces and dry in a salad spinner. (The lettuce can be prepared up to 2 days ahead. Store in the refrigerator in plastic bags.)

2. Meanwhile, preheat the oven to 375° F. Brush the bread slices lightly on both sides with ⅔ cup of the olive oil. Arrange in a single layer on a couple of baking sheets and bake, turning once, until golden brown, 8 to 10 minutes per side. Let cool, then rub with the cut garlic. Cut the bread into ½- to ¾-inch cubes. (The garlic croutons can be made up to a day ahead. Store in a sealed plastic bag or airtight container at room temperature.)

3. In a large salad bowl, mash the crushed garlic with half the anchovies, half the Roquefort cheese and the salt and black pepper. Stir in the lemon juice, Worcestershire and hot sauce. Blend in the remaining 1 cup olive oil. Add the lettuce and toss to coat.

4. Coarsely chop the remaining anchovies. Dip the eggs in boiling water for 30 seconds. Immediately crack into the salad and toss to blend. Add the chopped anchovies, Parmesan cheese and garlic croutons. Toss again and crumble the remaining Roquefort cheese on top. Serve at once.

HERBED ROAST PORK LOIN

16 SERVINGS

The last time I served this roast, I was greeted with the compliment, "I forgot how good a piece of meat can be." Juicy and tender and full of flavor, this simple roast can serve as a basis for the most elegant of meals. Best of all, it's one of the easiest ways I know to feed a crowd.

2 pork loins (6 pounds each), bones in, but cracked
*   by butcher for easy carving, fat trimmed to a*
*   thin layer and scored in a diamond pattern*
2 tablespoons coarse (kosher) salt
1 tablespoon plus 1 teaspoon chopped fresh
*   rosemary, or 2 teaspoons dried*
1 tablespoon plus 1 teaspoon black peppercorns
2 teaspoons thyme
6–8 garlic cloves, crushed through a press
¼ cup fresh lemon juice
¼ cup extra-virgin olive oil

1. If the butcher has left any thick pieces of fat, trim them to a thin layer and score to match the rest of the roast. Wipe the roast dry and place, bones down, in 1 or 2 roasting pans.

2. In a spice grinder or food processor, combine the salt, rosemary, peppercorns and thyme. Process until the peppercorns are coarsely ground. In a small bowl, mix together the seasoned salt with the garlic, lemon juice and olive oil. Smear this paste all over the pork loins. Set aside at room temperature for 3 to 4 hours.

3. Preheat the oven to 425° F. Roast the pork for 15 minutes. Reduce the oven temperature to 325° F. and roast for 1½ hours, or until the pork registers 155° to 160° F. Let stand for about 10 minutes before carving. (If you wish to serve the mustard sauce, prepare it while the roast is resting.)

MUSTARD SAUCE

MAKES ABOUT 3 CUPS

Pan drippings from roast pork loin
1 cup dry white wine
⅓ cup champagne vinegar or white wine vinegar
1 cup heavy cream
1 tablespoon plus 1 teaspoon Dijon mustard
1 tablespoon cornstarch dissolved in ¼ cup water
Salt and freshly ground pepper
4 tablespoons unsalted butter, cut into
*   tablespoons*

1. Pour the fat out of the roasting pan and put the pan over moderately high heat. Add the white wine and vinegar and bring to a boil, scraping up the brown bits from the bottom of the pan. Boil until the liquid is reduced by half. Add 1½ cups water and boil for 2 minutes.

2. Whisk together the cream and mustard until blended. Gradually whisk into the liquid in the pan. Boil for 2 minutes. Stir in the dissolved cornstarch and boil, stirring, until thickened. Season the sauce with salt and pepper to taste. Remove from the heat, whisk in the butter and serve.

OVEN-ROASTED GARLIC POTATOES

16 SERVINGS

These crisp flavorful potatoes are great for any large dinner or buffet because they don't require peeling, and all the messy preparation can be done a day ahead.

> 6 pounds baking potatoes, preferably Idahos
> 6 garlic cloves, peeled and cut in half
> ⅔ cup olive oil, preferably extra-virgin, or other vegetable oil
> 2 teaspoons coarse (kosher) salt
> ¾ teaspoon freshly ground pepper

1. Scrub the potatoes well and rub dry; do not peel. Cut lengthwise into long, ½-inch wedges. Dump the potatoes into a large pot of boiling salted water. Cover and bring to a boil over high heat, about 2 minutes. Uncover and cook for 5 minutes. Drain and rinse under cold running water. Drain well. Spread the potatoes out on a kitchen towel and let dry. (The recipe can be prepared to this point up to a day ahead. Refrigerate the potatoes in a covered container.)

2. Preheat the oven to 325° F. In a small, heavy saucepan, steep the garlic in the oil over low heat until the garlic just begins to color, 10 to 15 minutes.

3. Spread out the potatoes on a large baking sheet. Season with the salt and pepper. Drizzle the oil over the potatoes and toss gently to coat. (I cook the garlic cloves along with the potatoes and discard them before serving.) Bake, tossing with a spatula every 10 to 15 minutes, for 1 hour. Increase the oven temperature to 425° F. and bake, tossing once or twice, until the potatoes are browned and crisp, 15 to 20 minutes longer.

OVEN-ROASTING VEGETABLES

When we think of cooking vegetables, blanching them in a large pot of boiling water or steaming them usually come to mind first. But especially for large quantities, oven-roasting is an excellent, easy way to cook root vegetables such as potatoes, carrots, turnips and onions. Whole garlic cloves, roasted in their skins, are delicious when prepared this way, and asparagus becomes a completely new treat.

To oven-roast a vegetable, peel off the outer skin and, if large, cut in half or quarters. Toss with enough good olive oil, preferably extra-virgin, to coat lightly and season sparingly with coarse salt and freshly ground pepper. That's all there is to it. For a tender vegetable like asparagus, roast at a high temperature (450° to 500° F.) for about 10 minutes, tossing once or twice. Squeeze a little lemon juice over them before serving. Roast root vegetables for a longer time at a lower temperature in the same roasting pan as the meat or fowl for extra flavor. Turn once or twice for even browning.

Because roasting avoids large pots of water that need to be drained, I find it a convenient way to cook large quantities (5 pounds or more). I frequently use a disposable aluminum roasting pan for easy cleanup. In a pinch, the vegetables can be roasted ahead, set aside at room temperature and reheated in a hot oven for about 5 minutes just before serving.

For a large party, the presentation of the food means a lot. It sets the tone of the party as much as the decor of the room, flowers or music. In essence, the food is the theme of the party, and how you set it out reflects your expectations of what the event will be like. If you've pulled out your best china, silver and linen and set places formally around a table, guests will behave differently than if you've piled up the food informally in colorful bowls on a picnic table with stacks of paper plates.

I like party food to be plentiful, colorful and tasty. If the food looks wonderful to begin with, garnishes can be held to a minimum. However, a little color contrast always helps, especially with some foods that are not that great to look at. When a dish does need garnish, try to pick something appropriate. If you've used fresh tarragon or dill in a recipe, use that as your embellishment. Lemons, limes and radishes, sliced, carved or cut into wedges, as well as cherry tomatoes and olives, are common but indispensable adornments. Whenever possible, arrange the garnish so that it won't be destroyed as soon as the first person digs in. For large crowds I design my decorations around the rim of the platter rather than in the center.

Professionals offer other tricks. Restaurateur and corporate caterer Richard Lavin (of Lavin's and Sofi in New York) recommends simple geometric arrangements on dark platters for a stylish, dramatic effect. Caterer Timothy Maxim of Taste in San Francisco likes to use clear plastic blocks to create different heights on a buffet table, adding another dimension to the visual interest. Simply lining a bowl or platter with a contrasting colored leaf—green kale or red cabbage—can dress up a salad.

Try to keep dishes refilled and fresh looking throughout the party. One way to do this is to put out only half of what you have to serve. When the food has diminished less than halfway, or whenever it looks tired, whisk the bowl or platter into the kitchen and refill; at the same time, refresh it with a new garnish.

And if your party has a theme, play it to the hilt. Carry out the idea not only in the food itself and the way it's garnished and presented, but in the decorations and accessories you set around the room. And don't forget the music!

GREEN BEANS WITH LEMON BUTTER

16 SERVINGS

3 pounds green beans, trimmed and broken in half
6 tablespoons unsalted butter, cut into pieces
1½ teaspoons grated lemon zest
¼ cup fresh lemon juice
Salt and freshly ground pepper

1. In a large pot of boiling salted water, cook the green beans over high heat until tender, 5 to 7 minutes. Drain into a colander and rinse under cold running water, tossing, for 20 seconds; drain. (The green beans can be blanched and refreshed up to 6 hours before serving. Set aside at room temperature or cover and refrigerate for longer keeping.)

2. Either return the beans to the hot pot or, if you have done them ahead, add them to a large saucepan set over high heat. Toss over the heat until excess moisture is evaporated, about 1 minute. Add the butter and toss over the heat until the butter is melted and the beans are hot and coated with butter, about 2 minutes. Add the lemon zest and juice and toss. Remove from the heat and season with salt and pepper to taste; toss again and serve.

Hazelnut Roulade with Banana Cream and Hot Fudge Sauce

16 SERVINGS

The recipe for the flourless cake used in this dessert was given to me many, many years ago by Lenore Gordon, the mother of my good friend Linda Gordon (now Linda Wurzel of Cincinnati). She bakes it in a 10-inch springform pan for about 45 minutes to produce a stunning nut torte. I kept it a secret all this time, as she requested, but she's agreed to let me share it now.

The only trick to this easy cake, which is really a fallen soufflé, is to grind the hazelnuts with a nut grinder to produce a light, fluffy nut flour. The roulade can be assembled up to a day ahead. It will yield 16 slices, so be forewarned—no seconds here, unless you want to have a second dessert standing by.

½ pound hazelnuts (filberts)
9 eggs, separated
1 cup granulated sugar
½ teaspoon orange extract
½ teaspoon almond extract
1½ cups heavy cream
3 tablespoons confectioners' sugar
¾ teaspoon vanilla extract
4 to 5 medium bananas
Hot Fudge Sauce (page 46)

1. Preheat the oven to 375° F. Butter a 17 x 12-inch half-sheet or jellyroll pan. Line the pan with wax paper, allowing the long ends to extend over the side a little, and flour the entire pan; tap out any excess. Without skinning the hazelnuts, grind them in a nut grinder.

2. In a large bowl, beat the egg yolks lightly. Gradually beat in the granulated sugar and continue beating until the mixture is light in color and falls from the beater in a slowly dissolving ribbon, about 5 minutes. Beat in the orange and almond extracts.

3. Beat the egg whites until stiff but not dry. Sprinkle about one-third of the nuts over the egg yolk mixture. Scoop about one-third of the egg whites on top. Fold until partially blended. Repeat with half the remaining nuts and egg whites. Then add the remaining nuts and egg whites and fold just until the mixture is blended and no streaks are visible.

4. Turn the batter into the prepared pan and bake in the upper third of the oven for 12 to 14 minutes, or until the cake is puffed and browned and slightly springy to the touch. Let cool in the pan on a large rack for 5 minutes.

5. Set a slightly dampened clean kitchen towel on top of the rack. Invert the pan to unmold the cake onto the towel. Carefully peel off the wax paper. Cover with another dampened towel. Starting at one of the long sides, loosely roll up the cake in the towels. Let cool for 1 hour.

6. Meanwhile, beat the cream until it mounds softly. Add the confectioners' sugar and vanilla and beat until stiff. Cut the bananas crosswise on the diagonal into ¼-inch-thick slices.

7. After an hour, unroll the cake (if you wait longer, it will stiffen and may crack when you roll it). Remove the top towel and spread the whipped cream over the cake. Arrange the banana slices on top of the cream. Roll up again, using the edge of the towel to help, and set the cake, seam side down, on a large serving platter. Cover with plastic wrap and refrigerate for up to 24 hours before serving. (If you don't have a big enough platter, refrigerate the cake on the half-sheet pan and cut the slices in the kitchen.)

8. To serve, reheat the Hot Fudge Sauce, if necessary. Drizzle a little of the warm sauce decoratively over the top of the roulade. Cut the roulade into 1-inch slices and spoon Hot Fudge Sauce on top of each serving.

Couscous Party

FOR 16

Couscous with Lamb, Chicken and Sweet
Potatoes

Marinated Black Olives

Orange-Radish Salad

Pickled Turnips

Pita Bread

Mint Tea

.

Lemon Sorbet with Cointreau and Berries

There aren't a lot of restaurants where you can find a good couscous these days, and since it's festive one-dish party food, why not at your house? Couscous is one of those great Mediterranean dishes that is a meal in itself. Only a few colorful accompaniments are needed to create a veritable feast. The hot sauce, olives and tangy, refreshing salads that accompany it make a striking, tantalizing spread.

Paula Wolfert, author of *The Cooking of South-West France,* brought authentic couscous into the American kitchen in her delightful classic *Couscous and Other Good Food from Morocco.* I am indebted to her for the Orange-Radish Salad and for being so generous with her knowledge. Dorie Simon, owner of St. Mark's Gallery in New York, another excellent cook who lived in Tangiers, also showed me how this dish should be prepared. Nonetheless, I confess at the outset that for ease of preparation I have opted for the precooked couscous sold in supermarkets across the country. So that you can be as relaxed as your guests, cook the meat and vegetables for the couscous a day in advance. The couscous grain itself is prepared in stages the day of the party.

If oranges and radishes sound like an odd couple to you, you're in for a pleasant surprise. The bite of the radish and the refreshing sweetness of the orange match beautifully, as do their colors. Marinated Olives and pink Pickled Turnips add additional fillips of flavor.

For a lovely, simple dessert, appropriately light after the couscous, buy a good-quality lemon ice. Pack it into a metal ring mold, freeze it solid and unmold onto a platter (use a hot towel, if necessary, to unmold). Drizzle the Cointreau over the sorbet, which will help soften it enough to serve, and fill the center with fresh strawberries and/or blueberries.

Do-Ahead Planning

Up to 1 month in advance: Marinate the olives.

Up to 10 days in advance: Make the Pickled Turnips.

The day before the party: Prepare the Couscous with Lamb, Chicken and Sweet Potatoes through Step 4. Make the ring of lemon ice.

Up to 6 hours before serving: Give the couscous its first cooking and spread it out to dry.

Up to 3 hours before serving: Make the Orange-Radish Salad through Step 2.

About 30 minutes before serving: Steam the couscous. Finish the Couscous with Lamb, Chicken and Sweet Potatoes. Finish the Orange-Radish Salad. Unmold the sorbet ring and return to the freezer until ready to serve.

COUSCOUS WITH LAMB, CHICKEN AND SWEET POTATOES

16 TO 18 SERVINGS

For convenience, I use the precooked couscous that is sold in boxes in most supermarkets. If you own a couscousière, by all means use it, but the dish can be made in any large (at least 9-quart) pot, preferably an enameled cast-iron casserole or heavy stockpot. If you don't have a pot large enough, make the couscous in two smaller ones.

¼ pound (1 stick) plus 2 tablespoons unsalted
    butter
3 tablespoons olive oil
4 medium onions, thickly sliced
1 teaspoon ground ginger
1 teaspoon ground cinnamon
½ teaspoon grated nutmeg
½ teaspoon ground coriander
½ teaspoon freshly ground black pepper
¼ teaspoon cayenne pepper
¼ teaspoon turmeric
2 large pinches of saffron threads
4 pounds boneless lamb shoulder, trimmed of all
    excess fat and cut into 1½-inch pieces
1 can (28 ounces) Italian peeled tomatoes, cut in
    half, with their juices reserved
2 tablespoons sugar
2 teaspoons salt
8 medium carrots, peeled and cut crosswise on the
    diagonal into 1½-inch lengths
1 cup raisins
4 sweet potatoes (about 2 pounds), peeled, cut
    lengthwise in half and then into ¾-inch
    slices
3 pounds skinned and boned chicken breasts and/
    or thighs, cut into 1- to 1½-inch pieces
8 small zucchini (about 2 pounds), cut lengthwise
    in half and then into 1½-inch lengths
1 cup (4 ounces) slivered blanched almonds
2 tablespoons fresh lemon juice
2 teaspoons to 2 tablespoons harissa or sambal
    oolek, depending on how hot you like it
3 pounds couscous (recipe follows)

1. In a large flameproof casserole, melt the butter in the oil over moderate heat. Add the onions and cook, stirring occasionally, until they just begin to brown, 10 to 15 minutes.

2. Add the ginger, cinnamon, nutmeg, coriander, black pepper, cayenne, turmeric and saffron. Cook, stirring, for 1 minute to toast the spices.

3. Add the lamb and increase the heat to moderately high. Cook, stirring frequently, until the lamb is browned on the outside, about 10 minutes. Add the tomatoes and their liquid and enough water to barely cover the meat. Stir in the sugar and salt. Partially cover and simmer for 45 minutes.

4. Add the carrots and raisins and simmer for 45 minutes longer, or until the lamb is tender. (The recipe can be prepared to this point up to a day in advance. Let cool, then cover and refrigerate. Scrape off any surface fat and reheat before proceeding.)

5. Add the sweet potatoes and simmer for 5 minutes. Add the chicken and zucchini, the almonds, lemon juice and harissa to taste. Simmer until the chicken is cooked through but still moist and the vegetables are tender, about 10 minutes longer.

6. To serve, mound the cooked couscous on a large platter or in a shallow serving bowl. With a perforated skimmer or slotted spoon, transfer the meat and vegetables to the platter, arranging them around the couscous. Serve the broth in a separate bowl with a ladle; use to moisten the couscous. In a small bowl, mix some of the broth with additional harissa to taste to pass as a hot sauce.

Couscous

Couscous is Moroccan pasta—tiny grains of semolina wheat flour. (The word also refers to the entire dish of the cooked grain with whatever vegetables, meats and sauce are served with it.) Like any dried pasta, couscous expands when it is cooked. Traditionally, couscous is steamed three times. In between steaming it is dried and raked with the hands, so that when it is finally served, each grain is separate, light and fluffy. If you don't precook the couscous, it will expand in your stomach, giving you the uncomfortable feeling of having eaten too much.

These days, most couscous is precooked, which means it fluffs up much more with one cooking and can even be combined directly with liquid rather than being steamed. Even the couscous sold by the pound at health food stores and Middle Eastern groceries has most likely been precooked. For a crowd, I recommend this type of couscous. It needs only one or at most two steamings and is easy to handle.

I've experimented with cooking the couscous directly in the broth it will be served with and found it turned out leaden and heavy. There is plenty of flavor from the meat, vegetables and sauce. For a big party, cook the pasta in boiling salted water as directed in the recipe the morning of the party. Spread it out on a baking sheet or in a roasting pan and let dry, occasionally raking the couscous and breaking up any clumps with your fingers, until the grains are dry and not tacky to the touch. Cover with plastic wrap and a kitchen towel and set aside at room temperature. Shortly before serving, moisten the couscous, dump it into a colander and steam, uncovered, over boiling water or over the stew with which you are going to serve it for 20 minutes, until heated through. Then turn it out onto a platter or into a large bowl, top with a few tablespoons of butter and fluff up. Encourage guests to moisten the couscous with broth and/or hot sauce made from *harissa*, Middle Eastern chile paste, mixed with some of the broth.

Couscous

3 pounds couscous
3 tablespoons unsalted butter, cut into tablespoons

1. If you've bought the couscous loose, be sure it is precooked. For every cup of couscous, bring 1½ cups salted water to a boil. Add the couscous, stir, cover and remove from the heat. Let stand for about 5 minutes, or until all the liquid is absorbed. Spread out the couscous in a roasting pan and let dry, occasionally raking the couscous with your fingers and breaking up any lumps. When the couscous is no longer sticky, cover with plastic wrap and a kitchen towel and set aside at room temperature. (The recipe can be prepared to this point up to 6 hours before serving.)

2. About half an hour before serving, moisten the couscous with 1½ cups water. Dump into a colander set over a pot of boiling water (depending on the size of your colander, this may be easier to do in 2 batches). Steam the couscous, uncovered, for 20 minutes, or until hot. Transfer to a bowl, toss with the butter and serve.

MARINATED BLACK OLIVES

MAKES ABOUT 1½ QUARTS

You won't believe the difference a simple marinade makes for even an ordinary supermarket olive. Since these are so easy and only improve upon standing, I like to make a big batch.

2 pounds Moroccan or Mediterranean black olives
    (try at your deli counter or look for
    Peloponnese or Progresso brand on the shelf)
6 small dried hot red peppers
6 garlic cloves, smashed
2 tablespoons herbes de Provence
Extra-virgin olive oil

Put the olives in a stone crock or glass jar; use two if necessary. Add the hot peppers and garlic. Sprinkle on the herbes de Provence and stir to distribute. Pour in enough olive oil to cover and let stand at room temperature, loosely covered, for at least 1 week and up to 3 months before serving.

PICKLED TURNIPS

MAKES ABOUT 1½ PINTS

4 medium turnips (about 1 pound), peeled, cut in
    half and sliced
1 small beet, peeled, and quartered
2 garlic cloves, bruised
2 cups cold water
2 tablespoons coarse (kosher) salt
2 teaspoons sugar
1 tablespoon distilled white vinegar

1. Put the turnips and beet in a large glass jar. Tuck in the garlic cloves. Stir together the water, salt and sugar to dissolve the salt and sugar. Add the vinegar and pour over the vegetables. Let stand in a cool place for 3 days. Then cover and refrigerate for up to 2 weeks.

2. Drain the turnips and discard the beet before serving.

ORANGE-RADISH SALAD

16 SERVINGS

Paula Wolfert, author of *Couscous and Other Good Food from Morocco*, produces some of the tastiest food I have ever eaten. This attractive, unusual salad from that book is a refreshing accompaniment to other more highly seasoned dishes.

8 bunches of red radishes
⅓ cup sugar
⅔ cup fresh lemon juice
3 tablespoons orange flower water, optional but
    authentic
½ teaspoon salt
8 navel oranges
½ teaspoon ground cinnamon

1. Wash and trim the radishes. Using the shredding disk on a food processor (or the long holes on a hand grater), finely shred the radishes. Squeeze them gently to remove excess liquid. Put the radishes in a glass serving bowl and sprinkle with the sugar, lemon juice, orange flower water and salt. Toss to mix, cover and refrigerate for up to 3 hours.

2. Using a sharp paring knife, cut away the orange peel, removing all the bitter white pith. Holding the oranges over a bowl to catch the juices, slice down along both sides of each membrane to remove the orange sections. Put them in the bowl with the juice, cover and refrigerate for up to 3 hours.

3. Shortly before serving, add the oranges and their juice to the radishes. Toss lightly to mix and sprinkle with a dusting of cinnamon.

Noonday Brunch

FOR 16

Passion Fruit Mimosas

Cheese Straws (page 104)

Sour Cream and Two-Caviar Dip (page 133)
with Endive Spears and Other Crudités

Rich Liver Mousse with Toasted Hazelnuts

■

Baked Eggs with Mushrooms and Browned
Onions

Avocado, Strawberry and Orange Salad

Gougères

Grilled Marinated Quail

Gratinéed Tomatoes

■

Marbled Sour Cream Coffee Cake

Though it surprises me, the meal most people ask me advice about and for recipes for is brunch. Daytime entertaining is steadily growing in popularity. For parents and busy professionals, late mornings and afternoons are times when they have extra energy, the hour implies a more relaxed, casual form of entertaining, usually with less alcohol, and brunch ends early.

Planning a menu for brunch is fun because it allows such a wide range of food. It can be a breakfast-brunch, with a major egg dish along with accompaniments, a lunch-brunch with heavier afternoon food and perhaps more alcohol, or an all-day open house, with a substantial buffet as well as passed hors d'oeuvres. Since you will be serving early in the day, food that can be prepared in advance is all the more important.

Here's an excellent "noonish" brunch. Greet guests with Passion Fruit Mimosas. Pass the Cheese Straws. Have the caviar dip set out, surrounded by Belgian endive spears, with a basket of assorted crudités next to it. Accompany the liver mousse with rounds of toast or crackers.

I first encountered the pairing of avocados and strawberries aboard a sixty-five-foot Swan sailboat moored off Newport, Rhode Island, during the 1983 America's Cup race. The pastel combination was served as a composed salad at dinner, and it took us all by surprise. It was delicious. For a crowd, I've combined them here with oranges as well for a colorful and delightful starter.

I like these Baked Eggs with Mushrooms and Browned Onions for entertaining because the entire dish can be assembled the night before and baked at the last minute. Marinated quail make a tasty side dish and might be something of a conversation piece, but you can substitute your favorite sausage—broiled or grilled—if you prefer. Simple broiled tomato halves, topped with seasoned bread crumbs, provide a colorful accompaniment to brighten up the plates.

Gougères are traditional French savory pastries from the region of Burgundy. If you've never had them, you're in for a treat—puffs of crisp golden pastry loaded with nutty Gruyère cheese. Here they're served instead of bread and rolls. Formed into smaller puffs, they make great cocktail nibbles. These have the added convenience of being made in advance and frozen.

An easy dessert, the moist Marbled Sour Cream Coffee Cake serves 16 easily and keeps extremely well. If you prefer not to freeze it, you can still bake it five days in advance and store it in a cool place.

Do-Ahead Planning

Up to 2 months in advance: Bake and freeze the Cheese Straws, Marbled Sour Cream Coffee Cake and Gougères.

Up to 3 days in advance: Make the liver mousse. Cook the eggs, shell them immediately and store them in a bowl of cold water to cover in the refrigerator.

The day before the brunch: Make the caviar dip. Prepare the endive and other crudités. Assemble the Baked Eggs with Mushrooms and Browned Onions. Marinate the quail.

Up to 4 hours before serving: Prepare the oranges and strawberries for the salad. Prepare the bread crumb topping for the tomatoes.

About 1 hour before serving: Arrange the dip and crudités. Pour the orange juice and passion fruit liqueur into champagne flutes. Complete the Avocado, Strawberry and Orange Salad. Halve the tomatoes; cover with the topping.

About 30 minutes before you plan to serve: Bake the egg gratin. Bake the frozen Gougères to thaw and reheat them.

As soon as the eggs come out: Broil or grill the quail and the tomatoes.

PASSION FRUIT MIMOSAS

FOR EACH DRINK

In a champagne flute, combine 2 tablespoons (1 ounce, or a jigger) fresh orange juice and the same amount of Grand Passion passion fruit liqueur. Add a squeeze of lime wedge to each glass. Fill with brut Champagne and garnish with a thin slice of lime.

RICH LIVER MOUSSE WITH TOASTED HAZELNUTS

MAKES ABOUT 2½ CUPS

½ cup hazelnuts (filberts)
1 pound chicken livers
¼ pound (1 stick) plus 4 tablespoons unsalted butter
3 medium shallots, finely chopped (about ¼ cup)
½ cup Madeira
¾ teaspoon salt
⅜ teaspoon freshly ground pepper
⅛ teaspoon freshly grated nutmeg
1 tablespoon Cognac

1. Preheat the oven to 325° F. Spread the nuts out in a small baking pan. Toast in the oven, shaking the pan once or twice, until the skins are cracked and the nuts are golden brown, 10 to 15 minutes. Dump the nuts onto a clean kitchen towel and rub them around to remove most of the outer brown skins. Transfer to a food processor and coarsely chop.

2. Trim the livers, cutting off any yellow or green spots and large clumps of veins. Discard any livers that are particularly strong smelling. Cut each lobe in half.

3. Melt 1 stick of the butter. Let cool to tepid.

4. In a large skillet, melt the remaining 4 tablespoons butter over moderately high heat. Add the shallots and sauté, stirring frequently, until softened but not browned, about 1 minute. Add the livers and sauté, tossing, for about 2 minutes, until the livers are browned outside and slightly stiffened, but still rosy pink inside; do not overcook. Scrape the livers, shallots and pan juices into the food processor with the nuts.

5. Add the Madeira to the skillet and boil until reduced by half; remove from the heat. Puree the livers for 10 seconds. With the machine on, slowly pour in the cooled melted butter. Gradually add the Madeira through the feed tube. Scrape down the sides of the bowl. Add the salt, pepper, nutmeg and Cognac. Puree for at least 1 full minute, stopping several times to scrape down the sides of the bowl, until the mousse is as smooth as it can be.

6. Scrape into small crocks or a serving dish, cover and refrigerate for up to 3 days before serving.

Baked Eggs with Mushrooms and Browned Onions

16 SERVINGS

2 dozen eggs
¼ pound (1 stick) plus 6 tablespoons unsalted butter
3 tablespoons olive oil
1 pound mushrooms, sliced
1¼ teaspoons salt
½ teaspoon freshly ground black pepper
1 teaspoon lemon juice
5 medium onions, sliced
⅛ teaspoon (loosely packed) saffron threads
⅔ cup all-purpose flour
1 quart milk
⅛ teaspoon each: nutmeg, thyme, cayenne pepper
⅔ cup heavy cream or additional milk
⅔ cup shredded Gruyère or imported Swiss cheese

1. Put the eggs in a large saucepan or flame-proof casserole. Add cold water to cover by at least ½ inch. Bring to a boil, reduce the heat and simmer for 12 minutes. Remove from the heat and let stand for 5 minutes. Pour off the water and fill the pan with cold water. Peel the eggs immediately to avoid a dark ring around the yolk. (The eggs can be cooked and peeled up to 3 days in advance and refrigerated in a bowl of cold water.)

2. In a large skillet, melt 2 tablespoons of the butter in 1 tablespoon of the oil over moderately high heat. Add the mushrooms and sauté, tossing frequently, until lightly browned, about 10 minutes. Season with ¼ teaspoon of the salt, ¼ teaspoon of the black pepper and the lemon juice. Set aside.

3. In a large heavy saucepan or flameproof casserole, melt 1 stick of the butter in the remaining 2 tablespoons olive oil over moderately low heat. Add the onions, cover and cook slowly for 5 minutes. Uncover, increase the heat to moderate and cook, stirring occasionally, until deep golden brown, about 30 minutes.

4. Crumble the saffron over the onions. Add the flour and cook, stirring, for 2 minutes. Gradually whisk in the milk. Bring to a boil and cook, whisking, for 1 to 2 minutes, until thickened. Reduce the heat to a simmer and cook, stirring frequently, for 3 minutes. Season with the nutmeg, thyme, cayenne and remaining 1 teaspoon salt and ¼ teaspoon black pepper. Thin the sauce with the cream. Remove from the heat and set aside.

5. Use 2 tablespoons of the remaining butter to grease 2 large gratin or shallow baking dishes (or use a single dish if you have one large enough). Slice the eggs. Spread a thin layer of the onion-cream sauce over the bottom of each dish. Cover with a layer of half the egg slices, overlapping as necessary. Season the eggs lightly with additional salt and freshly ground pepper to taste. Spoon half the sauce over the eggs and cover with half the sautéed mushrooms. Arrange a layer of the remaining egg slices, season with salt and pepper and top with the remaining mushrooms and the remaining sauce. Sprinkle the cheese evenly over the top and dot with the remaining 2 tablespoons butter. (The recipe can be completely assembled to this point up to a day ahead. Set aside at room temperature for up to 3 hours or cover and refrigerate overnight.)

6. Preheat the oven to 375° F. Bake the gratins until bubbling hot and lightly browned on top, 15 to 20 minutes. Serve hot.

Avocado, Strawberry and Orange Salad

16 SERVINGS

4 navel oranges
3 pints strawberries
3 tablespoons balsamic vinegar
¼ cup avocado or corn oil
1 teaspoon coarsely cracked black pepper
4 ripe California avocados, preferably Hass
2 to 3 tablespoons fresh lemon juice

1. Cut the ends off the oranges and cut off the peel, removing all of the bitter white pith. Cut the oranges crosswise into ½-inch slices and then cut the slices into ½-inch pieces.

2. Hull the strawberries and halve or quarter them, depending on their size. In a medium bowl, combine the strawberries and oranges with the balsamic vinegar, avocado oil and pepper. Toss gently. (The recipe can be prepared to this point up to 4 hours ahead. Cover and refrigerate.)

3. Up to 2 hours before serving, peel the avocados and cut them off the pit lengthwise into ½-inch slices. Arrange around the rim of a large platter and brush all over with the lemon juice to prevent discoloration. Mound the strawberries and oranges in the center, cover with plastic wrap and let stand at room temperature until serving time.

Gougères

MAKES 32 TO 36

For this quantity of dough, a food processor is a great arm-saver, though you can beat the eggs into the dough with a wooden spoon if you prefer.

3 cups water
½ pound (2 sticks) plus 2 tablespoons unsalted butter, cut into tablespoons
2½ teaspoons salt
½ teaspoon freshly ground black pepper
⅛ teaspoon cayenne pepper
3 cups all-purpose flour
12 eggs, at room temperature
1 cup freshly grated Parmesan cheese (4 ounces)
½ pound Gruyère cheese, finely diced (about 2 cups)

1. Preheat the oven to 425° F. Butter 3 large, heavy baking sheets.

2. In a medium saucepan, combine the water, butter, salt, black pepper and cayenne. Bring to a rolling boil over moderately high heat. Add the flour all at once and beat with a wooden spoon over the heat until the dough is completely blended and masses together in the center of the pan.

3. Scoop one-third of the hot dough into the food processor. With the machine on, add 4 of the eggs through the feed tube, one at a time. Blend until smooth and satiny. Turn into a bowl. Repeat 2 more times with the remaining dough and eggs. (There's no need to wash the bowl in between batches.)

4. Add the Parmesan and Gruyère cheese to the dough and mix well with a wooden spoon to blend. Drop the dough by heaping tablespoons onto the buttered baking sheets, leaving about 2 inches in between. (If you have only 2 sheets, or room in your oven for only 2, bake one sheet after the others.)

5. Bake for 15 minutes. Reduce the oven temperature to 375° F. and bake for 20 to 25 minutes longer, until crusty and golden brown. Serve warm or at room temperature. (Gougères can be baked up to 2 months in advance and frozen.)

MINI-GOUGÈRES Prepare the dough as directed above, but drop by heaping teaspoons onto the baking sheets and bake at 425° F. for 10 to 15 minutes. Makes about 110.

GRILLED MARINATED QUAIL

SERVES 16

One quail each is enough for a side dish. If using this recipe as a main-course meat, serve two per person.

16 quail, split in half
¾ cup fresh lime juice
¾ cup extra-virgin olive oil
2 medium onions, sliced
3 bay leaves
2 teaspoons hot pepper sauce
1 teaspoon ground coriander
1 teaspoon ground cumin
1 ½ teaspoons salt
½ teaspoon freshly ground black pepper

1. Put the quail in a large shallow bowl. Add all the remaining ingredients and toss to coat well. Marinate, turning occasionally, for 2 hours at room temperature or, preferably, cover and refrigerate longer, overnight if you can.

2. Preheat the broiler or light the grill. Place the quail skin side away from the flame and grill for 6 to 8 minutes, until lightly browned. Turn skin side toward the heat and grill about 5 minutes longer, until the skin is browned and the meat is cooked through. Serve hot or at room temperature.

QUAIL

Until I was well over thirty I had never seen a quail except in the zoo. My husband, who is from a small town in the Midwest and was relatively unsophisticated about food when I first met him, grew up with them. He taught me a thing or two about game. At a fancy restaurant, he—not I—could determine with one bite whether a venison steak or supposedly wild pheasant had the pedigree it claimed. He knew because he'd hunted with his father from the time he could walk, and they ate whatever they shot. Now domesticated quail and wild game are appearing with increasing frequency on the menus of fine restaurants, in butcher shops and even prepackaged in the meat sections of supermarkets. To many suburbanites and city slickers like me, this boom in the distribution of game and game birds means we have to learn how to use these wonderful new meats.

Quail are tiny and weigh no more than four ounces each. They have a distinctive flavor that is not unpleasantly gamy. Like many other game birds, quail are best either cooked quickly under high heat or slowly with some moisture. Because the meat is dark, it can be dry and often benefits from an oil-based marinade—both for flavor and as a tenderizer. I like quail for entertaining because the little birds are so dressy and so easy to prepare. Though you can use a knife and fork, I like to pick them up with my hands. In this menu, I serve them—split in half, marinated and broiled—instead of sausage as an accompaniment to eggs. Prepared in exactly the same way and arranged on top of an interesting mix of tossed greens (allowing two per person), they would make a delicious, chic luncheon salad.

NOONDAY BRUNCH for 16 (clockwise
from bottom right): Grilled Marinated
Quail; Gratinéed Tomatoes; Avocado,
Strawberry and Orange Salad;
Gougères; Baked Eggs with
Mushrooms and Browned Onions

CHRISTMAS DINNER for 16 to 20 (counterclockwise from bottom left): Ham Braised in Port; Potatoes au Gratin; Zucchini Bread from the Inn at Thorn Hill; Glazed Carrots and Snow Peas; Maple-Butternut Bisque.

SOUTHWESTERN BUFFET for 16 to 20 (from left): Caviar Nachos; Spiced Nuts; Carrot and Jicama Salad; Corn, Rice and Bean Salad with Chile Vinaigrette; Barbacoa of Lamb with Tortillas; Fresh Tomato Salsa.

EASY SOUTHERN SHRIMP BOIL for 20 to 24 (clockwise from left): Shrimp Boil; Pesto Deviled Eggs; Cheese Straws; Summer Crudités with Two-Caviar Dip; Red and Yellow Cherry Tomatoes; Corn on the Cob; 24-Hour Salad.

THE ULTIMATE TAILGATE PARTY for 24 (clockwise from bottom): Potato Salad with Sweet Sausages and Mushrooms; Honey-Pecan Cake; Best Fudge Brownies; Grilled Marinated Flank Steak; olives; apples; Green Bean Salad with Roasted Red Peppers; Cheddar cheese; Chicken Pasta Salad with Lemon-Sesame Dressing.

Marbled Sour Cream Coffee Cake

16 SERVINGS

This recipe is from my last cookbook, *Tailgate Parties*, but it proved so popular, keeps so well and serves so many that I am repeating it here.

½ pound semisweet or sweet dark chocolate, broken into pieces
3 cups all-purpose flour
1½ teaspoons baking powder
1½ teaspoons baking soda
¼ pound (1 stick) unsalted butter, at room temperature
1½ cups sugar
3 eggs
1 tablespoon vanilla extract
2 cups (1 pint) sour cream

1. Preheat the oven to 325° F. Grease a 10-inch tube pan with a removable bottom. In a double boiler, melt the chocolate over hot water, stirring until smooth. Remove from the heat and set aside.

2. Combine the flour, baking powder and baking soda.

3. In a large bowl, beat the butter and sugar together until light and fluffy. Beat in the eggs, one at a time, blending well after each addition. Beat in the vanilla and sour cream until blended. Gradually beat in the dry ingredients. The batter will be very thick.

4. Stir about 1 cup of the batter into the melted chocolate. Turn half of the remaining vanilla batter into the tube pan. Spoon half of the chocolate batter on top. Repeat with the remaining vanilla batter and then top with the remaining chocolate. Stick a kitchen knife or spatula straight down into the center of the batter and pull it around the pan, weaving back and forth to swirl the chocolate through the cake. Smooth the top with a rubber spatula.

5. Bake in the center of the oven for 1 hour, or until the cake begins to pull away from the sides of the pan and a cake tester inserted in the center comes out clean, except perhaps for a little melted chocolate. Let stand for 5 minutes. Remove the outside of the pan. Let cool for 10 minutes. Then unmold and let cool completely on a rack before slicing. (Wrapped well, the cake will keep in a cool place for up to a week, or can be frozen for months.)

Clam Pie with Sage-Corn Crust

•

Maple-Butternut Bisque

•

Ham Braised in Port
Potatoes au Gratin
Zucchini Bread from the Inn at Thorn Hill
Glazed Carrots and Snow Peas

•

Thumbprints and Other Assorted Christmas
Cookies
Pineapple and Cherries Jubilee

Christmas Dinner

FOR 16 TO 20

Irving Berlin's "White Christmas" left me with an indelible childhood impression of what Christmas should be like. I don't care if the sun is shining, if I find myself blinking at date palms strung with colored lights across a harbor in San Diego or poinsettias grown to twelve feet in height on a remote island in the Bahamas. Come December 25, I hear sleigh bells ringing and see evergreen treetops glistening in the snow: Christmas is always in New England... and here are the dishes to prove it.

Clam Pie is a local favorite on Cape Cod. There are almost as many versions as there are cooks. This is a light rendering, with more vegetables and less starch in the clam filling than usual. Rather than enclose everything in a pie crust, only a cornbread topping is used. The clam filling can be made a day ahead. Then the pie can be freshly baked with little last-minute preparation just before serving. In a pinch, it reheats surprisingly well.

Because I love squash simply baked with butter and maple syrup, it occurred to me that the same combination of flavors would make a terrific easy soup—and it does. A bit of cayenne pepper adds a sophisticated counterpoint to the subtle sweetness of the squash and maple syrup.

Marinate the ham two days before you plan to serve it. Since the meat is precooked, it is braised only for the time it takes to heat through—about 1½ hours for an 8-pound ham—with another half hour to glaze the outside. In terms of scheduling, the easiest way is to put up the ham so that it is completely finished and out of the oven before you begin serving the clam pie. Just set it aside, loosely covered with aluminum foil. It will stay hot for at least 45 minutes, and ham is just as good, if not better, at room temperature.

Potatoes au Gratin are best made with the sharpest Vermont Cheddar you can find. Bake them along with the clam pie. Snow peas and carrots, lightly glazed with butter and sugar, make a colorful accompaniment that is slightly different.

The Inn at Thorn Hill in Jackson, New Hampshire, looks as if Bing Crosby slept there . . . or maybe it was Irving Berlin. It fits my image of a Christmas setting to a tee. So I couldn't resist including their excellent recipe for Zucchini Bread here. If you prefer to get your baking done well ahead, the bread freezes perfectly.

Plum pudding is *the* traditional Christmas dessert, but I never remember to make it far enough ahead. Since the drama of a flaming dessert is more appealing to me than the taste of the old-fashioned pudding, it seemed to me that cherries jubilee updated with fresh pineapple—a colonial symbol of welcome and warm hospitality—would make an excellent substitution. For the full effect, dim the lights and flambé the dessert in front of your guests. It sounds corny, but everyone loves it. Thumbprints, or your favorite Christmas cookies, will add a pleasing crispness over tea or coffee.

Do-Ahead Planning

Up to 3 days in advance: Bake the Zucchini Bread. Bake the Thumbprints; store in an airtight tin. (Or, bake them up to a month ahead and feeeze.)

No less than 2 days beforehand: Marinate the ham.

The day before Christmas: Prepare the Clam Pie through Step 6. Make the Maple-Butternut Bisque. Prepare the Potatoes au Gratin. Prepare the pineapple and cherry base for the jubilee.

About 2½ hours before you plan to begin serving Christmas dinner: Bake the ham. Blanch the snow peas and carrots.

About 30 minutes before dinner: Finish the Clam Pie with Sage-Corn Crust. Reheat the soup. Bake the Potatoes au Gratin.

Shortly before serving: Finish the snow peas and carrots. Complete the Pineapple and Cherries Jubilee just before carrying it in.

CHRISTMAS BASKETS

There's no gift as special as a homemade one, and every year I try to give Christmas baskets to those friends and associates I really care about. The best baskets are filled with little goodies, buried here and there with one or two larger gifts. I like to include some store-bought items and some homemade, some edible and some ornamental. The trick is to begin early in the year and collect things as you find them.

I use all kinds of baskets—woven rush, wicker, wooden mushroom crates. I collect them whenever I see them, often in antiques shops, country stores that sell dried flowers as well as fruits and vegetables, at five-and-dime stores and in markets that sell baskets from the Orient. I line them with a printed napkin or with colored tissue paper. Inside may go a bar of scented soap, a nutmeg grater with a few whole nutmegs inside, a bunch of cinnamon sticks tied with a ribbon, always at least one unusual handmade Christmas ornament. Something should be personalized. One year we included little notebooks, which my husband handpainted, a different design on the cover of each. I make decorated cookies and candies and sometimes preserves. If the basket is being personally delivered, you could include the Cranberry Chutney (page 27) in a small jelly jar with a piece of gingham around the top tied with a ribbon. Label "Refrigerate upon receipt" and mention there is something that needs refrigerating when you hand it over. Hot Fudge Sauce (page 46) would also make a lovely gift, or bake miniloaves of Zucchini Bread (page 83). Individually wrapped brownies (page 107) and Butter Pecan Turtle Squares (page 131) are guaranteed to be a hit.

When everything is assembled, I fill in with found objects—pinecones, sprigs of evergreen, holly, tiny toys. Colored tissue paper is tucked around everything, the basket covered with paper and a bow and card attached to the top. Merry Christmas!

CLAM PIE WITH SAGE-CORN CRUST

16 TO 20 SERVINGS

Unless you have a very large baking dish, use two, or, as I do, use a disposable heavy-duty aluminum roasting pan and dish out the individual portions in the kitchen. Normally I use canned or frozen corn in winter, but a new sweet hybrid, which is available year-round, has recently been introduced.

5 dozen large cherrystone clams
1½ pounds red potatoes
4 cups corn niblets—fresh, frozen or vacuum-
    packed
¼ pound (1 stick) plus 2 tablespoons unsalted
    butter
3 medium leeks (white and tender green), well
    rinsed and finely diced
3 celery ribs, cut into ¼-inch dice
1 large red bell pepper, cut into ¼-inch dice
1 large green bell pepper, cut into ¼-inch dice
½ cup all-purpose flour
2 cups half-and-half or light cream
2 cups clam juice (reserved from Step 1)
2 teaspoons fresh lemon juice
½ teaspoon freshly ground black pepper
½ teaspoon thyme
½ teaspoon minced fresh or ground dried sage
¼ teaspoon cayenne pepper
Sage Cornbread batter (recipe follows)

1. Scrub the clams under running water to remove any sand from their shells. If they still seem gritty, soak them in a bowl of water for about 1 hour. In a very large (9-quart), heavy flameproof casserole or stockpot, bring 1 cup of water to a boil. Add the clams and steam over high heat, stirring them up once or twice, until they open, 10 to 15 minutes. Begin checking them after 7 minutes and remove the clams with a slotted spoon as they open. Remove the meat from the shells and cut the clams into ⅜-inch dice. Strain the clam broth through a double thickness of dampened cheesecloth and reserve.

2. In a large pot of boiling salted water, cook the potatoes until tender, 15 to 20 minutes. Drain and let cool; then peel and cut into ⅜-inch dice.

3. If using fresh corn kernels, blanch them in a saucepan of boiling water for 1 to 2 minutes, to soften slightly. Drain and set aside.

4. In a large flameproof casserole, melt the 1 stick of butter over moderate heat. Add the leeks and celery, cover and cook for 5 minutes. Uncover and cook, stirring, until the vegetables are soft and the leeks are just beginning to color. Add the bell peppers and sauté until softened but still brightly colored, about 3 minutes.

5. Sprinkle the flour over the vegetables and cook, stirring, for 2 minutes. Gradually add the half-and-half, stirring to blend with the flour and vegetables. Add 2 cups of the reserved clam broth and bring to a boil, whisking until the liquid is smooth. Reduce the heat to moderately low and cook, stirring frequently, until the sauce has no trace of raw flour taste. Remove from the heat and stir in the lemon juice, black pepper, thyme, sage and cayenne.

6. Use the remaining 2 tablespoons butter to grease a 16½ x 13-inch baking dish (I use disposable aluminum). Add the clams, corn and potatoes to the cream sauce and stir to blend well. Turn into the baking dish. (The recipe can be prepared ahead to this point up to a day in advance. Cover and refrigerate. Let stand at room temperature for at least 1 hour before baking.)

7. About 30 minutes before you plan to serve the clam pie, preheat the oven to 425° F. Prepare the Sage Cornbread through Step 4. Pour the batter over the clam mixture and spread to cover evenly. Bake for 25 minutes, or until the crust is browned and a tester comes out clean. (This dish will keep warm for at least 15 minutes or, in a pinch, can even be reheated.)

SAGE CORNBREAD

16 TO 20 SERVINGS

4 cups stone-ground cornmeal
1½ cups all-purpose flour
¼ cup sugar
1 tablespoon plus 1 teaspoon baking powder
¾ teaspoon baking soda
1½ teaspoons salt
⅔ cup parsley sprigs (loosely packed)
5 fresh sage leaves, cut up, or 1½ teaspoons dried
¼ pound (1 stick) unsalted butter
4 eggs
2 cups milk
1 cup half-and-half or light cream

1. As far ahead as you feel like it, combine the cornmeal, flour, sugar, baking powder, baking soda and salt in a large bowl. Whisk to blend well.

2. Put 1 cup of the cornmeal mixture, the parsley and sage in a food processor and process until the herbs are minced. Add to the remaining dry ingredients and whisk to blend.

3. Preheat the oven to 425° F. Melt the butter and let cool to tepid.

4. Just before you're ready to cook the cornbread, whisk the eggs to blend them. Gradually beat in the milk and half-and-half. Add the liquid to the dry ingredients. Add the melted butter and mix just until blended.

5. Pour the batter into a buttered 16 x 13-inch baking dish and bake for 25 minutes, or until the cornbread is browned on top and a tester comes out clean.

MAPLE-BUTTERNUT BISQUE

16 TO 20 SERVINGS

This is one of my favorite winter soups. Baking the squash whole keeps them moist and flavorful.

6 pounds butternut or acorn squash
1½ sticks (6 ounces) unsalted butter
3 large onions, coarsely chopped
½ cup all-purpose flour
3 cups milk
3 cans (13¾ ounces each) chicken broth
⅜ teaspoon cayenne pepper
1½ teaspoons salt
1½ cups heavy cream
⅓ cup plus 1 tablespoon pure maple syrup
1½ cups pecans, toasted and coarsely chopped

1. Preheat the oven to 350° F. Pierce the squash in several places with a fork and bake until soft, 45 minutes to 1 hour. Remove and let cool slightly, then cut in half, scoop out and discard the seeds and stringy membranes and scoop the squash into a bowl.

2. In a large flameproof casserole or heavy stockpot, melt the butter over moderately low heat. Add the onions and cook, stirring occasionally, until golden brown, about 30 minutes.

3. Sprinkle the flour over the onions, increase the heat to moderate and cook, stirring, for about 2 minutes to make a roux. Whisk in the milk and chicken broth. Bring to a boil, stirring frequently. Season with the cayenne pepper and salt.

4. In batches in a blender or food processor, purée the baked squash with the soup base until smooth. Return to the pot, add the cream and maple syrup and simmer for 10 minutes to blend the flavors. Check the seasoning; if there is not a little bite to contrast with the slight sweetness of the squash and maple syrup, add more cayenne pepper to taste. (The soup can be made a day ahead and refrigerated, or weeks ahead and frozen.) Serve hot, garnished with a sprinkling of toasted pecans.

HAM BRAISED IN PORT

16 TO 20 SERVINGS

Ham has such a strong flavor that anything you add to it still plays second fiddle. However, I love the touch of sweetness and nuttiness that port imparts, and the resulting sauce is a nice addition to the holiday table.

>   1 boneless ham, about 8 pounds, such as Hormel
>   "Cure 81"
>   1 bottle port, such as Sandeman's Tawny Port or
>   Croft Distinction
>   1 cup (packed) dark brown sugar
>   1 tablespoon plus 1 teaspoon Dijon mustard
>   Cloves
>   1 tablespoon cornstarch
>   1 to 2 teaspoons lemon juice
>   Freshly ground pepper to taste

1. With a barbecue skewer, poke the ham all over at 1½- to 2-inch intervals. Put the ham in a heavy oval casserole or nonaluminum roasting pan. Pour the port over the ham, cover and marinate in the refrigerator, turning occasionally, for 2 days.

2. Preheat the oven to 325° F. Put the ham in the oven and braise, covered, basting with the port every 15 to 20 minutes, until the ham is just heated through, about 1½ hours. The internal temperature should measure about 125° F. Remove from the oven.

3. Increase the oven temperature to 375° F. Transfer the ham to a shallow roasting pan; reserve all the cooking juices. In a small bowl, combine the brown sugar, 1 cup of the cooking juices and 1 teaspoon of the mustard; blend well.

4. Score the ham in a diamond pattern and stud with cloves. Baste with the brown sugar mixture and return to the oven. Roast, basting frequently, for 30 minutes, or until the ham is heated through and nicely glazed. Remove to a carving board and cover with foil to keep warm.

5. Pour 3 cups of the cooking liquid into the roasting pan and bring to a boil on top of the stove, scraping up any brown bits from the bottom of the pan. Pour the juices into a small nonaluminum saucepan. Boil until the juices are reduced to 2 cups. Whisk in the remaining 1 tablespoon mustard. Dissolve the cornstarch in 2 tablespoons water and stir into the sauce. Bring to a boil, stirring until thickened and smooth. Season with the lemon juice and pepper to taste. Pour into a gravy boat and serve with the ham.

POTATOES AU GRATIN

16 TO 20 SERVINGS AT A
SIT-DOWN DINNER, 30 AS PART
OF A BUFFET

8 pounds red or other waxy potatoes
¼ pound (1 stick) plus 5 tablespoons unsalted
*   butter*
½ cup plus 2½ tablespoons all-purpose flour
6⅔ cups milk
3 garlic cloves, crushed through a press
2¼ teaspoons salt
½ teaspoon freshly ground black pepper
¼ teaspoon cayenne pepper
1 pound sharp well-aged Cheddar cheese,
*   shredded*

1. Put the potatoes in a large pot (or two if
necessary), cover with cold water and bring to a boil
over high heat. Boil for 15 to 20 minutes, or until
tender but not mushy; drain. When the potaotes are
cool enough to handle, peel them and cut into ½-
inch dice. Put in a large bowl.

2. Preheat the oven to 475° F. In a large sauc-
pan or flameproof casserole, melt 1 stick plus 3
tablespoons of the butter over moderate heat. Add
the flour and cook, stirring, for 2 minutes without
allowing the flour to color. Whisk in the milk. Bring
to a boil, whisking constantly, until smooth and
thickened. Add the garlic, salt, black pepper and
cayenne. Reduce the heat to low and simmer, whisking occasionally, for 10 minutes. Stir in all but ½ cup
of the cheese and cook, whisking, until the cheese is
melted and the sauce is smooth. The sauce should
be the consistency of thick molasses. If it seems too
thick, thin with a little additional milk. Add the
cheese sauce to the potatoes and toss to mix.

3. Turn the potatoes into 2 large buttered gratin
or shallow baking dishes. Sprinkle the remaining
cheese evenly over the top and dot with the remaining 2 tablespoons butter. (The recipe can be made to
this point up to a day ahead. Cover and refrigerate.)

4. Bake the potatoes, uncovered, for 15 to 25
minutes, or until they are bubbling hot and the top is
lightly browned.

ZUCCHINI BREAD FROM THE INN AT THORN HILL

MAKES 2 LOAVES

Chef Hoke Wilson credits another cook, George
Forney, with this scrumptious batter bread. No matter who created it, it has just the perfect balance of
sweetness, vanilla and spice. Serve as you would a
cranberry or nut bread, or enjoy it with coffee for
breakfast or at teatime.

For good results, you must use a metal loaf pan;
heatproof glass will not yield the same results, with
this or any other quick bread recipe.

3 medium zucchini
4 eggs
2⅔ cups sugar
1⅓ cups corn or other light vegetable oil
1 tablespoon vanilla extract
4 cups all-purpose flour
1 teaspoon baking powder
1½ teaspoons baking soda
1½ teaspoons cinnamon
⅛ teaspoon salt
1 cup walnut halves, broken into large pieces,
*   optional*

1. Preheat the oven to 350° F. Grease and flour
2 metal loaf pans, 9 x 5 x 3 inches.

2. Shred the zucchini; I use the grating disk on
my food processor. Measure out 2⅔ packed cups.

3. In a large bowl, whisk the eggs. Gradually
beat in the sugar; then slowly whisk in the oil and
add the vanilla. Stir in the zucchini.

4. In another bowl, combine the flour, baking
powder, baking soda, cinnamon and salt. Add the dry
ingredients to the egg mixture and beat with a
wooden spoon for 2 minutes, or until well blended.
Stir in the nuts.

5. Pour the batter into the 2 prepared loaf pans
and rap on the counter to settle any air bubbles.
Bake for 1 hour 15 minutes, or until a tester comes
out clean. Let cool in the pan for 10 minutes, then
unmold and let cool completely on a rack. Wrap well
and refrigerate for up to 2 days, or freeze for up to 2
months.

GLAZED CARROTS AND SNOW PEAS

16 TO 20 SERVINGS

2 pounds carrots
1 pound snow peas
3 tablespoons finely minced fresh ginger
(optional)
¼ pound (1 stick) unsalted butter, cut into
tablespoons
3 tablespoons sugar
Salt and freshly ground pepper

1. Peel the carrots and cut them into sticks about 2 inches long, ½ inch wide and ¼ inch thick. Trim the snow peas and pull off the strings.

2. In a large pot of boiling salted water, cook the carrots until just barely tender, about 5 minutes. Add the snow peas and drain immediately into a colander. Rinse under cold running water; drain well. (The vegetables can be prepared to this point up to 4 hours in advance. Set aside at room temperature.)

3. In a wok or large skillet, melt 4 tablespoons of the butter over moderately high heat. Add half the carrots and snow peas and 1½ tablespoons of the ginger if you have it. Sprinkle on 1½ tablespoons of the sugar and cook, tossing, until the sugar dissolves and the vegetables are hot, 2 to 3 minutes. Season with salt and pepper to taste. Turn into a large serving bowl; cover to keep warm. Repeat with the remaining ingredients.

THUMBPRINTS

MAKES 5 TO 6 DOZEN

These delicious butter nut cookies are best made with a small *sous-chef*, preferably under the age of five. Four-year-old David Bell has been helping his mother for at least two years, and by the next holiday season may be putting her to work for him.

½ pound (2 sticks) unsalted butter, softened
½ cup (packed) brown sugar
2 eggs, separated
1 teaspoon vanilla extract
2 cups all-purpose flour
½ teaspoon salt
1½ cups finely chopped pecans or walnuts
About ½ cup apricot, raspberry or strawberry jam
and/or blueberry jelly

1. Preheat the oven to 350° F. In a medium mixer bowl, beat together the butter, brown sugar, egg yolks and vanilla. Add the flour and salt and mix until blended.

2. With your hands, roll the dough by teaspoonfuls into small balls.

3. Beat the egg whites lightly with a fork. Set the nuts out on a plate or a sheet of wax paper. Dip each ball of dough first in the egg white and then in the chopped nuts to coat. Set 1 inch apart on ungreased cookie sheets.

4. Press your thumb gently into the center of each ball to make a well (this is where the small *sous-chef* comes in). Bake for 10 to 12 minutes, until crisp and lightly browned. Transfer to a rack and let cool.

5. Fill the center of each cookie with a dab of jam or jelly, using a variety of flavors if you wish.

PINEAPPLE AND CHERRIES JUBILEE

ABOUT 24 SERVINGS

Dramatically carried to the table with blue flames licking the edges, this old-fashioned standby, updated with fresh pineapple, proves why it's always been a favorite. Serve over scoops of vanilla ice cream.

> 2 bags (20 ounces each) individually quick-frozen
>   sweet cherries with no sugar added
> 2/3 cup kirsch
> 2/3 cup sugar
> 1 large ripe pineapple
> 2 tablespoons cornstarch
> 1/2 cup Cognac or brandy
> 4 to 5 pints vanilla ice cream

1. Up to 3 days before you plan to serve the fruit, thaw the cherries in the refrigerator. Dump them with their juice into a large bowl. Add the kirsch and sprinkle on 1/3 cup of the sugar; toss gently to mix. Cover and refrigerate.

2. Cut the top off the pineapple. Using a large sharp stainless steel knife, cut down along the sides to remove the thick skin and the spiny brown "eyes." Lay the pineapple on its side and cut into 1/2-inch-thick slices. Cut down around the core of each slice to make strips, and then cut the strips into 1/2-inch dice. Add the pineapple to the cherries. Cover and refrigerate overnight.

3. Drain the fruit, reserving the juice. Return the fruit to a heatproof glass serving bowl. Pour the juice into a small nonaluminum saucepan. Add the remaining 1/3 cup sugar and bring to a boil over moderate heat, stirring to dissolve the sugar. In a small bowl, combine the cornstarch with 2 tablespoons water; stir to dissolve. Stir the dissolved cornstarch into the sauce and boil, stirring, until thickened and smooth, 1 to 2 minutes. (The fruit topping keeps well in the refrigerator for up to 3 days.)

4. Just before serving, reheat the sauce and pour over the fruit. Add the Cognac to the same saucepan and heat for a few seconds, until just warm. Ignite with a match and pour over the fruit. Carefully make a grand entrance with the dramatic blue flames dancing over the fruit.

5. Scoop the ice cream into serving dishes and ladle the fruit and sauce on top.

Caviar Nachos

Spiced Nuts

Chipotle Chile Mayonnaise (page 49) with Crudités for Dipping

Golden Margaritas by the Batch and Cold Beer

.

Barbacoa of Lamb

Fresh Tomato Salsa

Warm Flour Tortillas

Chicken Cheese Tortilla Casserole

Carrot and Jicama Salad

Corn, Rice and Bean Salad with Chile Vinaigrette

.

Toasted Coconut Flan

Fresh Berries

South-western Buffet

FOR 16 TO 20

Like so many people, I've become addicted to the flavors of the American Southwest. This is food that truly deserves its popularity. Chock-full of taste, the piquancy of hot chiles, herbal astringency of fresh coriander, dusty pungency of toasted cumin and sweet tang of barbecue sauce satisfy our newfound craving for spices and seasonings. Cornmeal breads, mesquite-grilled meats and refreshing salads are all a part of this regional cuisine, borrowed from Mexico to the south and marked by the cattle country in which it was developed. Above all, it is cheerful food, reflective of the sun under which it was born, and perfect for a large party.

Caviar Nachos are a lot of fun. There is nothing serious about them. They are delicious and something of a conversation piece. Around the room, set out spiced nuts or store-bought highly seasoned pumpkin seeds, which are always good with cocktails.

Chipotle Chile Mayonnaise is made with both chipotle chiles, which are smoked jalapeños, and ancho chiles, the mildest and most flavorful of the hot peppers. It was Jerrie Strom, a San Diego cooking teacher whose recipe for Mexican barbecued lamb inspired my barbacoa, who taught me about chiles. I had read all I could, especially Jean Andrew's excellent book on peppers, but there is no substitute for experience. It was Jerrie who first led me by the hand through the Tijuana marketplace, stopping by each brick-red mountain of chiles to point out quality or explain the cooking properties and taste characteristics of each type of chile. I've been experimenting ever since. The spicy, earthy flavor of this mayonnaise works beautifully as a dip for fresh vegetables as well as a sauce for grilled meats and fish.

The Mexican-style barbecued lamb, salsa and tortillas are rolled up and eaten together like an enchilada. The lamb has to marinate for three days. It cooks very slowly in a low oven, so remember to put it in 3 or 4 hours before you plan to serve. You cannot overcook it; the meat is roasted until it is meltingly tender and falling off the bone. If you can manage to make up your salsa not more than a couple of hours in advance, do so, because tomatoes are always more flavorful if they're not refrigerated.

If you don't have a Latin market near you, chances are flour tortillas are available in the frozen food section of your supermarket. Defrost them in the package and warm them just before you bring them to the table. Serve them, Mexican-style, in a basket covered with a brightly colored cloth to keep them warm.

Chicken Cheese Tortilla Casserole, a guaranteed favorite, is one of those quintessentially Tex-Mex dishes that no one can stop eating. Completely assembled in advance, it's a great party dish. After so much highly seasoned food, the cool, crisp Carrot and Jicama Salad provides a welcome contrast.

My Toasted Coconut Flan is a creamy soft, light custard, unlike the traditional version made with condensed milk, and is pleasingly chewy. With its caramel sauce, it stands well on its own, but fresh berries always add a nice touch.

Do-Ahead Planning

Up to 5 days in advance: Make the Chipotle Chile Mayonnaise.

3 days in advance: Marinate the lamb. Make the Spiced Nuts.

Up to 2 days ahead: Assemble the Chicken Cheese Tortilla Casserole. Make the Toasted Coconut Flan.

The day before the party: Make the guacamole for the Caviar Nachos. Prepare the crudités. Make the Corn, Rice and Bean Salad with Chile Vinaigrette. Shred the vegetables for the Carrots and Jicama Salad.

About 4 hours before serving: Roast the lamb.

Up to 2 hours before the party starts: Squeeze the lime juice for the margaritas. Make the Fresh Tomato Salsa.

About half an hour before serving: Bake the Chicken Cheese Tortilla Casserole. Complete the Carrot and Jicama Salad.

CAVIAR NACHOS

MAKES ABOUT 4 DOZEN

The idea for these came from—who else?—a Texan, Ray Hertz of Dallas. Use inexpensive lumpfish or golden whitefish caviar for these whimsical hors d'oeuvres. Make the guacamole base up to a day ahead if you wish, but assemble the nachos, assembly-line fashion, shortly before serving, so the tortilla chips remain crisp.

2 ripe California avocados, preferably Hass
¼ cup minced onion
¼ cup fresh lime or lemon juice
1 tablespoon plus 1 teaspoon minced, seeded jalapeño peppers (if you can't get fresh jalapeños, substitute hot pepper sauce to taste)
½ teaspoon salt
¼ teaspoon freshly ground black pepper
1 bag (12 ounces) round tortilla chips (tostaditas)
1 cup sour cream
2 to 4 ounces salmon roe or red lumpfish or golden whitefish caviar

1. Mash the avocado in a bowl until fairly finely pureed. Add the onion, lime juice, jalapeño pepper, salt and black pepper. Blend well. (Guacamole is best fresh, but you can make this up to a day ahead. Cover with a piece of plastic wrap directly on the surface of the guacamole and refrigerate.)

2. To assemble the nachos, spoon about ½ tablespoon guacamole onto each of 48 tortilla chips. Top with a teaspoon of sour cream and garnish with ¼ to ½ teaspoon caviar.

SPICED NUTS

MAKES ABOUT 7 CUPS

Make these spicy nuts up to 3 days ahead and store in a tightly covered jar in a cool dark place, or refrigerate for up to a week.

2 pounds mixed shelled raw nuts, such as cashews, almonds, walnuts and pecans (available in health food stores)
1½ tablespoons vegetable oil
2 tablespoons chili powder
2 teaspoons ground cumin
½ teaspoon cayenne pepper
2 teaspoons salt

1. Preheat the oven to 350° F. In a large bowl, toss the nuts with the oil until they are evenly coated.

2. In a small bowl, combine the chili powder, cumin, cayenne and salt. Sprinkle this spice mixture over the nuts and toss to mix well.

3. Spread out the seasoned nuts on 2 large baking sheets and bake them in the preheated oven for 5 to 7 minutes, until lightly toasted. Let cool on paper towels. Serve at room temperature.

GOLDEN MARGARITAS BY THE BATCH

16 SERVINGS

It's easy to remember the proportions for a perfect margarita: one, two, three. That's one part fresh lime juice to two parts dry orange liqueur (Cointreau, Triple Sec or Curaçao) to three parts tequila. Golden tequila yields a much smoother drink, appropriate, I think, for the best of parties. The following amounts make a pitcherful to serve one (3-ounce) drink to sixteen people. If you remember the proportions, you can adjust this to your needs for any number.

1 cup fresh lime juice
2 cups Cointreau, Triple Sec or Curaçao
3 cups Cuervo Especial or other golden tequila

In a pitcher filled with ice, combine the lime juice, Cointreau and tequila. Stir for 1 to 2 minutes. Serve over plenty of ice (I use 3 cubes per glass).

BARBACOA OF LAMB

12 TO 16 SERVINGS

Because of the acidity of the marinade, be sure to use a nonaluminum pan for the Mexican-style lamb with warm flour tortillas and fresh tomato salsa.

> 1 whole leg of lamb or 2 shank halves (see Note)
> 5 large ancho chiles
> 1 can (13 ounces) whole tomatillos (Spanish green tomatoes)
> 2 medium onions, quartered
> 3 large garlic cloves, crushed
> 2 teaspoons cumin
> 1½ teaspoons salt

1. Trim off all excess fat from the meat. With a narrow knife, prick the meat deeply all over at 1- to 2-inch intervals. Place the leg of lamb in a heavy nonaluminum casserole with a tight-fitting lid, preferably enameled cast iron.

2. Lightly toast the ancho chiles on a dry griddle or over a gas flame for about 30 seconds per side, just to soften them. Cut open and remove the stem, seeds and ribs. Put in a bowl and pour on boiling water to cover. Let soak for about 15 minutes, until soft; drain.

3. Put the ancho chiles, tomatillos, onions, garlic, cumin and salt in a food processor or blender. Puree until smooth.

4. Lift up the lamb and smear some of the tomatillo-pepper puree over the bottom. Pour the remainder over the lamb and smooth it around to cover the meat entirely. Cover the pot and refrigerate for 2 to 3 days.

5. Preheat the oven to 300° F. Place the covered casserole of lamb in the oven and roast for 1 hour. Reduce the oven temperature to 275° F. and bake for 1 hour. Turn off the oven and leave the covered casserole untouched for at least 1 and up to 2 hours before serving.

6. To serve, thickly slice the meat from the bone and then cut or pull with a fork into thick shreds. Serve with warm flour tortillas and Fresh Tomato Salsa.

Note: It doesn't matter if you use a whole leg of lamb or 2 shank halves, but I find the 2 halves are often easier to fit into the proper casserole.

FRESH TOMATO SALSA

MAKES ABOUT 2½ CUPS

This is an unconventional recipe for salsa. Because I could not find chile peppers in my market, I made the sauce with some *sambal oolek*, Indonesian hot sauce, I had in the fridge. It worked beautifully, so I left it in. If you prefer finely minced serrano or jalapeño peppers, by all means use them.

> 3 large ripe tomatoes, finely diced
> 1 medium red onion, finely diced
> 1 tablespoon olive oil
> 1 tablespoon fresh lime or lemon juice
> ½ teaspoon salt
> Pinch of sugar
> 1 tablespoon sambal oolek or harissa (or more or less to taste)
> ¼ cup chopped fresh coriander, optional

1. In a medium bowl, combine the tomatoes, onion, olive oil, lime juice, salt and sugar. Stir in as much hot sauce as you like (the salsa should be piquant).

2. The salsa can be refrigerated, covered, for up to a day. Just before serving, stir in the coriander, if desired.

CHICKEN CHEESE TORTILLA CASSEROLE

16 TO 20 SERVINGS

6 skinned and boned chicken breast halves, about
    2 pounds total
1½ teaspoons salt
½ teaspoon freshly ground black pepper
3 dozen corn tortillas, 6 inches in diameter
About ½ cup corn oil
¾ pound Monterey Jack cheese
½ pound sharp white Cheddar cheese
3 cans (13 ounces each) tomatillo entero (whole
    green Spanish tomatoes)
1 jar (10¼ ounces) whole pickled jalapeño
    peppers, drained and tops trimmed off
4 large garlic cloves, crushed
2 medium onions, cut into eighths
4½ cups sour cream
2 cups milk
Sliced black olives, for garnish

1. Rinse the chicken breasts. Put them in a large saucepan or flameproof casserole and add water to cover by at least 1 inch. Add ½ teaspoon of the salt. Bring to a simmer over moderately high heat, reduce the heat and barely simmer for 20 to 30 minutes, until the chicken is just white throughout but still moist. Let cool in the water for 30 minutes. Remove the chicken and let cool completely; reserve the liquid for stock, if desired. (The chicken can be poached a day ahead. Wrap and refrigerate.)

2. Shred or very coarsely chop the chicken. Toss with the remaining 1 teaspoon salt and the black pepper.

3. Heat a medium skillet, preferably nonstick, over moderate heat. One at a time, lightly brush each tortilla with oil and cook for 15 to 20 seconds on each side, until softened. Stack as they are cooked and set aside.

4. In a food processor fitted with the shredding disk, grate the Monterey Jack and Cheddar cheese. Toss them together and set aside.

5. In the processor fitted with the metal blade (no need to rinse the bowl), combine the tomatillos, pickled jalapeños and garlic. Puree until smooth. Add the onions and turn the machine quickly on and off about 10 times, or until the onions are chopped. Scrape the green sauce into a bowl.

6. Rinse the work bowl of the processor and add the sour cream. With the machine on, add the milk through the feed tube, blending until smooth.

7. Using 2 large shallow baking dishes about 9 x 12 inches, or 1 very large dish, spread a thin film of green sauce over the bottom of each dish. Cover with a layer of tortillas. Scatter half the chicken over the tortillas. Drizzle on about one-third of the green sauce. Sprinkle on half the cheese and then spoon about one-third of the sour cream sauce over that. Repeat with another layer of tortillas, the remaining chicken, half the remaining green sauce, cheese and sour cream sauce. Top with the remaining tortillas. Spread the remaining green sauce on top of them, cover with the rest of the sour cream sauce and sprinkle what's left of the cheese on top of everything. Garnish with some sliced black olives. (The dish can be assembled up to a day ahead. Cover and refrigerate.)

8. Preheat the oven to 350° F. About half an hour before you plan to serve, put the casseroles in the oven and bake uncovered for 30 to 40 minutes, or until the cheese is melted and the dishes are sizzling hot throughout.

CHILES

Peppers are notoriously promiscuous and hot chiles are no exception. They breed like rabbits, and there's no telling what kind of a hybrid you'll end up with. To make matters worse, the same pepper can vary in hotness from field to field, and even from one end of the pepper to the other. On top of all that, people have a bad habit of giving the same pepper different names, depending on whether it's fresh or dried or where it comes from. Such confusion aside, the following are descriptions of some of the most common chile peppers you're likely to come across. Some of the heat of these hot chiles can be reduced by removing the seeds and inner ribs.

POBLANO This large, dark green pepper, bell-shaped with a tapering bottom, is the largest and one of the mildest of the chiles. With a deep aromatic flavor that is greatly enhanced by roasting, this is the pepper traditionally stuffed to make *chiles rellenos.*

ANCHO Brick red, the ancho is a dried poblano. Used as the basis for red enchilada sauce and mole, it is very flavorful, with an earthy taste. Usually mild, it can kick upon occasion.

ANAHEIM (also called California chile, Chile Verde, Long Green Chile, Big Jim). For all practical purposes, you can consider these chiles the same. They are usually semi-hot and, though frequently green, are sometimes red. Narrow and somewhat twisted, the long green chile is often chopped and added to dishes for hotness and flavor. It is probably the most common large chile found in American markets.

PASILLA This long, brownish pepper, known as *chile chilaca* in its fresh state, is usually used dried. Because of its dark color, the pasilla is sometimes called *chile negro*, or black chile. It is usually quite hot, with a dusky flavor, and is often used in combination with the ancho.

JALAPEÑO A small, blunt-nosed dark green chile, the jalapeño is very hot and flavorful. It is used fresh and pickled.

CHIPOTLE When dried and smoked, the jalapeño becomes the chipotle chile—light brown and wrinkled. It is extremely hot and has a distinctive smoky flavor, which adds a wonderful depth of flavor to sauces. The chipotle is frequently found canned in adobo sauce.

SERRANO The very small, narrow, dark green chile is extremely hot. It is usually very finely minced and should be used with discretion.

CARROT AND JICAMA SALAD

16 TO 20 SERVINGS

I learned to make this salad from a wonderful Mexican cook, Luisa (Lula) Bertran. It is pretty, crisp and refreshing. Served with spicy hot food, it provides contrast and relief.

2 pounds carrots, peeled
2 pounds jicama, peeled
2 tablespoons fresh lime juice
½ cup corn oil
½ teaspoon salt
2 dashes of cayenne pepper
⅔ cup chopped fresh coriander

1. Cut the carrots and jicama into very fine julienne strips. I use the fine julienne disk of my food processor or a mandoline; you can cut them by hand, but it is a lot of work. Rinse the jicama in a bowl of cold water, changing the water until the liquid runs clear. Soak the carrot and jicama in a bowl of ice water for at least 30 minutes, or overnight; drain well.

2. Shortly before serving, put the vegetables in a large serving bowl, preferably glass. Toss with the lime juice, corn oil, salt, cayenne and all but 2 tablespoons of the coriander. Sprinkle the remaining coriander on top.

CORN, RICE AND BEAN SALAD WITH CHILE VINAIGRETTE

16 SERVINGS

I love this salad in summer when fresh sweet corn is in season, but I make it all year in a flash with canned corn niblets. It has a nice sweet-sour tang with a bite that adds zest without scorching. A fine accompaniment to barbecued chicken or any kind of Mexican or southwestern-style meat, this is a great picnic salad, because there is nothing to spoil.

2 cups converted rice
3 teaspoons salt
2 cans (16 ounces each) pink beans, rinsed and
    drained
1 can (12 ounces) vacuum-packed corn niblets, or
    3 cups cooked fresh corn kernels
1 bunch of scallions, chopped (about ¾ cup)
⅔ cup safflower or corn oil
¼ cup fresh lime juice
2 tablespoons cider vinegar
2 tablespoons (packed) brown sugar
4 pickled jalapeño peppers, stemmed, seeded and
    quartered
2 teaspoons chili powder
1 teaspoon cumin

1. Cook the rice as directed on the package, using 5 cups of water and 1 teaspoon of the salt. (The rice can be made ahead.)

2. In a large bowl, combine the rice, beans, corn and scallions. Toss lightly to mix.

3. In a food processor, combine the oil, lime juice, vinegar, brown sugar, jalapeño peppers, chili powder, cumin and remaining 2 teaspoons salt. Process until the peppers are finely minced.

4. Pour the dressing over the salad and toss to coat. Let stand at room temperature, tossing occasionally, for up to 4 hours, or cover and refrigerate for up to 2 days. Serve at room temperature.

TOASTED COCONUT FLAN

16 TO 20 SERVINGS

This is a rich custard that forms a nice creamy finale to a spicy meal. Though you could make the entire flan in one large baking dish, I find two pie plates are easier in terms of unmolding and serving. This is a do-ahead dessert that should be served well chilled.

1 package (7 ounces) sweetened shredded (flaked) coconut
1½ cups sugar
1 quart milk
2 cups heavy cream
8 whole eggs
4 egg yolks
1 tablespoon vanilla extract

1. Preheat the oven to 300° F. Spread out the coconut on a large baking sheet and toast in the oven, tossing frequently, until light brown, 8 to 10 minutes. Don't worry if there is unevenness of color, but don't let the coconut burn. Turn out onto a plate or shallow bowl and let cool. (The coconut can be toasted several days before you make the flan and stored in the refrigerator in a covered container.)

2. Preheat the oven to 325° F. In a small heavy saucepan, combine 1 cup of the sugar with 3 table-spoons of water. Melt the sugar over moderate heat and continue to cook until the syrup turns a deep golden brown, 6 to 8 minutes. Immediately remove from the heat and pour half the syrup into each of two 10-inch glass pie plates. Swirl to coat the pie plates evenly with the caramel.

3. Heat the milk and cream together until hot but not boiling. In a large bowl, whisk the eggs and egg yolks until blended. Beat in the remaining ½ cup sugar. Very gradually at first and then in a slow stream, beat the hot milk and cream into the eggs. Reserve ½ cup of the toasted coconut for garnish. Mix the remainder of the coconut and the vanilla into the custard.

4. Divide the coconut custard between the 2 pie plates. Set them in a larger pan (remember those aluminum roasters if you have nothing else) with enough hot water to reach halfway up the sides and bake for 1 hour, or until the custard is set. Remove the flans from the water bath and let cool. Cover and refrigerate until chilled. (The flans can be made up to 2 days in advance.)

5. To serve, unmold the flans onto 2 round platters with lips. The caramel will form a sauce. Garnish the top of each with the reserved toasted coconut. Cut into wedges to serve.

Curried Carrot-Ginger Soup

∎

Roast Turkey with Pecan-Cornbread Stuffing

Giblet Pan Gravy

Gratin of Sweet Potatoes Flambéed with Bourbon

Wild Rice Risotto

Braised Fennel au Gratin

Buttered Peas

Cranberry Chutney (page 27)

∎

Easy Cream Cheesecake

Bittersweet Chocolate Truffle Torte

Thanks- giving for a Large Gathering

OF 16 TO 20

Thanksgiving has always been one of my favorite holidays—not surprising since it is one of the great feast days of the year. I took it as a special omen when on the very morning of the first Thanksgiving in my own home, some twenty years ago, with two dozen friends and family on their way, our pet cockatiels' egg hatched and their first-born son emerged. Needless to say, I named him "Thanks-a-lot," and we celebrated his birth all day.

The joy of this holiday continues to be a tradition in my home. Though families seem smaller than they used to be, Thanksgiving traditionally remains an extended affair. Increasingly, I find myself host to a groaning board set not only for family and friends, but for their children and their children's friends, with all the fun and disarray that such a crowd entails.

Imbued as it is with a spirit of excess to begin with, Thanksgiving calls for a large menu. I prefer to add more dishes for more guests, rather than to triple or quadruple quantities. Curried Carrot-Ginger Soup is a great starter. It's one of my favorite soups, made easily with canned broth, and its piquant flavor acts like an aperitif to whet the appetite. A grand turkey is called for, big enough to make everyone gasp with delight as it is hefted into the room. Three different vegetables, chosen for contrast of color, flavor and texture, a delectable wild rice casserole, cornbread stuffing, thick dark gravy and a jewel-red cranberry condiment make this a spectacular celebration indeed. It's fun to taste a little bit of a lot of things, and heaping plates are the order of the day. No doubt guests will offer to bring a dish—dessert, bread, whatever. Take them up on it!

Because there is so much food to follow, I never offer hors d'oeuvres before the Thanksgiving meal. If you serve dinner at 2 P.M., I don't think anything is required. If you celebrate in the late afternoon or early evening, you could put out some nuts and cheese to hold over the exceptionally hungry and the children, who cannot wait.

Both of the desserts suggested here can be made ahead and frozen, a tremendous boon when you have so much to attend to. Creamy and rich, they are the only part of the meal that is untraditional. My feeling is that everyone has a favorite recipe for apple and pumpkin pie, and if you're having such a large group for the holiday, someone is going to offer to bring a dessert. Ask the volunteers to bring the pies and you can skip the desserts I suggest, or have a fantastic dessert table. Multiple desserts do not fit my usual style of entertaining, but a big holiday like this provides a good excuse for a welcome exception.

Feeding a large group on this scale requires planning and organization. Because of the number of dishes, there's a lot to do, even if you've done most of the preparation in advance. For that reason, I suggest a checklist and timetable to keep you on track.

Do-Ahead Planning

Up to 1 month in advance: Make the Easy Cream Cheesecake and Bittersweet Chocolate Truffle Torte and freeze them.

Up to 2 weeks in advance: Make the Cranberry Chutney; store in the refrigerator. Bake the Sage Cornbread for the stuffing, cut into ¾-inch cubes and freeze.

Up to 2 days in advance: Make the Curried Carrot-Ginger Soup through Step 3. Make the Wild Rice Risotto. Partially cook the sweet potatoes for the gratin.

Up to 1 day ahead: Make the Pecan-Cornbread Stuffing. Make the turkey stock for Giblet Pan Gravy (this can be made months ahead and frozen if you use other turkey giblets). Assemble the Gratin of Sweet Potaotes. Braise the fennel. Prepare the crumbs for the topping.

Thanksgiving day—about 6 hours before you plan to start serving: Stuff the turkey and put it in the oven to roast.

Half an hour before the turkey is done: Put the Gratin of Sweet Potatoes in the oven. Bake the extra stuffing.

As soon as the turkey comes out of the oven: Cover loosely with foil and set aside in a warm place (the turkey will stay warm for at least 45 minutes). Increase the oven temperature to 450° F. and finish the Gratin of Sweet Potatoes. Gratinée the fennel. Make the Giblet Pan Gravy. Reheat, finish and serve the soup.

While someone else carves the turkey at table: Reheat the Wild Rice Risotto in a microwave (or set in the oven earlier). Make the peas, using 3 or 4 packages of frozen "tiny tender peas" and cooking them 1 minute less than directed on the package before tossing them with butter. Flambé the Gratin of Sweet Potatoes as you carry it to the table.

CURRIED CARROT-GINGER SOUP

18 TO 20 SERVINGS

Root vegetables sound humble, but this blend of sweet carrots, pungent fresh ginger and flavorful spices makes an exceptionally delicious soup. My only advice is—get help peeling the carrots! The type of curry powder you use will make an enormous difference in flavor. I use Sun Brand Madras.

> ¼ pound (1 stick) unsalted butter
> 3 tablespoons olive oil
> 4 medium onions, sliced
> ½ cup coarsely chopped fresh ginger
> 2 tablespoons Madras curry powder
> 1½ tablespoons ground cumin
> ½ cup all-purpose flour
> 1 large can (32 ounces) plus 1 small can (13¾ ounces) chicken broth
> 3 pounds carrots, peeled and thickly sliced
> 3 dashes of cayenne pepper
> Salt
> 1 cup sour cream
> 1 cup plain yogurt

1. In a large flameproof casserole, melt the butter in the oil over moderate heat. Add the onions and cook, stirring occasionally, until golden brown, about 10 minutes. Add the ginger, curry powder and cumin and cook, stirring, for 1 minute. Add the flour and cook, stirring, for 1 to 2 minutes without browning.

2. Add the chicken broth and bring to a boil, stirring frequently. Add the carrots, cayenne and 4 cups water. Simmer, partially covered, for 20 minutes, or until the carrots are tender. Remove from the heat.

3. Puree the soup, in batches, in a blender or food processor. (The recipe can be made to this point up to 2 days ahead. Cover and refrigerate.)

4. Reheat the soup. If it is too thick to your liking, thin with a little more water. Season with salt and additional cayenne to taste.

5. In a small bowl, blend the sour cream and yogurt. Ladle the hot soup into bowls and top with a dollop of the yogurt cream. Garnish with a sprinkle of cumin.

PECAN-CORNBREAD STUFFING

MAKES ABOUT 12 CUPS

Fill the turkey loosely with as much stuffing as it will hold (stuffing expands as it cooks). Spoon any extra into a buttered baking dish and bake it during the last 30 minutes the turkey roasts. Bake the cornbread a day before you prepare the stuffing so it has time to dry out.

> 1½ cups broken or coarsely chopped pecans
> 1 recipe Sage Cornbread (page 81)
> ¼ pound (1 stick) unsalted butter
> ⅓ cup olive oil
> 4 medium onions, chopped
> 3 celery ribs with leaves, chopped
> 5 garlic cloves, chopped
> 3 eggs
> ½ cup chopped parsley
> 1 teaspoon crumbled sage leaves
> 1 tablespoon salt
> 1 teaspoon coarsely cracked black pepper
> ⅛ teaspoon cayenne pepper
> 1½ teaspoons grated orange zest
> ½ cup fresh orange juice
> 1–1½ cups turkey or chicken stock

1. Preheat the oven to 325° F. Spread out the pecans on a baking sheet and toast in the oven for 8 to 10 minutes, or until lightly browned and fragrant. Pour onto a plate and let cool.

2. Cut the cornbread into ¾-inch cubes. Put them and any crumbs into a large bowl and let stand, tossing occasionally, for at least 6 hours, or overnight, to dry out.

3. In a large skillet or flameproof casserole, melt the butter in the oil over moderate heat. Add the onions, cover and cook for 5 minutes. Uncover, add the celery and cook, stirring occasionally, until the onions are golden, 15 to 20 minutes. Add the garlic and cook for 1 to 2 minutes longer, until fragrant. Scrape the vegetable mixture over the cornbread.

4. In a small bowl, beat the eggs with a fork until blended. Beat in the parsley, sage, salt, black pepper, cayenne and orange zest. Pour over the cornbread. Add the pecans and toss to mix. Add the orange juice and ½ cup of the stock and toss again. Add enough remaining stock so that the stuffing is moist but not soggy. Cover and refrigerate for up to a day before stuffing and roasting the turkey.

ROAST TURKEY WITH PECAN-CORNBREAD STUFFING

16 TO 20 SERVINGS

Order a fresh turkey from a good butcher if you can. This is a big bird, which will take a long time to roast. Allow at least 20 minutes after cooking for the juices to return to the meat. Since turkey can easily stay warm for 45 minutes before serving, play it safe and allow 5½ to 6 hours from the time the turkey goes into the oven until serving time.

1 turkey, 16 to 20 pounds, preferably fresh
1 large onion
1 tablespoon imported sweet paprika
1 tablespoon coarse (kosher) salt
1 teaspoon freshly ground black pepper
¼ teaspoon cayenne pepper
⅓ cup extra-virgin olive oil
Pecan-Cornbread Stuffing (recipe precedes)
¼ pound (1 stick) unsalted butter, cut into
   tablespoons

1. Remove the turkey from the refrigerator 1½ hours before roasting. Set the giblets aside for the stock and gravy; the liver is not used in this recipe. Pull out any excess fat from the large cavity. Rinse the turkey inside and out with cold running water and dry well with paper towels.

2. In a food processor, combine the onion with the paprika, salt, black pepper, cayenne and 2 table-spoons of the olive oil. Puree to a paste. Rub this seasoning paste all over the turkey, inside and out. Set the turkey in its roasting pan and let stand at room temperature, uncovered, for 1½ hours. When it's time, preheat the oven to 425° F.

3. Fill the turkey loosely with the Pecan-Cornbread Stuffing; it will hold 6 to 7 cups. Pack the remainder into a buttered baking dish, cover and refrigerate. Truss the turkey.

4. In a small saucepan, melt the butter in the remaining olive oil. Dip a doubled-up rectangle of cheesecloth (at least 4 layers thick) into the melted butter. Drape over the turkey breast.

5. Roast the turkey for 30 minutes. Baste the legs and thighs with some of the butter left in the saucepan. Reduce the oven temperature to 325° F. and roast the turkey for 3 to 4 hours, or until the meat in the thickest part of the thigh registers 155° to 160° F. on an instant-reading thermometer. Remove the cheesecloth, baste the turkey all over and roast, basting every 20 minutes, for about 1 hour longer, or until the thigh registers 175° to 180° F.

6. Remove the turkey to a carving board. Loosely cover with foil and let stand for at least 20 minutes before carving.

GIBLET PAN GRAVY

MAKES ABOUT 3 CUPS

Turkey giblets (heart, gizzard and neck), reserved
  from Turkey Stock
Drippings from Roast Turkey
2 large shallots, minced
⅓ cup all-purpose flour
3½ cups Turkey Stock
3 tablespoons unsalted butter
Salt and freshly ground pepper to taste

1. Cut the cooked heart and gizzard into ¼-inch dice. Pull the meat off the neck bone and cut it into small pieces if the shreds are long. (Do this ahead of time.)

2. As soon as your turkey is done, set it aside on a carving board, loosely covered with foil to keep warm. Pour off and reserve the juices, leaving about ¼ cup of fat in the roasting pan. Set the pan on top of the stove, add the shallots and sauté over moderate heat for 1 to 2 minutes, until softened. Sprinkle on the flour and cook, stirring frequently, for 2 minutes. Pour in the stock and bring to a boil, scraping up the brown bits from the bottom and sides of the pan with a wooden spoon. Reduce the heat and simmer for 2 to 3 minutes, stirring occasionally.

3. Remove from the heat and whisk in the butter, 1 tablespoon at a time. Season with salt and pepper to taste. Pour into a sauceboat and pass with the turkey.

TURKEY STOCK

MAKES 3½ CUPS

Turkey neck, wing tips and giblets
1 large onion, thickly sliced
1 large carrot, thickly sliced
2 garlic cloves, smashed
1 celery rib, quartered
8 parsley stems
2 ounces fresh mushrooms, sliced, or mushroom
  trimmings (optional)
12 black peppercorns
¼ teaspoon thyme
1 imported bay leaf

1. Rinse off the turkey neck; cut it into 1- to 1½-inch pieces. Trim off the fat from the heart and gizzard.

2. Put all the ingredients in a heavy medium saucepan. Add 6 cups water or more to cover. Bring to a boil over moderately high heat, skimming off the foam occasionally. Reduce the heat to low and simmer, adding water as needed to keep the ingredients covered, for 2 hours. Strain and skim off the fat.

3. Pour the stock into a clean saucepan and boil until reduced to 3½ cups.

GRATIN OF SWEET POTATOES FLAMBÉED WITH BOURBON

16 TO 20 SERVINGS

This easy dish is formed just like a French apple tart—minus the pastry. It is only slightly sweet and can make a grand entrance if you choose to flambé it in front of your guests. For best presentation, use a very large, round ovenproof dish—I use my 15-inch paella pan—though it can be prepared in one or even two baking dishes of any sort.

6 pounds large sweet potatoes
¼ pound (1 stick) plus 2 tablespoons unsalted
    butter, softened to room temperature
½ teaspoon salt
½ teaspoon freshly ground pepper
¼ cup sugar
½ to ⅔ cup bourbon, to taste

1. Put the potatoes in a large pot of cold water. Bring to a boil over moderately high heat and cook for about 20 minutes, until about 1 inch of the potatoes are tender around the edges but they are still firm in the center. Drain and rinse with cold water. When they are cool enough to handle, peel the potatoes with a knife—the skins will come off easily. (The potatoes can be cooked a day ahead. Wrap in plastic wrap and refrigerate.)

2. Use 1 tablespoon of the butter to grease a large baking dish, preferably 15 inches round. Cut the sweet potatoes into ¼-inch rounds. Arrange the slices, overlapping, in the dish in concentric circles, as you would a French apple tart. The finished arrangement should look something like a rose. Smear the remaining softened butter all over the potatoes, covering them as well as you can. Season with the salt and pepper. Sprinkle the sugar evenly over the potatoes. (The recipe can be prepared ahead to this point. Set aside at room temperature for up to 3 hours, or cover and refrigerate overnight. Let return to room temperature before proceeding.)

3. Preheat the oven to 325° F. Bake the sweet potatoes, uncovered, for 30 minutes. Increase the heat to 450° F. and bake for 15 to 20 minutes, or until the potatoes are tender and lightly glazed.

4. Pour the bourbon into a small nonaluminum saucepan. Warm over low heat for 20 to 30 seconds. Carefully ignite the bourbon with a match and drizzle the flaming liquid over the sweet potatoes.

WILD RICE RISOTTO

18 TO 24 SERVINGS

3 ounces imported dried mushrooms
1½ pounds wild rice (3¼ cups)
4 tablespoons unsalted butter
1½ tablespoons olive oil
2 medium onions, chopped
2 medium celery ribs with leaves, finely diced
2 medium carrots, finely diced
3 garlic cloves, minced
⅓ pound thickly sliced Black Forest or baked
    ham, finely diced
2 cans (13¾ ounces each) chicken broth
1 can (13¾ ounces) beef broth
1½ tablespoons soy sauce
¾ teaspoon thyme
½ teaspoon freshly ground pepper

1. Put the mushrooms in a medium bowl. Pour on 4 cups boiling water and let soak for 20 minutes, or until soft. Remove the mushrooms from the liquid, squeeze dry and finely dice. Strain the soaking liquid through a double layer of dampened cheesecloth and reserve 2½ cups.

2. Rinse the rice well. Boil in a large saucepan of salted water for 10 minutes; drain.

3. Preheat the oven to 350° F. In a large flameproof casserole, melt the butter in the oil over moderate heat. Add the onions and cook for 5 minutes. Add the celery, carrots, garlic and ham and cook, stirring occasionally, until the onions are golden and the other vegetables are softened, 5 to 10 minutes longer.

4. Add the rice and diced mushrooms and stir to blend with the oil and vegetables. Add the chicken broth, beef broth, reserved mushroom liquid, soy sauce, thyme and pepper. Cover and bake for 50 minutes. (The rice can be made ahead up to 2 days in advance. Transfer to a bowl and refrigerate, covered. Before serving, microwave to heat through or reheat in a covered casserole in a 350° F. oven for 20 to 30 minutes.)

Braised Fennel au Gratin

16 SERVINGS

This dish combines the deep, toasted flavor of long-braised fennel with the pleasant crunch of a crisp browned topping.

- ½ cup plus 2 tablespoons extra-virgin olive oil
- 5 large fennel bulbs, cut lengthwise into ½-inch slices, plus ½ cup coarsely chopped fennel top greens
- 8 garlic cloves, unpeeled
- Salt and freshly ground pepper
- 2 cups chicken stock or water
- 3 slices firm-textured white bread
- ¼ cup freshly grated Parmesan cheese

1. Preheat the oven to 375° F. In a large heavy skillet, heat ¼ cup of the oil. Fry the fennel slices with the garlic in batches over moderately high heat until the fennel is lightly browned, 1½ to 2 minutes per side. Leave the garlic in until it is softened, but do not let it brown. Add more oil as needed; it will probably take another ¼ cup. Transfer the fennel and garlic to a large gratin or baking dish and season with salt and pepper.

2. Pour the stock into the skillet. Bring to a boil, scraping up any browned bits from the bottom of the pan, and pour over the fennel. Cover the dish tightly with foil and bake for 10 minutes. Uncover the pan and bake for 15 to 20 minutes, basting once or twice with the liquid in the pan, until the fennel is just tender. (The recipe can be prepared to this point up to a day ahead. Let stand at room temperature for up to several hours, or cover and refrigerate.)

3. Tear the bread into a food processor. Add the fennel tops and the cheese. Process until the bread is ground into crumbs and the mixture is well blended.

4. Preheat the oven (or increase the temperature) to 450° F. Sprinkle the bread-crumb topping all over the fennel and drizzle on 2 tablespoons of olive oil. Bake until the fennel is heated through and the topping is crisp and golden brown, 15 to 20 minutes.

Easy Cream Cheesecake

12 TO 16 SERVINGS

If you have a mental image of what great soft cheesecake tastes like, this is it—absolutely classic! And it is made with no fuss in a food processor.

- ⅓ box (⅓ pound) graham crackers, broken up
- 1¼ cups plus 2 tablespoons sugar
- ¼ pound (1 stick) unsalted butter, cut into tablespoons
- 2 pounds cream cheese (4 packages, 8 ounces each), at room temperature
- 6 eggs
- 1¾ teaspoons vanilla extract
- 1 pint (2 cups) sour cream
- Fresh raspberries or strawberries, for garnish, optional

1. Preheat the oven to 375° F. In a food processor, grind the graham crackers to crumbs along with 2 tablespoons of the sugar.

2. Melt the butter. (I like to put it in a glass bowl and melt it in the microwave.) Add the graham cracker crumbs and mix to moisten evenly. Dump this mixture into a 10-inch springform pan. With your fingers, pat it evenly all over the bottom and about 1 inch up the sides.

3. In a large bowl, beat the cream cheese with an electric mixer until light. Gradually beat in 1 cup of the sugar. Beat in the eggs, 1 at a time, until well blended. Beat in 1½ teaspoons of the vanilla. Pour into the prepared springform and smooth the top.

4. Put on a baking sheet or piece of aluminum foil to catch any drips and bake for 15 minutes. Reduce the oven temperature to 325° F. and bake for 25 minutes longer.

5. Meanwhile, in a bowl, blend together the sour cream with the remaining ¼ cup sugar and ¼ teaspoon vanilla.

6. Remove the cheesecake from the oven and let cool on a rack for 10 minutes. Leave the oven on. Spoon the sour cream topping over the cheesecake, spreading evenly to the edges. Return to the oven and bake for 10 minutes. Let the cheesecake cool completely in the pan. Cover the pan and refrigerate until chilled, at least 6 hours, or overnight.

7. Before serving, run a knife around the edge of the cake and remove the side of the springform. Garnish the cheesecake with fresh berries, if desired.

Bittersweet Chocolate Truffle Torte

12 TO 16 SERVINGS

Bittersweet rather than cloying, and just a little bit different from any other deep chocolate dessert you've tasted, this rich creation is from pastry chef Jean-Marc Burillier of the Lafayette restaurant in New York.

3 eggs
1 cup sugar
¼ cup all-purpose flour
2 tablespoons cake flour
2½ tablespoons unsweetened Dutch-process cocoa powder, preferably imported
½ cup fraise de Bourgogne, framboise or Grand Marnier
9 ounces best-quality bittersweet, sweet or semisweet chocolate
2½ ounces unsweetened chocolate
2 cups heavy cream
Cocoa powder, for garnish

1. Preheat the oven to 375° F. Butter an 8½- or 9-inch cake pan or springform. Dust with flour and tap out any excess.

2. In a metal bowl, beat the eggs with ½ cup of the sugar. Place over a pan of barely simmering water and whisk until the mixture is very warm, 3 to 5 minutes. Remove from the heat and beat with an electric mixer until the mixture is cold and falls back in a slowly dissolving ribbon, 3 to 5 minutes.

3. Sift together the all-purpose flour, cake flour and cocoa. One-third at a time, fold the cocoa and flour into the egg mixture. Turn the batter into the prepared cake pan and bake for 15 to 20 minutes, until a cake tester comes out dry and the edges are just beginning to pull away from the sides of the pan. Unmold onto a rack and let cool completely. The cake is best made a day ahead, or bake it weeks or even months ahead and freeze; it is supposed to be dry.

4. To assemble the torte, cut the cake horizontally in half; you need only one half for this recipe. (Freeze the second half or make 2 tortes if you need them.) Put the cake, cut side up, in the center of the bottom of a 10-inch springform pan. If you don't like to serve off the bottom of the springform, line it with a round of cardboard first.

5. In a small saucepan, combine the remaining ½ cup sugar with ½ cup water. Bring to a boil, stirring to dissolve the sugar. Boil for 1 minute; remove from the heat. Add the liqueur. Brush this syrup all over the cake; it will be very moist.

6. In a small heavy saucepan, melt the bittersweet and unsweetened chocolate in ⅓ cup of water over low heat, stirring frequently, until smooth. Remove from the heat and let cool until almost room temperature and slightly thickened.

7. In a large bowl, beat the cream until fairly stiff. Whisk about one-third of the cream into the chocolate to lighten it. Fold the chocolate into the remaining cream just until no streaks show. Pour this ganache, or chocolate cream, over the cake, filling in the gap around the edge of the springform. Smooth the top. Cover and freeze for 1 to 2 hours until set, or refrigerate overnight. To unmold, run a knife around the edge; remove the side of the springform. Dust with additional cocoa before serving.

Easy Southern Shrimp Boil

FOR 20 TO 24

Pesto Deviled Eggs

Cheese Straws

Summer Crudités with Sour Cream and Two-Caviar Dip (page 133)

■

Shrimp Boil with Creole Butter Dipping Sauce

24-Hour Salad

Corn on the Cob

Red and Yellow Cherry Tomatoes

Portuguese or French Bread

■

Brownie Sundaes

Margaret Hess's Best Fudge Brownies

Fresh Strawberry Sundaes with Strawberry Sauce

When I was young, we spent summers in a big stone house on a hill overlooking the ocean. Our neighbor's rock garden, a patchwork of brilliant colors abuzz with dragonflies and bees, led down to the beach path, lined with milkweed and wild roses. Above, a line of white pine and seckel pear trees hemmed in our lawn. During the week, when we were there alone, the yard seemed as vast as the shore. But on weekends, with company milling all about, it barely contained the crowd. Anyone with a country house or even a comfortable backyard knows this phenomenon. Wherever you are, summer weekends bring guests—usually lots of them—and they're not always expected.

For those times when you're entertaining a couple of dozen good friends and you'd rather be outdoors in the sun than indoors cooking, here's a delightful backyard spread that's perfect for large-scale casual entertaining—a down-home, southern-style shrimp boil. A combination of Cajun spice, Mediterranean freshness and good old-fashioned food highlights this menu, which is easy to serve and fun to eat. Just spread out plenty of newspapers all over your backyard picnic table, set down a tall pile of paper napkins at either end, dump these tasty shrimp in the middle and let everyone go at 'em.

The appetizers range from frozen ahead to easy-to-make to store-bought. Tangy cheese and a bit of hot pepper make these cheese straws irresistible nibbles. Fresh basil and toasted pine nuts bring the flavor of pesto to a traditional deviled egg. For the crudités, scour your local farmer's market, or raid your own garden, for the prettiest, most unusual seasonal vegetables you can find. Serve them raw or lightly blanched, as their texture dictates, with the easy Two-Caviar Dip.

You'll need at least two big pots—10 gallons or more—for the shrimp and corn (borrow or rent an extra if you need it). Both cook quickly at the last moment. Allow ⅓ to ½ pound shrimp and 2 ears of corn per person, and get help shucking. Guests shell their own shrimp as they eat them. Pile up the cherry tomatoes in large baskets, lined with dark green grape leaves if you have any growing near you.

The 24-Hour Salad, a classic American recipe found at more than one family reunion and church supper, is called that because it is assembled a day ahead. There's nothing fancy about it, but everyone loves it. Be sure you have a garage full of iced beer before you start, and one or two large, clean, plastic-lined garbage cans for easy cleanup.

For dessert, just set out the components for the sundaes—brownie squares, vanilla ice cream, chocolate sauce, walnuts, sliced strawberries, strawberry sauce and whipped cream, and let all your guests help themselves. It is, after all, the informal, self-serve aspect of this food that makes it so light-hearted.

Do-Ahead Planning

Up to a month in advance: Make the Cheese Straws and freeze them. Bake the brownies and freeze them.

Several days in advance: Cook the eggs, shell them immediately and store them in the refrigerator in a bowl of cold water to cover. Make the Creole Butter Sauce and refrigerate.

The day before the party: Stuff the Pesto Deviled Eggs; cover and refrigerate. Prepare the crudités. Make two recipes of the 24-Hour Salad, except for the bacon. Make the Strawberry Sauce for the sundaes.

Several hours in advance of the party: Arrange the crudités on platters or in baskets; cover with a damp cloth. Make the Two-Caviar Dip. Make the court bouillon for the Shrimp Boil. Cook the bacon for the 24-Hour Salad. Slice the berries for the Strawberry Sundaes. Whip the cream for the sundaes; cover and refrigerate.

Shortly before serving: Boil the shrimp. Reheat the Creole Butter Sauce. Cook the corn on the cob. Add the bacon to the salad and toss. Reheat the Hot Fudge Sauce.

PESTO DEVILED EGGS
MAKES 48 PIECES

½ cup pine nuts (pignoli)
2 dozen extra-large eggs
1 large bunch of basil
1 tablespoon plus 1 teaspoon Dijon mustard
1 tablespoon red wine vinegar
1 teaspoon hot pepper sauce
½ teaspoon salt
½ teaspoon freshly ground pepper
3 garlic cloves, crushed through a press
½ cup extra-virgin olive oil

1. Preheat the oven to 300° F. Put the pine nuts on a small baking sheet and toast in the oven for about 8 minutes, until golden brown. Immediately transfer to a plate to cool. (The nuts can be toasted up to 3 days ahead and stored in the refrigerator in a covered container.)

2. Put the eggs in a large heavy pot and add water to cover by at least 1 inch. Bring to a simmer over moderately high heat, reduce the heat and simmer for 12 minutes. Drain and rinse under cold water until cool. Peel the eggs immediately to avoid a dark ring around the yolk. (The eggs can be cooked and peeled up to 2 days in advance. Put in a bowl, cover with cold water and refrigerate.)

3. Split the eggs in half lengthwise and remove the yolks. Wash and dry the basil. Set aside 48 small leaves for garnish. Coarsely cut up enough basil to measure ⅔ cup loosely packed. (Reserve the remainder for another use.)

4. In a food processor, combine the egg yolks, basil, mustard, vinegar, hot sauce, salt, pepper and garlic. Turn the machine quickly on and off until the mixture is blended and the basil is coarsely chopped. Reserve 1 tablespoon of the pine nuts for garnish. Add the remaining nuts to the yolk mixture. With the machine on, add the olive oil through the feed tube until it is incorporated and the nuts are coarsely chopped.

5. Fill the egg white halves with heaping teaspoonfuls of the egg yolk-basil filling. Garnish each egg half with a small basil leaf and a couple of toasted pine nuts. Cover and refrigerate for up to a day before serving.

CHEESE STRAWS

MAKES ABOUT 12 DOZEN

These are irresistible; there is no way anybody can eat just one...or two...or...This recipe makes a large batch, but you'll be surprised at how fast they disappear. And they freeze beautifully.

¼ pound (1 stick) plus 4 tablespoons unsalted
   butter
¼ pound extra-sharp white Cheddar cheese
¼ pound imported Parmesan cheese
2 cups all-purpose unbleached flour
1 teaspoon salt
⅛ teaspoon cayenne pepper
1 egg yolk blended with 3 tablespoons cold water

1. Preheat the oven to 375° F. Set out 4 tablespoons of the butter to soften.

2. With the shredding disk on a food processor, grate the Cheddar cheese; transfer to a medium bowl.

3. With the metal blade on the processor, finely grate the Parmesan cheese. Add the Parmesan to the Cheddar and toss to mix.

4. Put the flour in the same processor bowl (no need to rinse). Add the salt and cayenne and process for 5 seconds to blend. Add the 1 stick cold butter, cut into tablespoons. Pulse (turn the machine quickly on and off) 12 times. Add half of the mixed cheeses. Pulse 6 times. Add the remaining cheese and pulse 6 more times. The dough should be evenly mixed, but it will remain granular. Add the egg yolk and water and blend until the dough is evenly moistened, about 10 seconds.

5. Divide the dough in half and press each into a ½-inch-thick rectangle. Wrap one half in plastic and refrigerate. On a lightly floured surface, roll out the other half of the dough to an 8 x 12-inch rectangle, about ¼ inch thick. Spread 2 tablespoons of the softened butter over the dough. Fold in thirds like a letter, dust with flour and roll out again. Fold in thirds a second time. (You can use the dough now or give it a couple more turns if you'd like it to be more puffed. If it becomes too soft to work with, refrigerate it for 10 to 15 minutes until it firms up. This is not a delicate dough, so feel free to pat and patch wherever necessary.)

6. To form the straws, roll out the dough to a rectangle about 8 inches wide and ⅛ to ¼ inch thick. Using a fluted rolling wheel cutter or a small sharp knife, cut the dough into straws 3½ to 4 inches long and ¼ to ⅜ inch wide. Use a pastry scraper or wide spatula to transfer them to lightly buttered baking sheets. Repeat with the remaining dough and butter. Place each sheet in the freezer for 10 to 15 minutes.

7. Bake the straws for 10 minutes, or until they are golden and crisp. Transfer to a rack and let cool. Store in an airtight container at room temperature for up to 5 days, or freeze for longer storage.

SHRIMP BOIL

20 TO 24 SERVINGS

*7 to 8 pounds medium shrimp (25 to 30 per
    pound) in the shell*
⅓ cup mustard seeds
¼ cup coriander seeds
¼ cup allspice berries
2 tablespoons black peppercorns
2 tablespoons crushed hot red pepper flakes
12 whole cloves
6 blades of mace
3 imported bay leaves, broken in half
2½ tablespoons coarse (kosher) salt
3 onions, thickly sliced
2 celery ribs, thickly sliced
6 garlic cloves, smashed
1 lemon, sliced
½ cup fresh lemon juice

1. Rinse the shrimp very well but do not shell.
Drain and set aside.

2. Fill a stockpot with 6 to 8 quarts of water.
Add all the remaining ingredients. Bring to a boil,
reduce the heat and simmer for 15 minutes. (The
court bouillon can be made several hours ahead.)

3. Just before you are ready to serve the shrimp,
bring the court bouillon to a boil. Dump about one-
third of the shrimp into the pot and boil for 2 to 3
minutes, until pink, loosely curled and opaque
throughout. Remove with a skimmer or slotted
spoon and transfer to a bowl. (The shrimp in their
shell will stay hot for a good 5 to 10 minutes.) Repeat
twice with the remaining shrimp. Serve with Creole
Butter Dipping Sauce.

CREOLE BUTTER DIPPING SAUCE

MAKES 3 CUPS

1½ pounds unsalted butter
¼ cup fresh lemon juice
1 tablespoon Worcestershire sauce
2 to 3 teaspoons hot pepper sauce, to taste
1½ teaspoons salt

1. In a heavy medium-size saucepan, melt the
butter over low heat. Skim the white foam off the
top. Pour the clear butter into another saucepan or
bowl, discarding the thick milky residue at the bottom of the pan. (This "clarified" butter can be made
up to 2 weeks ahead and stored in a covered jar in the
refrigerator.)

2. Whisk in the lemon juice, Worcestershire,
hot sauce and salt. (The flavored butter can be made
up to 2 days ahead. Refrigerate in a covered jar.)
Reheat over low heat or in the microwave until hot
before serving.

CRUDITÉS

Nothing brightens up a buffet table or is more welcome to a group of nibblers than a colorful assortment of crudités with a tasty dip. Short of flowers, fresh vegetables are the most attractive thing you can put on a table. For that reason, it pays to give them some thought. Which will be more effective, creating large areas of color or a mix of contrasting light and dark together? Plan your design, thinking of your container as well. Will everything be standing up in a basket or piled in mounds on a platter? A lot of what you decide will depend on seasonal availability. Try to choose one or two unusual vegetables, along with the more standard carrots, bell peppers, broccoli, cauliflower, radishes, zucchini and cherry tomatoes. Perhaps steamed artichokes, asparagus stalks, sticks of crisp jicama or bunches of tiny, white enoki mushrooms.

Though the French word *crudité* implies raw-ness, I am very opinionated on that subject. Some vegetables are wonderful raw—carrots, peppers and tomatoes, to name a few. Others, such as broccoli, cauliflower, asparagus and green beans require at least momentary blanching in boiling water both to heighten their flavor and to soften them to a pleasing crunch rather than woody toughness. For display purposes, blanching also performs the important service of greatly intensifying the color of the vegetable. The boiling water breaks up tiny air bubbles under the skin, brightening the color underneath. After blanching, be sure to rinse vegetables under cold running water to stop the cooking and set the color.

24-HOUR SALAD
12 TO 14 SERVINGS

In Texas, folks do a lot of large-scale entertaining. This ranch recipe, from Betty Jo Conlee of Bryan, Texas, is one she uses frequently at barbecues and picnics. It's a great boon to any busy cook because the salad is prepared a day ahead and just tossed together before serving. I like to add the bacon when I toss the salad with the dressing so that it stays crisp. Make a double recipe in two bowls for this menu.

> 1 pound spinach, stemmed, rinsed, dried and torn into large bite-size pieces
> 1 medium red bell pepper, cut into 1½ x ¼-inch strips
> 3 scallions, cut into ½-inch lengths
> 1 large head of romaine lettuce, rinsed, dried and torn into large bite-size pieces
> ½ red onion, very thinly sliced
> ½ pound Swiss cheese, shredded
> 1 package (10 ounces) frozen peas
> 4 hard-cooked eggs, sliced
> 1⅓ cups sour cream
> ⅔ cup mayonnaise
> ½ cup chopped parsley
> ⅓ cup minced fresh chives
> 2 garlic cloves, crushed through a press
> 1 tablespoon fresh lemon juice
> 1 tablespoon red wine vinegar
> 2 teaspoons Dijon mustard
> ½ teaspoon salt
> ¼ teaspoon freshly ground pepper
> 1 pound sliced bacon, cooked until crisp and crumbled

1. Up to 24 hours before you plan to serve the salad, layer in a large bowl in the exact order given—first the spinach, then the red pepper, scallions, half the romaine lettuce, the red onion, the remaining lettuce and the Swiss cheese. Scatter the frozen peas on top. Cover with a layer of the egg slices.

2. In a bowl, combine the sour cream, mayonnaise, parsley, chives, garlic, lemon juice, vinegar, mustard, salt and pepper. Whisk to blend well. Spread the dressing over the top of the salad to cover it completely. Cover the bowl with plastic wrap and refrigerate for up to 24 hours.

3. Shortly before serving, toss the salad with the dressing until coated. Save about ½ cup bacon. Add the rest to the salad and toss. Sprinkle the reserved bacon on top.

BROWNIE SUNDAES

12 SERVINGS

This dessert is a guaranteed crowd pleaser for guests of all ages. For a dozen sundaes, you'll need only a half-recipe of brownies, but I'd make the whole batch, put them all out and freeze the extras, if you are fortunate enough to end up with any. For a crowd, it's probably easiest just to put out all the fixings and let guests help themselves.

*½ recipe Margaret Hess's Best Fudge Brownies
    (recipe follows), cut into 3-inch squares
2 to 3 pints good-quality vanilla ice cream
Hot Fudge Sauce (page 46)
Whipped cream and broken walnuts*

For each sundae, set a brownie on a plate. Top with a ½-cup scoop of vanilla ice cream. Drizzle a couple of spoonfuls of the Hot Fudge Sauce over the ice cream and top with a dollop of whipped cream and a sprinkling of walnuts.

MARGARET HESS'S BEST FUDGE BROWNIES

MAKES 2 DOZEN 3-INCH OR 4 DOZEN 1½-INCH BROWNIES

These moist brownies are as rich as they come. The better the quality of chocolate you use, the better the brownies will taste.

*2 pounds semisweet chocolate, cut up
1 pound unsalted butter, cut up
7 eggs
2 cups sugar
1 tablespoon vanilla extract
2½ cups all-purpose flour
1½ teaspoons salt
¾ pound walnuts, optional*

1. Preheat the oven to 350° F. In a large double boiler, or a large bowl placed in a skillet of water, melt the chocolate and butter together over simmering water, stirring until smooth. Remove from the heat.

2. In a mixing bowl, beat the eggs and sugar until they are light in color and begin to ribbon, about 2 minutes. Beat in the chocolate mixture and the vanilla. Mix until well blended, about 1 minute. Add the flour and salt and beat until just blended, 30

to 60 seconds. Stir in the walnuts, if you're adding them.

3. Pour the batter into an 18 x 13-inch half-sheet pan lined with wax paper. Spread to even thickness and bang the pan on the table two or three times to release any air bubbles.

4. Bake the brownies for 35 minutes. Let cool on a rack for 15 minutes before cutting into 3- or 1½-inch squares.

FRESH STRAWBERRY SUNDAES WITH STRAWBERRY SAUCE

12 SERVINGS

*4 pints fresh strawberries
¼ cup sugar
3 tablespoons Fraise de Bourgogne (French
    strawberry liqueur), framboise (raspberry
    brandy) or kirsch
2 teaspoons arrowroot or cornstarch
2 to 3 pints good-quality vanilla ice cream, such as
    Haagen-Dazs
Vanilla-flavored sweetened whipped cream,
    optional*

1. Rinse the strawberries by dunking them in a bowl of cold water. Lift them out into a colander and drain well. Hull the berries. Reserve 12 of the most attractive berries for garnish. Halve or quarter 3 cups of the berries, depending on their size. Puree the remaining berries until smooth; strain through a sieve to remove the seeds.

2. Put the cut berries in a bowl. Sprinkle with the sugar and Fraise de Bourgogne and toss gently. Let stand at room temperature for at least 2 hours.

3. In a small nonaluminum saucepan, bring the pureed strawberries to a boil over moderate heat. Drain the juice from the macerated strawberries into a small bowl and stir in the arrowroot until it is smooth and blended. Stir into the hot puree and cook, stirring, until the sauce thickens. Remove from the heat.

4. For each sundae, put a scoop of vanilla ice cream in a dessert bowl. Top with about ⅓ cup of the cut berries. Then spoon on about 3 tablespoons of the strawberry sauce. If you're including whipped cream, spoon a dollop on top and garnish the sundae with a whole strawberry.

Elegant Evening Buffet

FOR 20 TO 24

Niçoise Swordfish Salad in Endive Cups
(page 151)

Coriander Chicken Rolls

Rich Liver Mousse with Toasted Hazelnuts
(page 65)

Olives and Nuts

∎

Smoked Chicken Torte

Karen Lee's Gingered Side of Salmon

Asparagus and Mushrooms with
Sesame-Orange Dressing

Romaine, Radicchio and Fennel Salad

Ila's Wild Rice Salad

French Bread

∎

Truffled Brie

Basket of Grapes

∎

Bourbon-Peach Trifle

Chocolate Mints

Buffets are frequently the butt of bad jokes. There's something about that endless table laden with platters of garishly garnished food that brings out the beast in people. We've all been there, dressed in evening clothes, standing in line, balancing plate, napkin, silverware and wineglass like a trained seal, while fending off friends who begin jockeying for position as soon as dinner is announced.

There is, however, nothing quite as breathtaking as a glorious display of food, and a buffet can be not only the most practicable way to serve a crowd, but the best way. All you need are a few tricks to avoid traffic jams and turn what could be a free-for-all into an elegant, civilized way for guests to help themselves. Here are a few dos and don'ts that I guarantee will make a spectacular, smooth-flowing buffet:

Choose attractive, colorful food. A buffet should be as inviting to look at as it is to eat.

Avoid dishes with fancy little garnishes in the center that will be destroyed as soon as guests help themselves. Decorate around the rims of platters.

Replenish platters when they start looking worn down. Always carry them out to the kitchen and refill them out of sight of the guests.

Don't put all the food in one place. Allow at least

one station for every ten or twelve guests so that lines are kept to a minimum. Divide recipes between two bowls or platters where appropriate.

Put the bar in a separate place. If possible, help guests to drinks after they are seated with their food.

Be sure that there is somewhere for everyone to perch his or her glass.

Don't serve a lot of hot food. Limit yourself to one or two hot dishes, perhaps as the centerpiece of the meal. Choose accompaniments that are appropriate chilled or at room temperature.

Choose recipes that can be prepared ahead.

This particular menu for an elegant evening buffet is especially easy on the cook. It offers one individual cold hors d'oeuvre—Niçoise Swordfish Salad in Endive Cups—and one hot hors d'oeuvre—Coriander Chicken Rolls, little filo packets filled with an Oriental-flavored, coriander-flecked chicken. They are fabulous and can be prepared and frozen well before the party. They're so good, in fact, that you may want to make a double recipe. These and a simple liver mousse spread and nuts and olives are all you need to accompany cocktails.

A great dish for entertaining, the Smoked Chicken Torte, colorfully layered with bright red peppers, green spinach, ivory smoked chicken and yellow cheese and egg, can be assembled completely up to two months ahead and frozen. The salmon does need to be cooked at the last moment, but since it is excellent at room temperature, you could broil or grill it just before guests arrive. Since the salmon is richly flavored, I've chosen wild rice as an accompaniment. This delicious salad, studded with diced red, yellow and green peppers, improves when made a day ahead. Also colorful, the Romaine, Radiccho and Fennel Salad is shredded so that it is easy to serve and relatively compact on the plate. Asparagus and Mushrooms—button and shiitake—provides another luxurious touch. While this dish can be served hot, I prefer it as a room-temperature salad on a buffet.

For a crowd of this size, you'll need two Smoked Chicken Tortes. Make a double recipe of Ila's Wild Rice Salad, likewise, the Romaine and Radicchio Salad. Obviously, this menu halves easily to serve twelve.

No matter how much food you put out, everyone will still be looking forward to dessert, and Peach-Bourbon Trifle won't disappoint them. While fresh peaches are, of course, a tremendous treat, I make this cold dessert year-round, using individually quick-frozen peach slices with no added sugar when fresh are out of season.

Do-Ahead Planning

Up to 1 month in advance: Assemble and freeze two Smoked Chicken Tortes. Assemble and freeze one or two recipes of the Coriander Chicken Rolls.

4 days before the party: Prepare the Truffled Brie.

Up to 3 days ahead: Make the Rich Liver Mousse with Toasted Hazelnuts.

The day before the party: Make the swordfish salad. Separate the endive spears; rinse and dry them and refrigerate in a plastic bag. Make two recipes of Ila's Wild Rice Salad. Prepare a double amount of romaine, radicchio and fennel for the salad. Cook the asparagus. Prepare the peaches and the pastry cream for the trifle.

The morning of the party: Assemble the Bourbon-Peach Trifle.

About 4 hours in advance: Assemble the Niçoise Swordfish Salad in Endive Cups, arrange on a platter, cover and refrigerate. Make the Asparagus and Mushrooms with Sesame-Orange Dressing; let stand at room temperature. Remove the Truffled Brie from the refrigerator.

At least 2 hours before you plan to serve the buffet: Bake the frozen Smoked Chicken Tortes.

About 1 hour ahead: Marinate the salmon.

Just before guests arrive: Broil or grill two sides of salmon. Let stand at room temperature for up to 1½ hours before serving.

Shortly before serving: Bake the frozen Coriander Chicken Rolls. Toss the Romaine, Radicchio and Fennel Salad.

CORIANDER CHICKEN ROLLS

MAKES ABOUT 50

Rosa Ross, New York cooking teacher and caterer (Wok on Wheels), gave me this terrific recipe. It is based on the classic Chinese paper-wrapped chicken, which Rosa used to serve. But when she saw too many people popping the paper into their mouths, she realized it was time for a change and cleverly chose filo dough, thin as parchment but edible.

Provided you keep the dough covered so it doesn't dry out, filo is easy to work with. Don't open the package until you are ready to begin wrapping, keep the sheets covered with a towel or sheet of plastic wrap and pull them out as you need them. Don't worry about tears and rips; they can be patched with a little oil.

¾ pound skinned and boned chicken breasts
2 tablespoons hoisin sauce
1 tablespoon Chinese dark soy sauce
1 tablespoon dry sherry
1 tablespoon cornstarch
2 teaspoons Oriental sesame oil
2 garlic cloves, smashed and minced
¼ cup minced scallion
¼ cup finely chopped fresh coriander (cilantro) or
*   flat-leaf parsley*
⅛ teaspoon salt
¼ teaspoon freshly ground pepper
1 box (8 ounces) filo pastry sheets
About ⅓ cup safflower or corn oil

1. Trim any excess fat or gristle from the chicken. With the knife at an angle, cut the chicken crosswise into thin slices. (This is easier to do if the chicken is partially frozen.) Then stack the slices and cut the chicken into very thin slivers.

2. In a bowl, combine the slivered chicken, hoisin sauce, soy sauce, sherry, cornstarch, sesame oil, garlic, scallion, coriander, salt and pepper. Toss to mix well.

3. Remove one-third of the filo dough from its package. Reroll the remainder and keep it wrapped. Cut the filo sheets lengthwise in half to measure rectangles about 10 inches long and 3 to 4 inches wide. Stack the strips and keep them covered. One by one, remove a strip of filo and set it down lengthwise with one of the short ends in front. Brush the top half of the pastry with oil, fold up the bottom to double the sheet and scoop a scant teaspoon (use a measuring spoon) of the chicken filling onto the center of the bottom edge. Roll up twice, fold in the sides about ½ inch at each edge and paint the top ½ to 1 inch of the pastry with oil. Roll up all the way to form a packet about 1 x 2 inches; it will self-seal. Repeat to use up all the filo and filling. (The recipe can be prepared to this point up to 3 months in advance. Layer the packets in an airtight container with wax paper between the layers and freeze.)

4. Preheat the oven to 350° F. Bake the chicken packets (unthawed if frozen) on an ungreased cookie sheet for 10 to 15 minutes, until golden brown. Serve hot.

SMOKED CHICKEN TORTE

10 TO 12 SERVINGS

I love this recipe because it can be made completely ahead and frozen. When you want to serve it, pull it out of the freezer and bake it without even defrosting. Colorful and tasty, this dish was developed by Robert Willson of Parties Plus, a top caterer in Los Angeles.

3 large red bell peppers
Salt and freshly ground pepper
2 pounds fresh spinach
5 tablespoons unsalted butter
2 tablespoons olive oil
2 medium shallots, minced
2 garlic cloves, minced
¼ teaspoon nutmeg, preferably freshly grated
6 eggs
1 tablespoon minced fresh parsley
2 teaspoons minced fresh chives
1 teaspoon minced fresh tarragon, or ½ teaspoon dried
1 pound frozen puff pastry, thawed
¾ pound Gruyère or Swiss cheese, shredded
¾ pound thinly sliced smoked chicken breast

1. Roast the peppers directly over a gas flame or under a broiler as close to the heat as possible, turning, until they are charred all over. Put in a bag and let steam for 10 minutes. Rub off the blackened skin and remove the stems, seeds and ribs. Rinse under cold running water and pat dry. Season liberally with salt and freshly ground pepper. Set aside.

2. Stem the spinach leaves; rinse well and dry. In a large flameproof casserole or wok, melt 2 tablespoons of the butter in the oil. Add the shallots and garlic and sauté over moderate heat until softened but not browned, 1 to 2 minutes. Add the spinach and sauté, tossing, until the spinach is wilted but still bright green. Turn into a colander and drain well, pressing out all excess liquid with the back of a spoon. Season with the nutmeg, ¼ teaspoon salt and ⅛ teaspoon pepper. Set aside.

3. In a medium bowl, beat 5 of the eggs with the parsley, chives, tarragon, ¼ teaspoon salt and ⅛ teaspoon pepper. In a large skillet, melt 1 tablespoon of the butter. Add half the egg mixture and cook over moderately low heat until the eggs are almost set, about 3 minutes. Flip the omelet over and cook until the bottom is set, about 1 minute. Remove to a plate and set aside. Repeat with another tablespoon of butter and the remaining eggs.

4. Grease a 9-inch springform pan with the remaining 1 tablespoon butter. Roll out about ¾ pound of the puff pastry to ¼-inch thickness. Line the pan, fitting the dough against the bottom and sides without stretching. Let the extra dough hang over the rim. Refrigerate for 5 to 10 minutes if the dough is very soft.

5. To assemble the torte, put one of the omelets into the bottom of the pastry-lined pan. Layer on half the spinach, half the shredded cheese, half the chicken, all the roasted red peppers, the remaining chicken, cheese, spinach and, finally, the second omelet.

6. Roll out the remaining dough. Arrange on top of the torte and trim the overlap to ½ inch. Beat the remaining egg with 1 tablespoon of water to make a glaze. Paint the edges of the dough with the egg glaze, fold over and crimp to seal. Paint the top of the torte with the egg glaze. Cut out some decorations from any scraps of dough and arrange them as a garnish on top. Paint with another wash of egg glaze. Refrigerate for at least 2 hours, or overnight, before baking, or freeze for up to 2 months.

7. Preheat the oven to 375° F. Put the torte on a cookie sheet to catch any drips and bake for 1½ hours; if the crust begins to brown too much before that time, cover loosely with aluminum foil. Remove from the oven and let the torte cool on a rack for at least 15 minutes. Remove the sides of the springform and slide the torte onto a platter. Serve warm or at room temperature.

KAREN LEE'S GINGERED SIDE OF SALMON

16 TO 20 SERVINGS

This dish is delicious at room temperature, but if you prefer to serve it hot, simply broil as directed in Step 3 for 5 minutes only. Just before serving, pop into a 450° F. oven for about 10 minutes, until the salmon is heated through and just opaque throughout.

> 1 whole salmon, preferably Norwegian, about 8
>   pounds (see Step 1)
> 1/3 cup unhulled sesame seeds
> 1 cup medium-dry sherry
> 1/3 cup dark soy sauce
> 1/3 cup Oriental sesame oil
> 1/4 cup minced fresh ginger
> 1 1/4 cups thinly sliced scallions
> 2 tablespoons minced garlic
> Slices of lemon and scallion brushes or sprigs of
>   parsley, for garnish

1. Ask your fishmonger to remove the head and to fillet both sides of the salmon, leaving the skin attached. You will have 2 sides of salmon fillet, about 3 pounds each. Rinse the salmon under cold running water; pat dry.

2. Put the salmon, skin side down, into 2 shallow nonaluminum roasting pans, roughly 12 x 17 inches each. Combine the sesame seeds, sherry, soy sauce, sesame oil, ginger, scallions and garlic and pour half over each piece of fish. Let marinate at room temperature for 1 hour.

3. Adjust your broiler so that the rack is about 4 inches from the heat. Preheat the broiler for at least 10 minutes. Place one side of salmon on the broiler rack, skin side down, and broil without turning for 10 to 12 minutes, or until it is just cooked through but still moist and juicy. Set aside loosely covered with foil and repeat with the remaining side of salmon. (If the salmon is so thick that it doesn't cook in this time, transfer to a 450° F. oven for about 5 minutes to finish off.) Serve garnished with lemon slices and scallion brushes or sprigs of parsley.

ASPARAGUS AND MUSHROOMS WITH SESAME-ORANGE DRESSING

ABOUT 16 SERVINGS

Reheated at the last moment, this makes an elegant vegetable to serve with almost any simple chicken or roast. Left at room temperature, it makes a fabulous salad or buffet side dish, ready ahead and even better upon standing.

> 3 pounds asparagus
> 1/3 cup safflower or corn oil
> 2 large shallots, minced
> 2 large garlic cloves, minced
> 1 pound medium mushrooms, trimmed and
>   quartered
> 1/2 pound shiitake mushrooms, stemmed, caps
>   sliced about 1/4 inch thick
> 1/2 cup fresh orange juice
> 2 tablespoons fresh lemon juice
> 2 tablespoons soy sauce
> 1 tablespoon plus 1 teaspoon Oriental sesame oil
> 1/2 teaspoon coarsely ground pepper

1. Trim off the bottom 1/4 to 1/2 inch of the asparagus. Bring 2 inches of salted water to a boil in a tall narrow stockpot or asparagus steamer. Stand the asparagus up in the pot, cover and steam until barely crisp-tender, 3 to 4 minutes. Remove and rinse under cold running water to stop the cooking; drain well. (The asparagus can be cooked a day ahead and refrigerated.)

2. Trim the tough, white ends off the asparagus and discard. Cut the asparagus crosswise on the diagonal into 1-inch lengths.

3. In a wok or a large frying pan, heat the safflower or corn oil. Add the shallots, garlic, quartered mushrooms and sliced shiitakes. Sauté over moderate heat until tender, 3 to 5 minutes. Add the orange juice, lemon juice, soy sauce, sesame oil and pepper; reduce the heat and simmer for 5 minutes. Add the asparagus and toss to mix. Either cook until the asparagus is heated through, about 2 minutes, and serve hot; or transfer the asparagus, mushrooms and dressing to a serving dish and let stand, tossing occasionally, until cool and serve at room temperature.

Romaine, Radicchio and Fennel Salad

12 TO 16 SERVINGS

Pretty with its strips of red, white and green, this salad looks especially nice in a glass bowl. Because it's shredded, it is easy to serve and eat at a buffet.

2 heads of romaine lettuce
1 large head of radicchio
2 large fennel bulbs
¼ cup sherry wine vinegar
¾ cup extra-virgin olive oil
Salt and freshly ground pepper to taste

1. Separate the lettuce leaves and rinse well. Drain and dry.

2. Stack the lettuce and radicchio leaves and shred fine. Sliver the fennel bulbs as fine as possible.

3. In a large salad bowl, combine the romaine, radicchio and fennel. Drizzle on the vinegar and then the oil. Toss to coat with the dressing. Season with salt and pepper to taste and toss again.

Ila's Wild Rice Salad

12 SERVINGS

This terrific party salad, the creation of Ila Stanger, editor-in-chief of *Food & Wine* magazine, tastes much better if made the day before (and lasts well for a day after that). It just needs an hour out of the refrigerator to allow it to return to room temperature before serving.

1 pound (2⅓ cups) wild rice
1 cup currants
4 carrots, peeled and finely diced
5 celery ribs, finely diced
1 small red bell pepper, finely diced
1 small yellow pepper (or use another red), finely diced
1 large red onion, finely diced
⅔ cup chopped flat-leaf parsley
1 large shallot, minced
1 cup extra-virgin olive oil
¼ cup balsamic vinegar
½ teaspoon freshly ground pepper

1. Rinse the rice well under cold running water. Place it in a large saucepan with 10 cups of water. Cover and bring to a boil. Remove the cover, reduce the heat and simmer until the rice is tender but still pleasantly chewy, about 40 minutes. Drain and let cool.

2. Meanwhile, put the currants in a bowl and cover with warm water for 20 to 30 minutes until they are plump; then drain.

3. In a large bowl, combine the wild rice, currants, carrots, celery, bell peppers, red onion and parsley, tossing to mix. In a small bowl, combine the shallot, olive oil, vinegar and pepper; whisk to blend the dressing well. Pour the dressing over the salad and toss to coat. Serve at room temperature.

Truffled Brie

24 TO 30 SERVINGS

This dish is expensive, but worth it. Choose the best brie you can, ripe but not ammoniated. The rind should have some light brown striations and, even when cold, it should be no harder than a grapefruit.

8½-inch wheel of brie (about 2 pounds)
½ pound mascarpone
1 fresh white truffle (1 to 1½ ounces), finely minced, or 1 tube (2 ounces) white truffle paste

1. With a long sharp knife, split the brie horizontally in half. In a small bowl, blend the mascarpone and white truffle. Spread it in an even layer over the cut side of the bottom half of the brie to about ¼ inch from the edge. Set the top of the brie in place and press gently to sandwich the layers. If any filling squeezes out, use your finger or a narrow spatula to smooth it in place.

2. Wrap the brie in plastic wrap. If you've saved the wooden container it came in (I always do), set it back in the container. Refrigerate for 4 days to allow the flavors to develop. Let stand at room temperature for at least 3 hours before serving.

BOURBON-PEACH TRIFLE

24 SERVINGS

Made with store-bought pound cake, a trifle is one of the easiest desserts to serve to a large group. When peaches are out of season, opt for the individually quick-frozen ones without sugar rather than a rock-hard tasteless fruit.

4 pounds ripe peaches, or 5 packages (12 ounces each) individually quick-frozen peach slices with no sugar added
⅓ cup bourbon
2 tablespoons peach schnapps or Pêcher Mignon
1 tablespoon plus ½ teaspoon fresh lemon juice
1⅔ cups plus 3 tablespoons granulated sugar
9 egg yolks
⅔ cup all-purpose flour
3 cups hot milk
1 tablespoon plus 1 teaspoon vanilla extract
2 pound cakes (12 ounces each)
2½ cups heavy cream
1 tablespoon confectioners' sugar
1 cup chopped or slivered toasted almonds

1. In a large pot of boiling water, blanch the peaches for 2 minutes, or until the skins peel off easily; drain. Peel and pit the peaches and cut them into ½-inch wedges over a bowl to catch their juice. (If using frozen peach slices, just let them defrost and be sure to include all their juice.) Put the fruit with any of its juices into a large bowl. Add the bourbon, peach schnapps, 1 tablespoon of the lemon juice and 3 to 4 tablespoons of the granulated sugar, depending on the sweetness of the peaches. Toss gently and let stand for at least 3 hours; the peaches will exude some of their juice. (The peaches can be prepared a day ahead. Cover and refrigerate; toss occasionally.)

2. In a medium bowl, whisk the egg yolks to break them up. Gradually beat in ⅔ cup of the sugar. Whisk until the mixture turns pale yellow and forms a ribbon, 2 to 3 minutes. Beat in the flour. Gradually whisk in the hot milk and ½ cup of the juices from the peaches.

3. Pour the custard mixture into a heavy saucepan, preferably enameled cast iron. Cook over moderately high heat, whisking frequently, until the pastry cream is smooth and thick, 3 to 5 minutes. Reduce the heat to moderate and continue to boil, whisking, until the mixture relaxes and thins out slightly and loses any trace of a raw flour taste, about 3 minutes longer. Scrape into a bowl and whisk in 1 tablespoon of the vanilla. Cover with a piece of plastic wrap directly on the surface to prevent a skin from forming. Refrigerate until chilled. (The pastry cream can be made a day in advance.)

4. Trim the brown edges off the pound cakes. Cut them into ½-inch slices and then into pieces about 2 x 1 inch. Set aside.

5. Up to 6 hours before serving, whip the cream in a large bowl until it forms soft peaks. Transfer half to a medium bowl. Whisk about one-third of the cream from the large bowl into the pastry cream to lighten it. Turn the lightened pastry cream into the large bowl and fold in the remaining whipped cream in that bowl. Cover and refrigerate.

6. Add the confectioners' sugar and remaining 1 teaspoon vanilla to the whipped cream in the medium bowl and beat until stiff peaks form. Cover and refrigerate.

7. When you are ready to assemble the dessert, have on hand a large (5-quart) glass serving bowl, the peaches, pastry cream and nuts; then make the caramel. In a small saucepan, combine the remaining 1 cup sugar and ½ teaspoon lemon juice with ⅓ cup water. Cook over moderately low heat, swirling the pan, until the sugar melts and the liquid is clear. Increase the heat to moderate and boil until the liquid caramelizes to a golden brown. It will continue to cook after you remove it from the heat, so don't wait too long. (You'll only use about two-thirds of the caramel, but I find it easier to work with a larger amount.)

8. Immediately arrange a layer of cake pieces in the bottom of the glass bowl. Cover with a single layer of the peach slices and their juice and, with a spoon, drizzle the hot caramel in a thin lacy pattern over the peaches; if you're heavy-handed, you'll end up with hard globs of caramel. Add a light sprinkling of almonds and spoon on about a 1-inch layer of the pastry cream. Repeat the layers until you use all the ingredients except the caramel, 5 or 6 peach slices and a couple of tablespoons of the nuts, which should be reserved for garnish. When you're through, spoon or pipe the whipped cream onto the top, drizzle on a little caramel and garnish with the reserved peaches and almonds. Cover and refrigerate for up to 6 hours before serving.

Chicken Pasta Salad with Lemon-Sesame Dressing

Grilled Marinated Flank Steak

Lentil Salad with Goat Cheese and Sun-Dried Tomatoes

Potato Salad with Sweet Sausages and Mushrooms

Giovanna's Shocking Pink Rice Salad

Green Bean Salad with Roasted Red Peppers (page 154)

Italian Bread

•

Honey-Pecan Cake

Sharp Cheddar Cheese and Tart Apples

Margaret Hess's Best Fudge Brownies (page 107)

The Ultimate Tailgate Party

FOR 24

Picnics and tailgate parties are perfect for potluck. No one should have to work hard on a lovely sunny day, and everyone enjoys a party more when they pitch in. While it is fun to be eclectic at a large event and the food should be varied, you do want to keep the menu balanced. That's why I suggest one person act as coordinator. If you're organizing the day, let everyone else know you're handing out recipes, first choice to the first caller. Assign noncooks the task of buying apples, bread, cheese, beverages and paper plates and plastic utensils, if you need them. As Phillip Schulz, author of *Cooking with Fire & Smoke*, suggested in an article on picnics in *Food & Wine* magazine, have everyone be responsible for the serving dishes and utensils for the dishes that they are making.

All of the following recipes allow for advance preparation and all will hold up well out-of-doors, though for safety's sake I suggest carrying the food in a cooler, even if it ends up being served at room temperature. Since this is potluck, the number of people these dishes serve will depend in part on the number of different dishes brought to the party. Assume a recipe that serves 12 will serve 24 if you have a large assortment of food. If only a dozen friends are getting together, four of the main course recipes, with the bread, fruit, cheese and dessert will be plenty, and be sure to halve the bean salad. If three dozen are coming, make all the recipes and double the lentil and potato salads.

POTLUCK

These days potluck makes more sense than ever, especially for entertaining a crowd. No one has as much time as he or she needs, and everyone enjoys themselves more when they contribute something to the party. For a picnic or tailgate, when the attention is on the out-of-doors and having fun, get the cooking done ahead and spread out the chores. If you are playing host, you might design the menu in detail, or outline it and let friends fill in the blanks with their favorite recipes. Be sure one person coordinates, though, so you don't end up with three chicken salads and two chocolate cakes. Once the menu is planned, consider sending around a mimeographed sheet with all the recipes listed, as well as where and when you are assembling. It will serve as a reminder and raise enthusiasm for the event. I've been at potluck parties where all the recipes were distributed to everyone who brought something— a nice souvenir and a great way to add to your repertoire. Chances are if a friend loves a recipe and finds it doable, you will too.

People who don't like to cook or who won't be around beforehand can bring bread, cheese, beverages, etc. As coordinator, make sure there is a grill, if you need one, as well as charcoal and matches. Make sure there are serving utensils, coolers and plenty of ice. If it's paper plates, napkins and plastic utensils, make sure you have extra, and throw in a couple of large plastic garbage bags for cleaning up.

Potluck suppers can make great charity fundraisers. For a special potluck party—indoors or out—consider a theme (Italian, Chinese, seafood or something sillier like South Seas, black and white, the Fifties—come as you were) with appropriate props and dress. Sometimes it's fun to go all out with flowers, silver, china and evening dress, if you are so inclined.

Do-Ahead Planning

Up to a month in advance: Bake the brownies and the Honey-Pecan Cake and freeze them.

Up to 3 days ahead: Roast the red peppers for the green bean salad. Refrigerate them in a bowl, covered with olive oil.

The day before the picnic: Cook the chicken, pasta and broccoli and make the lemon-sesame dressing. Make the Lentil Salad with Goat Cheese and Sun-Dried Tomatoes. Make the Potato Salad with Sweet Sausages and Mushrooms. Make Giovanna's Shocking Pink Rice Salad. Cook the green beans.

The morning of the picnic: Make the marinade for the steak. Transport the meat in the marinade in a tightly covered container and grill it at the picnic site. (Alternatively, grill the steak the night before and bring it already sliced.) Toss the Green Bean Salad with Roasted Red Peppers and the Chicken Pasta Salad with Lemon-Sesame Dressing just before leaving the house.

CHICKEN PASTA SALAD WITH LEMON-SESAME DRESSING

12 TO 16 SERVINGS

My friend Irene Thomas, of Lebanese descent, taught me this fabulous dressing, which can be used on broiled or grilled fish and on vegetables, or as a dip with toasted pita bread.

1½ to 2 pounds skinless, boneless chicken breasts
1 pound pasta shells, preferably imported
Salt and freshly ground pepper
3 tablespoons extra-virgin olive oil
⅔ cup plus 1 tablespoon fresh lemon juice
1 large shallot, minced
1 large bunch of broccoli (about 1½ pounds)
4 medium garlic cloves, crushed through a press
1 cup tahini
⅛ teaspoon cayenne pepper
1 large red bell pepper, cut into ½-inch squares
½ cup thinly sliced scallions

1. Rinse the chicken breasts under cold running water and put them in a medium to large saucepan. Add lightly salted water to cover by at least 1 inch. Bring to a simmer, reduce the heat to moderately low and cook at a bare simmer, partially covered, for 20 minutes, or until the chicken is still juicy but white throughout; do not allow to boil. Let the chicken cool in the cooking liquid.

2. Meanwhile, in a large pot of boiling salted water, cook the pasta until it is tender but still slightly firm to the bite, about 12 minutes. Drain, rinse in a bowl of cold water and drain well. Put the pasta in a large bowl and toss with 2 tablespoons of the olive oil and ¼ teaspoon each salt and pepper.

3. Remove the chicken from its cooking liquid (which can be saved for stock) and trim off any cartilage or bits of fat. Cut the chicken into ¾-inch cubes. In a medium bowl, toss the chicken with the remaining 1 tablespoon olive oil, 1 tablespoon of the lemon juice, the minced shallot and ⅛ teaspoon each salt and pepper.

4. Separate the top of the broccoli into 1- to 1½-inch florets. Peel the stems and cut them cross-wise on the diagonal into ½-inch-thick slices. Steam the broccoli over boiling salted water until just tender but still bright green, about 5 minutes. Rinse immediately under cold running water; drain well. (The chicken, pasta and broccoli can all be prepared a day ahead. Cover the bowls, put the broccoli in a plastic bag and refrigerate separately.)

5. In a medium bowl, combine the crushed garlic with 1 teaspoon salt; mash to a paste. Blend in the tahini and remaining ⅔ cup lemon juice. Gradually whisk in 1 cup hot water and the cayenne pepper. (The dressing can be made a day ahead. Cover and refrigerate. Thin with additional water if necessary.)

6. To assemble the salad, add the chicken, broccoli, red bell pepper and scallions to the pasta. Toss lightly to mix. Drizzle on the dressing and toss to coat. Season with additional salt and pepper to taste. (The salad can be assembled up to 3 hours ahead.) Serve slightly chilled or at room temperature.

GRILLED MARINATED FLANK STEAK

12 TO 16 SERVINGS

1 cup soy sauce
¼ cup (packed) dark brown sugar
12 black peppercorns
3 star anise pods
2 imported bay leaves
1 small dried hot red pepper, optional
2 tablespoons vegetable oil
2 tablespoons Oriental sesame oil
3 large garlic cloves, crushed through a press
5 pounds flank steak, trimmed of excess fat

1. In a small nonaluminum saucepan, combine the soy sauce, brown sugar, peppercorns, star anise, bay leaves, hot pepper and vegetable oil. Bring to a boil, stirring to dissolve the sugar. Reduce the heat to low and steep the marinade for 5 minutes. Remove from the heat, add ⅓ cup water and let cool.

2. Stir the sesame oil and garlic into the marinade. Put the flank steak into 1 or 2 large glass baking dishes (so that the meat lies in a flat layer). Pour the marinade over the meat and turn the steaks to coat. Marinate at room temperature, turning every 20 or 30 minutes, for at least 45 minutes and up to 3 hours.

3. Light the fire or preheat the broiler. Grill the steak, turning once, for 3 to 5 minutes per side, until rare (you can cook it longer, but flank steak is best rare—juicy and tender). Let stand, loosely covered with foil, for 5 to 10 minutes before slicing. Serve warm or at room temperature.

Lentil Salad with Goat Cheese and Sun-Dried Tomatoes

12 SERVINGS

1 pound lentils
1/3 cup plus 3 tablespoons extra-virgin olive oil
2 medium onions, finely diced
2 medium carrots, peeled and finely diced
2 celery ribs, finely diced
Bouquet garni: 5 sprigs of parsley, 3 sprigs of fresh
    thyme, or 1/2 teaspoon dried, and 1 small bay
    leaf tied in cheesecloth
1/2 teaspoon salt
2 pinches of hot pepper flakes
1/2 cup red wine vinegar
8 large sun-dried tomato halves (about 3 ounces),
    finely diced
1/2 large red onion, diced (1 cup)
1 teaspoon coarsely cracked black pepper
1/2 log (4 1/2 ounces) Montrachet or other mild goat
    cheese
1/3 cup chopped parsley
3 large beefsteak or 6 large plum tomatoes, cut
    into wedges

1. Rinse the lentils and pick over to remove any grit. In a large flameproof casserole, heat 3 tablespoons of the oil. Add the onions, carrots and celery and sauté over moderate heat until the onions are just beginning to color. Add the lentils and 6 cups of water. Tuck the bouquet garni into the lentils and season with the salt and hot pepper flakes. Bring to a simmer over moderate heat and cook, partially covered, stirring occasionally, until the lentils are just tender and almost all the liquid is evaporated, 20 to 25 minutes. (It will take slightly longer if the lentils are old.) Boil for a few minutes if necessary to evaporate excess liquid.

2. Turn into a large bowl and drizzle on the remaining 1/3 cup oil and the vinegar and toss lightly. Add the sun-dried tomatoes, red onion and black pepper. Crumble half the cheese into the salad, add the parsley and toss again. Season with additional salt to taste. Let stand, tossing occasionally, until cooled to room temperature.

3. Turn into a serving bowl or deep platter. Crumble the remaining goat cheese over the top. Surround with the tomato wedges. Serve at room temperature or slightly chilled.

Potato Salad with Sweet Sausages and Mushrooms

12 SERVINGS

This hearty salad, from Convito Italiano, a chic Chicago Italian food shop, restaurant and catering firm, is unusual in that it is made with no vinegar. Consequently, it is full of flavor, but easy to eat—lots of. It can be served as a side dish or as one of a number of offerings on a buffet. But my favorite way to eat it is as a main course salad, along with some well-dressed arugula and tomato.

3 pounds small red potatoes
2 pounds sweet Italian sausages
1/2 cup dry red wine
2/3 cup plus 2 tablespoons extra-virgin olive oil
1 pound mushrooms, sliced
1 teaspoon fresh lemon juice
Salt and freshly ground pepper
3/4 cup chopped scallions
1 1/2 tablespoons Dijon mustard
1/3 cup dry white wine
1/3 cup chicken stock or canned broth

1. In a large saucepan of boiling water, cook the potatoes until tender, 15 to 20 minutes. Let cool slightly, then slice. Put the potatoes in a large bowl.

2. Meanwhile, preheat the oven to 350° F. Put the sausages in a single layer in a baking dish and prick them several times with a fork. Bake for 15 minutes. Turn and bake for 15 minutes. Add the red wine to the pan, turn the sausages and bake for 8 minutes. Turn the sausages once more and bake for 7 minutes longer. Remove the sausages to a dish and let cool. Slice into rings and add to the potatoes.

3. In a large skillet, heat the 2 tablespoons olive oil. Add the mushrooms and sauté over moderately high heat, tossing, until they give up their liquid and most of it evaporates, about 5 minutes. Sprinkle on the lemon juice and season lightly with salt and pepper. Add to the potatoes and sausages. Add the scallions. Toss lightly to mix.

4. In a food processor or blender, combine the mustard, 1 teaspoon salt, 1/2 teaspoon pepper, white wine and stock. Blend to mix well. With the machine on, slowly add the remaining 2/3 cup olive oil. Pour the dressing over the salad and toss to coat. Serve warm or at room temperature, or cover and refrigerate overnight.

GIOVANNA'S SHOCKING PINK RICE SALAD

12 TO 16 SERVINGS

Perhaps because she is married to one of Italy's premier wine makers, Giovanna Folinari Ruffino prides herself on her food and enjoys entertaining with elegance. This tasty salad has enough ham, cheese and vegetables to serve as a lovely first course, especially in summer when something cool is welcome, but because of its striking color, I like to present it as part of a buffet. Giovanna garnishes the top with a pink rose from her garden.

2½ cups long-grain white rice
2 tablespoons fresh lemon juice
5 tablespoons extra-virgin olive oil
1 cup diced cooked beets, fresh or canned
1½ tablespoons red wine vinegar
Salt and freshly ground pepper
1½ tablespoons capers, rinsed and drained
1 cup diced cooked ham
1 cup diced Emmentaler Swiss cheese
⅓ cup sliced cornichon pickles
⅓ cup pitted green olives, sliced
⅓ cup peas, cooked fresh or thawed frozen

1. In a large saucepan of boiling salted water, cook the rice until tender but not mushy, about 15 minutes. Drain and rinse with cold running water; drain well. Put the rice in a large bowl and toss with the lemon juice and 3 tablespoons of the olive oil.

2. Meanwhile, marinate the beets with the vinegar, ⅛ teaspoon each salt and pepper and the remaining 2 tablespoons of the oil.

3. One at a time, add the capers, ham, cheese, pickles, olives and peas to the rice, tossing to mix each ingredient thoroughly. Add the beets with their marinade, ¼ teaspoon salt and ⅛ teaspoon pepper and toss to blend well. Let marinate at room temperature, tossing once or twice, for at least 15 minutes before serving.

HONEY-PECAN CAKE

12 SERVINGS

1 cup milk
1 tablespoon distilled white vinegar
2 cups sifted all-purpose flour
1 tablespoon baking powder
1 teaspoon baking soda
1 teaspoon ground cinnamon
¼ teaspoon ground cloves
1 cup corn or safflower oil
1½ cups sugar
3 eggs
1 teaspoon vanilla extract
½ cup chopped pecans
¼ cup honey, preferably wildflower
1 tablespoon fresh lemon juice

1. Preheat the oven to 350° F. Grease a 10-inch bundt pan.

2. In a small cup, combine the milk and vinegar. Set aside; the milk will thicken slightly.

3. Sift together the flour, baking powder, baking soda, cinnamon and cloves.

4. In a large mixer bowl, beat the oil with the sugar until creamy. Beat in the eggs and vanilla. Beat on medium speed for 1 minute. In three batches, alternately add the dry ingredients and the sour milk to the batter. Beat for 1 minute longer. Stir in the nuts.

5. Turn the batter into the greased bundt pan and bake for 40 to 45 minutes, or until a tester inserted in the center of the cake comes out clean. Let stand for 10 minutes.

6. Meanwhile, in a small nonaluminum saucepan, combine the honey and lemon juice with 1 tablespoon water. Bring to a boil, stirring to dissolve the honey. Remove from the heat.

7. Unmold the cake and set it on a rack over a baking sheet to catch any drips. Gently prick the top of the cake with a fork and drizzle the hot honey syrup over the hot cake. Let cool before serving.

Texas-Style Barbecue

FOR 24 TO 30

Pepper-Pecan Cornbread

Guacamole and Fresh Tomato Salsa (page 89) with Taco Chips

Barbecued Carnitas with Chipotle Chile Mayonnaise (page 49)

·

Mesquite-Smoked Barbecued Brisket of Beef

Mesquite-Grilled Chicken and Sausages (page 41)

Creole Coleslaw

Egg and Potato Salad with Roasted Red Peppers

Bacon and Brandy Baked Beans (page 136)

·

Strawberry Corn Shortcakes

A "crowd" in Texas can be as oversized as the state. They know how to have a good time out there and don't even blink at a guest list that might fill a football stadium elsewhere. I've scaled things down a bit for this big old barbecue, but I've kept the exuberant flavors and relaxed style that typifies Western outdoor entertaining. It's a menu that works well anywhere and requires nothing more than a barbecue grill and a warm smile to guarantee a great party.

If you look carefully, you'll notice that cornmeal is used three times in this menu. I couldn't resist. Pepper-Pecan Cornbread, which contains whole kernels of roasted corn as well, is wonderful for nibbling. At San Simeon, a restaurant in Dallas, the cornbread is brought warm to your table as soon as you order. Corn flavors the taco chips, served here with guacamole from the Caviar Nachos recipe on page 88, tripled for this crowd. It also appears in the cloudlike biscuits for the dessert shortcake.

I must confess, I am proud of this Mesquite-Smoked Barbecued Brisket of Beef. My pal Sara Caron, who hails from Dallas, tells me it tastes just like the real thing. I smoke it for two hours, in a smoker or a covered grill, and then bake it slowly in the oven until it shreds with a fork. For a fiesta this size, you'll want to make two of the briskets and a double recipe of the Texas-Style BBQ Sauce. To make things easier with everyone milling about, marinate and grill the chicken and blanch the sausages a day ahead. Then reheat them in the oven or on the grill at the last minute.

While the Egg and Potato Salad can be made a day ahead, it has a fresher, creamier taste if the components are prepared in advance and the salad is assembled only several hours before serving. Remember to begin the Bacon and Brandy Baked Beans three days ahead, especially if you plan to soak the beans overnight. With all this food, one recipe should be enough, but do make a double recipe of the Creole Coleslaw. It will look like a lot at first, but it shrinks down. Since it contains no mayonnaise, it can stand at room temperature for hours with no ill effect; in fact, it will improve in flavor.

With dessert for this many, I suggest you pile up the light, fluffy corn shortcakes in baskets, with a serrated knife to split them. Put out bowls of the strawberries and whipped cream and let everyone help themselves. With a pretty cloth and maybe some wildflowers, it will make a lovely presentation. If you're having more than two dozen guests, make an extra half-recipe of dessert; there will be extras, but I'm sure they'll disappear.

Do-Ahead Planning

Up to 1 month in advance: Bake the Pepper-Pecan Cornbread and the Corn Shortcakes. Freeze both.

Up to 5 days in advance: Make a double recipe of the Chipotle Chile Mayonnaise.

Up to 3 days before the barbecue: Smoke and bake 2 beef briskets. Soak the beans overnight. Roast the bell peppers and make the mayonnaise for the Egg and Potato Salad. Make the Bacon and Brandy Baked Beans.

The day before the barbecue: Make a triple recipe of the guacamole. To prevent discoloration, cover the top with a film of mayonnaise thinned with lemon juice, cover the bowl with plastic wrap and refrigerate. Stir to blend well before serving. Marinate a double recipe of pork for the Barbecued Carnitas. Make the Texas-Style BBQ Sauce. Marinate the chicken (and grill it if you wish). Precook the sausages. Boil the potatoes for the salad.

The day of the barbecue, up to 6 hours in advance: Make a large bowl of Fresh Tomato Salsa. Assemble the Egg and Potato Salad; cover and refrigerate. Make the Creole Coleslaw through Step 3.

About 3 hours before guests arrive: Finish the Creole Coleslaw. Macerate the strawberries and whip the cream for the Strawberry Corn Shortcakes.

Shortly before serving: Reheat the Pepper-Pecan Cornbread in the oven. Grill the carnitas. Reheat the Mesquite-Smoked Brisket in the oven and the Texas-Style BBQ Sauce on top of the stove. Adjust the seasoning of the sauce if necessary. Reheat the chicken in the oven if it's precooked, or grill it. Grill the sausages until browned. Reheat the baked beans in the oven for 30 to 40 minutes.

PEPPER-PECAN CORNBREAD

From San Simeon in Dallas, Texas.

MAKES 5 DOZEN 1¼-INCH
SQUARES

4 ears of corn
1 cup plus 1 tablespoon corn oil
2 large red bell peppers
2 large green bell peppers
1 cup pecans, coarsely chopped
4 eggs
1⅓ cups sugar
2½ cups milk
2 teaspoons salt
5½ cups all-purpose flour
2½ cups cornmeal
¼ cup baking powder
6 tablespoons honey

1. Preheat the oven to 375° F. Grease 2 rectangular baking pans, 8½ x 14 inches.

2. Brush the corn with 1 tablespoon of the oil. Roast the corn and the red and green bell peppers directly over a gas flame or under a hot broiler as close to the heat as possible, turning, until the corn is roasted to a light brown and the peppers are charred all over, 5 to 10 minutes for the corn and 10 to 15 minutes for the peppers. Put the peppers in a bag and steam for 10 minutes. Remove the blackened skins and the stems, seeds and ribs and cut the peppers into ½-inch dice. Cut the corn off the cob.

3. In a large, dry cast-iron skillet, sauté the peppers, corn and pecans over moderately high heat for about 5 minutes. Set aside.

4. In a large mixing bowl, beat the eggs. Gradually beat in the sugar and then the milk and salt. Beat on medium-high speed for 2 minutes. Scrape down the sides of the bowl. Gradually beat in the flour, cornmeal and baking powder. Beat for 3 minutes. Gradually beat in the remaining 1 cup oil and the honey. Mix until smooth. Reserve ½ cup of the peppers, corn and pecans; stir the rest into the batter.

5. Turn the batter into the greased pans. Sprinkle ¼ cup of the reserved mixture over the top of each pan. Bake for 30 minutes, or until a tester comes out clean and the cornbread is beginning to pull away from the sides of the pan. Let cool slightly before cutting into squares.

DRY MARINADES

Most of us are familiar with oil and vinegar or wine-based marinades for grilling. They tenderize the meat and add moisture as well as extra flavor. Dry marinades, or spice mixtures, are not as commonly used, but they, too, tenderize and add flavor in a different way. A dry marinade is not completely dry; it is frequently moistened to a paste with onion and a little oil and vinegar or citrus juice. Rubbed into meat, it is like a short-term curing process, which works extremely well with foods to be barbecued. As demonstrated in this chapter, it turns chicken into instant barbecue, with no sauce needed. It's also great on roast pork and is a prerequisite for an authentic smoked barbecued brisket.

Any dry marinade begins with salt and pepper. For this purpose, I prefer coarse (kosher) salt. It has no additives and works well for this purpose. Don't be alarmed at the amount of coarse salt called for; because of the size of the crystals, 1 teaspoon of coarse salt is equivalent to about ½ teaspoon of ordinary table salt. The pepper should be freshly ground in a pepper mill. For flavor, I prefer Tellicherry, which can be found in specialty food shops, but any kind will do. Cayenne pepper is another must. Believe it or not, even cayenne pepper can lose its fire if it's old enough. If yours has been on the shelf for over a year and it's a dusty brick brown rather than bright red, buy a new jar. (These days, many spice companies label their hot red pepper as such, rather than calling it cayenne. They can be used interchangeably.)

Other spices and herbs in the dry marinade can vary, but for barbecue I always add a hefty dose of ground cumin and frequently oregano, Mexican if you can get it. Paprika produces appealing color. I am partial to the imported sweet Hungarian paprika; it has fine flavor as well as a nice color. Experiment, if you like, with your favorite herb, perhaps thyme or tarragon in place of oregano, and with different meats and cuts—lamb chops, steaks, pork chops, roasts, and ribs.

Here is my basic dry marinade, which you can mix up and set aside in a covered jar in a cool, dark place for whenever you need it. When you're ready to marinate the meat, for every 5 pounds, put 2 to 3 tablespoons of the Basic Spice Blend in a food processor. Add 1 medium onion cut up, 2 garlic cloves, 2 tablespoons olive oil and 2 tablespoons lemon or lime juice and puree. Smear over the meat and let marinate in the refrigerator overnight or at room temperature for 2 to 3 hours before grilling.

Basic Spice Blend

½ cup coarse (kosher) salt
2 tablespoons coarsely cracked black peppercorns
¼ cup sweet Hungarian paprika
1 to 1½ tablespoons cayenne pepper, to taste
1½ tablespoons crumbled oregano
1 tablespoon ground cumin

MESQUITE-SMOKED BARBECUED BRISKET OF BEEF

12 TO 16 SERVINGS

1 whole brisket of beef, 9 to 10 pounds
2 tablespoons coarse (kosher) salt
2 teaspoons coarsely cracked black pepper
2 teaspoons sweet Hungarian paprika
1 teaspoon cayenne pepper
1 teaspoon crumbled oregano, preferably Mexican
½ teaspoon ground cumin
Texas-Style BBQ Sauce (recipe follows)

1. Ask the butcher to trim the brisket, leaving a thin layer of fat all over. The meat will weigh 7 to 8 pounds after trimming. Put the brisket in a large glass baking dish.

2. Combine the salt, black pepper, paprika, cayenne, oregano and cumin and rub into both sides of the meat. Let stand at room temperature for about 2 hours.

3. If you are using a smoker, follow the manufacturer's instructions for mesquite smoking. If you are using a covered grill, soak enough mesquite chunks to cover the bottom of your grill in water for 45 minutes. Meanwhile, in a covered grill or smoker, start a charcoal fire. When the coals are covered with white ash, add the mesquite. When the fire is hot, put the brisket on the grill rack. Grill for 5 minutes, then turn and cook for 5 minutes longer. If the fire flares while grilling, splash the coals with water.

4. When you are through searing the meat, splash the coals with water so that only a red glow remains. Cover the grill. If it is gas, turn to the lowest setting. If it is a kettle grill, adjust the vents so that the fire is as slow as possible. Smoke the brisket for 1 hour. Turn and smoke for 1 hour longer. Check the grill several times during smoking to be sure the wood is smoking. Splash the fire with water or open the vents or turn up the heat, if necessary, to keep the smoking going without charring the meat (it will finish cooking in the oven).

5. After 2 hours, remove the brisket from the grill or smoker. Wrap well in 2 layers of heavy-duty aluminum foil. Place in a 250° F. oven and bake for 4 hours. If baked ahead, let cool a bit without unwrapping, then refrigerate for 2 or 3 days before serving.

6. To reheat, place the wrapped brisket in a 300° F. oven and bake until heated through, 1 to 1½ hours (if it's coming straight from the refrigerator). Drizzle with a little barbecue sauce and pass the remainder on the side. Thinly slice the brisket, crosswise on the diagonal. It will be so tender, it will almost shred.

TEXAS-STYLE BBQ SAUCE

MAKES ABOUT 2½ CUPS

To obtain the drippings, unwrap the brisket after baking. If it has been chilled, the drippings will be jellied.

1¼ cups cider vinegar
¾ cup ketchup
3 tablespoons (packed) dark brown sugar
2 tablespoons Worcestershire sauce
2 tablespoons drippings from Barbecued Brisket, optional
1 tablespoon soy sauce
1 medium onion, minced
1 teaspoon ground cumin
1 teaspoon powdered mustard
1 to 2 teaspoons hot pepper sauce, depending on whether you like your sauce spicy or hot

In a small nonaluminum saucepan, combine all the ingredients. Stir to blend well. Bring to a boil, reduce the heat to low and simmer uncovered, stirring occasionally, for 45 minutes. (The sauce can be made up to 2 days ahead.)

CREOLE COLESLAW

10 TO 12 SERVINGS

Creole mustard has a pleasing bite and slightly coarse texture. Zatarain's, made in New Orleans, is the only brand I have ever seen. It is sold in many supermarkets. A coarse-grained French mustard, such as Pommery, can be used instead, though the flavor will not be quite the same.

1 green cabbage, about 2 pounds
6 large carrots
2 teaspoons coarse salt
2 tablespoons distilled white vinegar
2 teaspoons sugar
1½ tablespoons Creole or coarse-grained French
  mustard

1. Shred the cabbage using the slicing blade, preferably thin, on a food processor. Transfer to a large bowl.

2. Without rinsing the processor bowl, grate the carrots, using the shredding disk. Set aside in a separate bowl; cover and refrigerate.

3. Sprinkle the salt over the cabbage and toss. Set aside at room temperature for at least 1 and up to 3 hours. Pour off the liquid that exudes from the cabbage. (If the cabbage looks very wet, use some paper towels to absorb more of the moisture.)

4. In a small bowl, combine the vinegar and sugar; stir to dissolve the sugar. Blend in the mustard.

5. Add the carrots to the cabbage and toss lightly to mix. Add the mustard dressing and toss well to coat.

EGG AND POTATO SALAD WITH ROASTED RED PEPPERS

24 SERVINGS

This rich salad can be served as a side dish or as a luncheon main course with an interesting green salad on the side.

2 dozen eggs
4 pounds red potatoes
3 medium red bell peppers
2 cups mayonnaise, preferably homemade
3 tablespoons white wine vinegar
3 tablespoons tiny (nonpareil) capers
1½ cups finely chopped red onion
2 dozen anchovy fillets (preferably bottled),
  drained, rinsed and coarsely chopped
3 tablespoons chopped parsley
3 tablespoons chopped fresh basil
2 tablespoons Dijon mustard
Salt and freshly ground pepper to taste

1. Put the eggs in a large flameproof casserole. Add cold water to cover by 1 inch. Bring to a boil, reduce the heat and simmer for 12 minutes. Remove from the heat and let stand for 5 minutes. Drain and let cold water run into the pan to cool the eggs. Peel immediately. (The eggs can be prepared up to a day ahead and refrigerated in a bowl, covered with cold water, but I prefer them freshly cooked in this salad.)

2. Put the potatoes in a large pot, cover with cold salted water and bring to a boil over moderately high heat. Cook for 15 to 25 minutes, or until tender. Drain, let cool, then peel. Cut the potatoes into ½-inch dice.

3. Roast the peppers directly over a gas flame, or under a broiler as close to the heat as possible, turning, until charred and blackened all over, 7 to 10 minutes. Seal in a bag and let steam for 10 minutes. Peel the peppers, discarding the stems, seeds and ribs. Cut the peppers into ½-inch dice.

4. Put the mayonnaise in a large bowl. Blend in the vinegar, capers, onion, anchovies, parsley, basil and mustard. Coarsely chop the eggs and add to the mayonnaise. Add the potatoes and peppers and toss to mix. Season with salt and pepper to taste. Cover and refrigerate until serving time.

STRAWBERRY CORN SHORTCAKES

24 SERVINGS

5 pints strawberries
¾ cup sugar
¼ cup fraise de Bourgogne (strawberry liqueur),
    optional
1 tablespoon grated orange zest
4 cups (1 quart) heavy cream
½ cup confectioners' sugar
1½ tablespoons vanilla extract
24 Corn Shortcakes (recipe follows)

1. Set aside 24 perfect berries in a separate bowl for garnish. Thickly slice the remaining berries. With a potato masher or fork, lightly crush the sliced berries. Sprinkle on ½ cup sugar, the strawberry liqueur, if you have it, and the orange zest. Taste and add the remaining sugar if needed. Cover and set aside for at least 1 hour.

2. In a chilled bowl with chilled beaters, whip the cream until it mounds softly. Add the confectioners' sugar and vanilla and beat the cream until firm but not stiff. Cover and refrigerate for up to 4 hours before serving.

3. To serve, split the shortcakes horizontally in half. Lay the bottom on a dessert plate or in a shallow bowl and cover with crushed strawberries and their juice. Put the top on, add a generous dollop of the whipped cream and garnish with a whole berry.

CORN SHORTCAKES

MAKES 24

Partially prepared in a food processor, these take only minutes to assemble. Unless you have an extra-large bowl, make the dough in two batches without rinsing out the bowl in between.

4½ cups all-purpose flour
2¼ cups yellow cornmeal
⅔ cup sugar
¼ cup baking powder
1 teaspoon baking soda
1 teaspoon salt
Zest from ½ orange, removed with a swivel-
    bladed vegetable peeler
½ pound (2 sticks) cold unsalted butter, cut into
    tablespoons
3½ cups heavy cream

1. Preheat the oven to 450° F. Grease 2 large baking sheets.

2. In a food processor (in two batches if necessary), combine the flour, cornmeal, sugar, baking powder, baking soda, salt and orange zest. Process until the orange zest is minced.

3. Add the butter and turn the machine quickly on and off until the mixture resembles coarse meal, about 20 times.

4. Turn the dough into a large bowl. If there are any large clumps of butter, pinch them into the dough with your fingers. Stir in the cream just until mixed. Turn out and knead lightly to complete the blending.

5. If you made all the dough at once, divide in half and form one half at a time. On a lightly floured surface, pat out half the dough to a 9 x 7-inch rectangle. Cut into 2¼-inch squares. Using a pastry scraper or wide spatula, transfer the corn cakes to one of the baking sheets.

6. Bake the corn cakes for 10 to 12 minutes, or until golden brown on top. Repeat with the remaining dough. (You can first form all the cakes and then bake them together, but you'll get more even results with one sheet in the oven at a time.) Let cool for at least 20 minutes before splitting. Store in an airtight container for up to 1 day before serving, or freeze for longer storage. Defrost no more than 3 hours before serving.

Cranberry-Raspberry Mousse
Chocolate Pecan Fruit Tart
Easy Cream Cheesecake (page 100)
Rose Levy Beranbaum's Chocolate Party
Cake
Fresh Lemon Roulade
Butter Pecan Turtle Squares

■

Fresh Fruit Basket
Cheese Platter with Crisp Crackers
Chilled Brut Champagne or Sparkling Wine
Coffee and Tea

Dessert and Champagne Party

FOR 36

What could be more elegant than a gorgeous array of glamorous desserts and glittering iced champagne! Picture a table covered with confections of chocolate, raspberry, lemon, caramel and nuts. To the many who look forward to the end of a meal so they can delve into dessert, a buffet of sweets is the stuff of which fantasies are made. Such indulgence provides the perfect excuse for dressing up and putting out your fine china, best linen, bouquets of flowers, cut crystal and polished silver.

Everything should be made ahead, whether it is frozen, refrigerated or just set aside in a covered container. Don't worry about each dessert serving every person in the room. Since sampling is de rigueur at a party like this, a dessert that serves sixteen will serve at least thirty-two. In total, there will be more than enough to go around. Serving amounts listed with the recipes are for that single dessert alone.

On the invitations, do be sure to indicate that this is a dessert party, so that guests will know to eat beforehand. Unless you hold the party after lunch on a Saturday or Sunday, I recommend that it not begin before eight-thirty or nine o'clock at night.

Since some people will eat only a light supper and because a few people in any crowd cannot eat refined sugar, I like to put out a small cheese platter with crackers and an attractive fruit basket. Choose appropriate dessert cheeses, such as Bel Paese, walnut-flavored gourmandise and perhaps a fresh young goat cheese.

Champagne is a great crowd pleaser, and these days you can get those tingly bubbles in a variety of styles and prices. Aside from the finest French brut Champagne, there are excellent sparkling wines available from the United States, Spain and Italy. For a pretty change, consider a pink champagne, fragile as a rose.

You can pour six to eight glasses from one bottle. Allow an average of three glasses per person. For thirty-six people, that would mean a case and a half. But remember, it's always better to have extra than to run out. About an hour before the party starts, put the champagne on ice. For this volume, I use a tub or plastic trash can, discreetly hidden away or draped with a tablecloth. Recently I've seen some inexpensive plastic party coolers that are not unattractive. Open each bottle only when you're ready to pour, which means that somebody—you, your spouse, a friend or hired help—should be delegated this important job. Have a big urn of coffee and a pot of tea as well as plenty of club soda for those who prefer a nonalcoholic beverage.

Do-Ahead Planning

Up to 1 month in advance: Bake and freeze the Easy Cream Cheesecake, the layers for the chocolate cake and the Butter Pecan Turtle Squares.

Up to 1 week in advance: Make and freeze the Fresh Lemon Roulade.

The day before the party: Make the pastry for the fruit tart. Make the Cranberry-Raspberry Mousse. Defrost the chocolate cake layers.

The morning of the party: Complete the Chocolate Party Cake. Defrost the cheesecake, lemon roulade and turtle squares.

About 3 hours before serving: Complete the Chocolate Pecan Fruit Tart. Arrange the fruit basket and cheese platter.

About 1 hour before the party starts: Put the champagne on ice. Remove all the desserts from the refrigerator and arrange them on the buffet. Get the coffee urn ready to go.

CRANBERRY-RASPBERRY MOUSSE

30 TO 36 SERVINGS

A glorious rose color, this frothy dessert is as lush to look at as it is to eat. For a smaller group, the recipe can be halved exactly.

1 envelope (¼ ounce) unflavored gelatin
2 packages (12 ounces each) cranberries, fresh or frozen
2½ cups sugar
1 package (12 ounces) individually quick-frozen raspberries with no sugar added
6 egg whites
¼ teaspoon cream of tartar
3 cups heavy cream

1. In a small bowl, sprinkle the gelatin over ¼ cup cold water. Let stand to soften.

2. In a large heavy saucepan, combine the cranberries with 1½ cups of the sugar and 1½ cups of water. Bring to a boil over moderately high heat, reduce the heat to moderate and cook, stirring frequently, for 5 minutes. Remove from the heat, stir in the softened gelatin and let cool slightly.

3. Pass the cranberries through the medium disk of a food mill or puree in a food processor and then strain to remove the skins. Let cool to room temperature.

4. Puree the raspberries in a food processor. Work through a mesh sieve with a rubber or plastic spatula to remove the seeds. (There will be about 1¼ cups puree.) Combine the cranberry and raspberry purees in a large bowl and mix well to blend.

5. Beat the egg whites and cream of tartar with an electric mixer on high speed until stiff. Gradually beat in the remaining 1 cup sugar.

6. Beat the cream until fairly stiff. (Tip: The cream will mount much faster if you put the cream, mixer bowl and beaters in the freezer for 10 minutes before beating.)

7. Fold about one-third of the cream into the berry puree to lighten it a little. Fold in the remaining cream and then the egg whites, until the mousse is even in color and no white streaks show. Turn into a large serving bowl, preferably glass, cover with plastic wrap and refrigerate until chilled and set, at least 6 hours, or overnight.

CHOCOLATE PECAN FRUIT TART

20 SERVINGS

Pecan Pastry (recipe follows)
6 ounces dark sweetened chocolate—semisweet, sweet or bittersweet—coarsely chopped
2 tablespoons unsalted butter
¼ cup heavy cream
1 pint strawberries, halved if large
2 bananas, cut crosswise on the diagonal into 20 pieces and tossed with 1½ tablespoons fresh lemon juice
3 dozen seedless green grapes, cut in half
20 canned apricot halves (16-ounce can), well drained

1. Prepare the pastry sheet as detailed in the recipe that follows. Let cool to room temperature.

2. In a small heavy saucepan, melt the chocolate and butter, stirring until smooth. Blend in the cream and let cool slightly.

3. Spread the chocolate cream over the pastry crust in a light, even layer to the edges. (The recipe can be prepared to this point up to 6 hours in advance. Set aside at room temperature.)

4. Up to 3 hours before serving, arrange the fruit decoratively on top of the chocolate, grouping the design within the squares outlined. Set aside at room temperature. If the fruit begins to dry out, cover with damp paper towels.

PECAN PASTRY

MAKES A 14 x 16-INCH SHEET

⅔ cup pecans
2 tablespoons sugar
2½ cups all-purpose flour
¼ teaspoon salt
½ pound (2 sticks) cold unsalted butter, cut into ⅜-inch dice
2 tablespoons chilled heavy cream
¼ cup cold water

1. In a food processor, chop the pecans and sugar as fine as possible.

2. In a medium bowl, toss together the ground pecan mixture, flour and salt. Add the pieces of butter and toss to coat them with flour. Rub with your fingertips to cut in the butter; undermix rather than overblend.

3. Tossing with a fork, sprinkle on the cream and then 2 tablespoons of the water. Gather the pastry into a mass, pressing to help it adhere. Turn out onto a light floured surface. If dry flour mixture remains in the bowl, sprinkle on the remaining water and toss to moisten. Add to the pastry.

4. With the heel of your hand, smear a bit of the pastry away from you. Repeat to blend all the pastry. Gather it together into a ball and repeat. Gather into a ball again, flatten into a disk, wrap and refrigerate for at least 30 minutes. (The pastry can be made a day ahead.)

5. Preheat the oven to 375° F. Butter a heavy cookie sheet 16 x 14 inches. Put the dough on the sheet and roll or pat it out almost to the edges. Prick the pastry all over with a fork. With a small knife, score the pastry into 20 squares, 3 inches each.

6. Butter the bottom of another sheet and lay it on top of the pastry. Bake for 15 minutes. Remove the top baking sheet to uncover the pastry, prick any bubbles with a fork and bake for 10 to 15 minutes longer, until the pastry is dry and just beginning to color lightly.

ROSE LEVY BERANBAUM'S CHOCOLATE PARTY CAKE

16 TO 20 SERVINGS

Dessert is Rose's middle name, as her cookbooks and articles testify. This deep chocolate double layer cake with its rich dark frosting reminds me of the kind of chocolate cake I used to dream about as a child. Thankfully, some dreams never fade.

If you want to ready this dessert ahead, bake the layers up to two months in advance and freeze them. After thawing, frost the cake and store in the refrigerator for up to three days before serving.

> 1 cup Dutch-process unsweetened cocoa powder, such as Droste or Poulain
> 1 2/3 cups boiling water
> 5 large eggs, at room temperature
> 1 tablespoon plus 1 teaspoon vanilla extract
> 4 cups sifted cake flour
> 2 1/2 cups sugar
> 1 tablespoon plus 2 teaspoons baking powder
> 1 1/4 teaspoons salt
> 3/4 pound (3 sticks) plus 2 tablespoons unsalted butter, at room temperature
> Chocolate Cream Frosting (recipe follows)

1. Grease two 10-inch-round cake pans. Line the bottoms with a round of parchment or wax paper and grease the paper. Flour the pan; tap out any excess. Preheat the oven to 350° F.

2. In a medium bowl, whisk together the cocoa and boiling water until smooth. Let cool to room temperature.

3. In another bowl, lightly beat the eggs. Whisk in the vanilla and 1/2 cup of the cooled cocoa mixture.

4. In a large mixing bowl, combine the flour, sugar, baking powder and salt. Whisk to blend. Add the butter and the remaining cocoa and beat on medium speed with a stationary mixer, or on high speed with a hand mixer, for 2 minutes. Scrape down the sides of the bowl.

5. Gradually beat in the egg mixture, one-third at a time, beating well for about 20 seconds after each addition and scraping down the sides of the bowl as necessary.

6. Scrape the batter into the prepared pans and smooth the tops. Tap the pans lightly on the counter to settle any air bubbles. Bake the cakes for 25 to 30 minutes, or until a tester inserted near the center comes out clean and the edges of the cake have begun to pull away from the side of the pan. Let cool for 15 minutes; then unmold onto a lightly greased rack and let cool completely. Carefully peel off the paper.

7. To assemble, spread about one-quarter of the frosting over one of the layers. Put the second layer on top and cover with the remaining frosting, swirling it decoratively with the back of a spoon.

CHOCOLATE CREAM FROSTING

ENOUGH FOR ONE 10-INCH DOUBLE LAYER CAKE

> 1 pound sweetened dark chocolate—sweet, semisweet or bittersweet
> 1 1/2 cups heavy cream
> 6 tablespoons unsalted butter, at room temperature
> 3 tablespoons Cognac, optional

1. Grate the chocolate in a food processor. Scald the cream. With the machine on, pour the cream through the feed tube; process until blended. Pour the chocolate cream into a large bowl and let cool slightly.

2. Whisk the butter and Cognac into the chocolate cream just until blended. Let stand until the chocolate begins to firm up. Whisk to fluff up the frosting.

FRESH LEMON ROULADE

12 TO 16 SERVINGS

Sometimes a light dessert is the best dessert. This one is melt-in-your-mouth and refreshing with a triple dose of tart fresh lemon. You can use any good raspberry jam, but I like the fresh fruit flavor of the new low-sugar fruit spreads.

> 5 eggs, separated
> ⅓ cup sugar
> 3 tablespoons fresh lemon juice
> Grated zest from 1 large lemon
> ¼ teaspoon salt
> ½ cup sifted all-purpose flour
> ¾ cup raspberry jam
> Fresh Lemon Cream (recipe follows)
> Confectioners' sugar

1. Preheat the oven to 375° F. Butter an 18 x 13-inch jellyroll or half-sheet pan. Line the bottom with a sheet of wax paper; butter the paper. Dust the pan with flour and tap out any excess.

2. In a medium bowl, beat the egg yolks. Gradually beat in the sugar. Add 1 tablespoon of the lemon juice, the lemon zest and salt. Beat until the mixture is thick enough to fall from the whisk or beaters in a slowly dissolving ribbon, 3 to 5 minutes.

3. Beat the egg whites until stiff but not dry. Scoop about one-third of the egg whites onto the egg yolk mixture and partially fold in. Return the flour to the sifter and sift about one-third over the batter. Fold until just blended. Scoop half the remaining egg whites onto the batter. Sift half the remaining flour onto the egg whites. Fold into the batter until just blended. Repeat with the remaining egg whites and flour.

4. Turn the batter into the prepared jellyroll pan. With a rubber spatula, spread to fill evenly. Bake for 15 to 20 minutes, until the cake is puffed and lightly browned and the edges have begun to pull away from the sides of the pan. Let cool for 5 minutes.

5. Lay a damp kitchen towel over a rack. Invert the jellyroll pan to unmold the cake onto the towel. Carefully peel off the wax paper. Combine the remaining 2 tablespoons lemon juice with 2 tablespoons water and sprinkle evenly over the cake. Starting with a long side, fold one edge up about 2 inches. Continue to roll up the cake in the towel,

with the material between the layers. Let stand until completely cool, at least 15 minutes but no longer than 1 hour.

6. Unroll the cake. Cover with a thin, even layer of the raspberry jam. Scrape the lemon cream onto the cake and spread evenly. Again roll up the cake (without the towel this time, of course), allowing 2 to 3 inches for the first fold. Wrap in plastic wrap and refrigerate for up to 2 days before serving. (After the filling is completely cold and set, you can freeze the roulade for up to 2 months. Thaw in the refrigerator.)

7. Just before serving, sprinkle confectioners' sugar generously over the roulade to coat.

FRESH LEMON CREAM

> 3 egg yolks
> ¼ cup white wine
> Grated zest of 1 lemon
> ¼ cup fresh lemon juice
> 1 teaspoon unflavored gelatin dissolved in 2
>   tablespoons of cold water
> ½ cup heavy cream

1. In a heavy nonaluminum saucepan, combine the egg yolks, wine, lemon zest and lemon juice. Whisk over moderate heat until the mixture is frothy and hot and thick enough to leave a trace as the whisk moves through it, about 10 minutes. Beat in the dissolved gelatin and whisk over the heat for about 30 seconds to blend completely. Strain into a bowl. Cover and put in the freezer for about 10 minutes, stirring twice, or stir over a bowl of ice and water, until cold.

2. Meanwhile, whip the cream until it is stiff. Scrape the lemon mixture onto the whipped cream and fold until blended. Cover and refrigerate until almost set before using. (If too set, whisk to soften.)

Butter Pecan Turtle Squares

MAKES ABOUT 100

An incredibly decadent recipe from my editor, Harriet Bell, these are guaranteed to disappear...fast! The cookie-candies freeze remarkably well.

2 cups all-purpose flour
1½ cups (packed) dark brown sugar
½ pound (2 sticks) plus 3 tablespoons unsalted
*   butter*
1½ cups pecans, coarsely chopped
1½ cups chocolate chips

1. Preheat the oven to 350° F. In a food processor, combine the flour, 1 cup of the brown sugar and 1 stick of the butter. Process until sandy; the dough will not form a ball. Pat the dough firmly into an ungreased 13 x 9 x 2-inch baking pan. Sprinkle the pecans evenly over the dough.

2. In a heavy medium saucepan, combine the remaining 1 stick plus 3 tablespoons butter and ½ cup brown sugar. Bring to a boil over moderate heat, stirring to dissolve the sugar. Boil the caramel for 30 seconds, stirring constantly.

3. Pour the hot caramel over the nuts in the baking pan. Bake for 20 minutes. Remove from the oven and immediately sprinkle the chocolate chips evenly over the top. Let melt slightly, then spread lightly, leaving some of the chips whole. Let cool completely before cutting into 1-inch squares.

How to Open a Bottle of Champagne

To my ear, the popping of a champagne cork is just about the prettiest sound in the world. For many years, I sat back and listened; the idea of opening a bottle myself was unthinkable. I played helpless. To be honest, it scared me. Then one day, at a champagne tasting I was attending, a sommelier explained exactly how it should be done—for ease, for safety purposes (to avoid shooting the cork across the room) and to preserve all the bubbly. When they asked for volunteers, I impulsively raised my hand. It was with great trepidation that I opened my first bottle, and with great pride, I poured. I was liberated forever. Here's how easy it is:

Set out the glasses ahead—tall, narrow flutes are the shape connoisseurs prefer to maximize the effect of the effervescence. Be sure the champagne has been resting for at least a couple of hours; shaking up the bottle before opening is for locker rooms only. The wine should be well chilled, in the refrigerator or in a bucket of ice and water for 45 minutes to 1 hour.

First remove the outer foil wrappings from the top of the bottle. Then loosen the wires around the neck. Do not peer over the top as you do this, because occasionally a cork will spontaneously eject. Leaving the wire loose but still over the cap, grip the cork, using a folded kitchen towel to help you and, holding the bottle at a 45-degree angle, slowly twist, *not* the cork, but the bottle. Continue to hold the cork with the towel to restrain it if necessary as you twist. You'll feel the cork partially ease up out of the bottle before it pops open. Immediately put down the cork and pour, filling the glasses slowly and only part way until the initial foam subsides, then top them off. Salud!

Sour Cream and Two-Caviar Dip, served with Crudités

Louisiana Shrimp

Gingered Eggplant Spread

Olives and Assorted Nuts

■

Baked Ham

Potatoes au Gratin (page 83)

Red and Green Coleslaw with Blue Cheese Dressing

Bacon and Brandy Baked Beans

Sourdough and Pumpernickel Bread

■

Baskets of Apples and Grapes

Bags of Halloween Candy

Butter Cookies

No matter how old I get, I still love to celebrate Halloween. A large costume party has become an annual event at our house, and this menu has proved perfect for the occasion. Minus the jack-o'-lanterns and Halloween candy, it also works beautifully for any fall or winter party.

Dips and spreads are easy and don't take a lot of time. For the crudités to accompany the Sour Cream and Two-Caviar Dip, choose easy-to-prepare vegetables like Belgian endive leaves, strips of sweet red pepper, carrot and zucchini sticks, cherry tomatoes and cauliflorets. The Louisiana Shrimp is even better when allowed to marinate for a day. Line a serving bowl with dark green, curly kale to make a striking background for the pink shellfish, and pass toothpicks for skewering. Accompany the Gingered Eggplant Spread with rounds of toasted French bread or Melba toast.

As for the main-course buffet, the ham can be warm or at room temperature. My only advice is— buy a good ham! Baked beans and tangy Potatoes au Gratin accompanied by Red and Green Coleslaw with Blue Cheese Dressing make this a hearty, savory spread.

For a large party like this, I rarely bother with a homemade dessert. Store-bought butter cookies and an attractive assortment of fresh fruit are all you need. Loot bags of Halloween candy will carry the theme through and are guaranteed to cause everyone to wax nostalgic.

A Halloween Party

FOR 36 TO 48

To ensure success, don't forget decor. For Halloween, my husband, who is an artist, carves out half a dozen or more little jack-o'-lanterns, which we light with small votive candles and set out on serving tables and windowsills around the room. A big pumpkin presides over the coffee table, and a canopy of twisted orange and black crepe paper covers the ceiling.

Do-Ahead Planning

Up to 3 days in advance: Soak the beans.

Up to 2 days in advance: Make the Bacon and Brandy Baked Beans. Boil the potatoes.

The day before the party: Prepare the crudités. Briefly blanch hard vegetables. Make the Gingered Eggplant Spread. Make the Louisiana Shrimp. Assemble the Potatoes au Gratin.

The morning of the party: Make the Sour Cream and Two-Caviar Dip; refrigerate. Toast rounds of French bread brushed with olive oil for the eggplant spread. Make the Red and Green Coleslaw with Blue Cheese Dressing; refrigerate until serving time.

About half an hour before serving: Reheat the beans in the oven. Bake the Potatoes au Gratin.

SOUR CREAM AND TWO-CAVIAR DIP

MAKES ABOUT 3½ CUPS

This dip is particularly good with Belgian endive leaves, assorted raw or partially cooked vegetables and even low-salt potato chips.

> 3 cups (1½ pints) sour cream
> 2 ounces salmon caviar
> 2 ounces golden whitefish caviar
> ¼ cup minced fresh chives, or 3 tablespoons
>   freeze-dried

Stir together all the ingredients. Cover and refrigerate until serving time. Serve chilled.

LOUISIANA SHRIMP

36 SERVINGS AS AN HORS D'OEUVRE, 12 TO 16 AS A FIRST COURSE

> ½ cup Creole mustard
> ¼ cup imported sweet paprika
> 2 to 3 teaspoons cayenne pepper
> 2 teaspoons salt
> ¼ cup fresh lemon juice
> ¼ cup white wine vinegar
> 1¼ cups olive oil
> 1¼ cups corn or safflower oil
> 1 cup chopped scallion green
> 1 cup chopped red onion
> 1 cup chopped celery
> 1 cup chopped parsley
> 1½ tablespoons chopped fresh tarragon, or 1
>   teaspoon dried
> 4 pounds medium shrimp (25 to 30 per pound),
>   shelled and deveined
> 1 head iceberg lettuce, shredded, optional

1. In a large bowl, combine the mustard, paprika, cayenne, salt, lemon juice and vinegar. Whisk to blend well. Gradually beat in the olive and corn oil to make a thick sauce. Stir in the scallion green, onion, celery, parsley and tarragon.

2. Bring a large pot of salted water to a boil. Add the shrimp and boil for about 3 minutes, until pink, loosely curled and opaque throughout. Drain.

3. Add the warm shrimp to the sauce and stir to coat. Refrigerate, stirring occasionally, for at least 4 hours, or overnight. Serve with toothpicks as an hors d'oeuvre or over a bed of lettuce as a chilled first course.

GINGERED EGGPLANT SPREAD

MAKES ABOUT 5 CUPS (ENOUGH FOR 6 DOZEN CANAPÉS)

This rich northern Chinese eggplant dish, loaded with fresh ginger, is from Bruce Cost, a California caterer and food writer and author of *Ginger East to West*. He serves it on toasted French bread, sprinkled with sesame seeds. Also great as a vegetable side dish, it can be made the night before but should be allowed to return to room temperature and stirred up before serving.

⅓ cup unhulled sesame seeds (available in health food stores and Oriental markets)
Peanut oil
3 pounds small, thin Asian eggplants, unpeeled, cut crosswise on the diagonal into ½-inch slices
3 tablespoons soy sauce, preferably dark
3 tablespoons sugar
1½ tablespoons distilled white vinegar
1 tablespoon pale dry sherry or shao hsing wine
2 tablespoons finely minced ginger
1 tablespoon finely minced garlic
1 teaspoon Oriental sesame oil
Toasted slices of French bread or Melba toast

1. In a dry heavy skillet, toast the sesame seeds over moderate heat until fragrant and lightly browned, about 3 minutes. Set aside in a covered jar. (The sesame seeds can be toasted days or even weeks ahead and stored in the refrigerator or freezer.)

2. In a wok or large skillet, heat about 1 inch of peanut oil over moderately high heat to 375° F. Fry the eggplant in batches without crowding, turning, until golden brown, 3 to 5 minutes per batch. As they are cooked, spread out on paper towels to drain. (When you are through, the cooking oil can be strained and reused, if desired.)

3. In a small bowl, combine the soy sauce, sugar, vinegar and sherry. In a clean wok or large skillet, heat 2 tablespoons of peanut oil over moderately high heat until it just begins to smoke. Add the ginger and garlic and stir-fry for about 10 seconds, until fragrant. Add the soy sauce mixture and stir briefly. Add the fried eggplant and stir quickly to coat all the slices with sauce. Remove from the heat and transfer to a bowl. Drizzle the sesame oil over the eggplant and stir gently to mix. Let cool to room temperature before serving. (The eggplant can be made a day ahead and refrigerated, covered. Let return to room temperature before serving.)

4. To serve, stir up the eggplant, mashing some of the slices. Stir in 3 tablespoons of the toasted sesame seeds. Mound in a serving bowl. Sprinkle the remaining sesame seeds on top and accompany with the toasted bread.

HAMS

That a great big succulent ham is terrific for feeding a crowd is not a statement that will arouse much controversy. But *which* ham—well, that is another matter. If you're from the South, ham usually means Smithfield or some other country ham that has been dry-cured and hung for up to a year before being lightly smoked. Aside from the fact that these hams need to be soaked for several days and then scoured to remove the mold from the outside before being cooked, most Yankees find country hams too salty for their taste. Southerners will counter with the argument that a country ham belongs sliced paper thin, sandwiched within a beaten biscuit and nowhere else.

Given that we're talking about serious eating, not nibbling, and that the aim is to avoid as much work as possible, I recommend a brine-cured, lightly smoked, precooked ham that needs only to be heated through if you so desire. I'll even go a step further and say that for a crowd, I recommend you purchase a ham that is presliced as well, so you have absolutely nothing to do but put it out on the table. My favorite is Honeybaked, a no-water-added ham with a convenient spiral cut; it doesn't even need heating. The flavor is excellent and not overly salty. The largest ham is sixteen pounds, which will serve up to fifty people. You can order it by phone or mail anywhere in the United States: Honeybaked Foods, Inc., P.O. Box 7043, Troy, MI 48007-7043, 1-800-892-HAMS. Other excellent hams are available from McArthur's Smokehouse, Litchfield on the Green, P.O. Box 190, Litchfield, CT 06759, (203) 567-4593 and Roi Ballard for mahogany-smoked ham, P.O. Box 1387, Bishop, CA 93514, (619) 873-5311.

RED AND GREEN COLESLAW WITH BLUE CHEESE DRESSING

20 TO 24 SERVINGS

This coleslaw holds up surprisingly well after a day in the refrigerator; if anything, the flavor improves. Just let stand at room temperature for about an hour and toss again before serving.

1 head of green cabbage (2 to 2½ pounds)
1 head of red cabbage (2 to 2½ pounds)
4 large carrots, peeled
1½ teaspoons coarse (kosher) salt
1 large bunch of scallions (about 6), thinly sliced
¼ cup red wine vinegar
1 tablespoon Dijon mustard
½ teaspoon coarsely cracked black pepper
⅔ pound Roquefort cheese
⅔ cup extra-virgin olive oil

1. In a food processor with the slicing disk, shred the green and red cabbages. Separately, with the shredding disk, shred the carrots.

2. Put the shredded cabbage in a large bowl, sprinkle on the salt and toss. Let stand at room temperature, tossing occasionally, for at least 1 and preferably 2 hours.

3. With your hands, transfer the cabbage to another large bowl, squeezing gently to remove as much of the salty liquid as possible. Add the carrots and scallions and toss lightly to mix.

4. In a blender or food processor, combine the vinegar, mustard, pepper and half the cheese. Mix until almost smooth. With the machine on, gradually add the oil through the feed tube.

5. Crumble the remaining cheese over the salad. Drizzle on the dressing and toss well. Let stand at room temperature for at least 30 minutes or up to 2 hours. Cover and refrigerate for longer storage.

BACON AND BRANDY BAKED BEANS

16 TO 20 SERVINGS

2 pounds California small white beans
⅔ pound slab bacon, in 1 piece
1 cup ketchup
1 cup molasses
2 tablespoons Dijon mustard
2 tablespoons powdered mustard
4 medium onions, chopped
1 cup brandy (I use a fruity California brandy)
2 cups boiling water
2 teaspoons cider vinegar
2 teaspoons salt
1 teaspoon freshly ground pepper
⅛ teaspoon hot pepper sauce

1. Rinse the beans and pick them over to remove any grit. Soak the beans overnight in 3 inches of cold water to cover, or bring them to a boil, boil for 2 minutes and then simmer for 30 to 40 minutes, until tender but not mushy. Drain the beans.

2. Preheat the oven to 250° F. Cut the rind off the bacon and reserve. Cut the bacon into 1 x ¼-inch lardons.

3. In a large beanpot or casserole, combine the beans, bacon, ketchup, molasses, Dijon mustard, powdered mustard, onions and brandy. Stir to mix. Add the boiling water, cover and bake for 2½ hours.

4. Season the beans with the vinegar, salt, pepper and hot sauce. Add more boiling water if they appear dry. Continue to bake, covered, for at least 3½ hours longer, checking every hour or so and adding water, about ½ cup at a time, as needed. The beans can be eaten after 6 hours, but they are even better after 8, or after being reheated the next day.

Nuts and Olives

Spaghetti Torta with Parmesan Cheese Sauce

Cobb Salad

Meat Loaf from the Waldorf

Baked Ham

Rye, Pumpernickel and French Bread

Assorted Mustards, Pickles and Relishes

Swiss, Brie and Cheddar Cheese

Triple-Mustard Potato Salad

Dilled Pasta Salad with Scallops and Smoked Salmon

Lydie Marshall's Ratatouille with Goat Cheese

■

Assorted Pastries and Cookies

Red and White Wine and Beer

Nonalcoholic Party Punch

Afternoon Open House

FOR 50 OR MORE

When I was married and living in student housing at the University of Chicago many years ago, our neighbors down the hall threw a huge open house. We received an invitation when we moved in, just as I was cooking my way through the first volume of Julia Child's *Mastering the Art of French Cooking.* I had fallen in love with cooking—permanently as it turned out—and I knew this couple had spent a year in France. Seeing how they entertained was going to be like touching the holy grail.

To my naive surprise, the spread she put out, though delicious, was quite casual. There were pâtés and cold meats, wheels of cheese and big bowls of assorted salads. The house glowed with the soft light of thick tallow candles, and everyone had a wonderful time. Our hostess remained relaxed and quick to smile all evening.

I think she had learned something important. Even if you're a fabulous cook, entertaining fifty-odd guests dropping in at unexpected intervals during the day will keep you busy enough—greeting everyone, taking coats, making necessary introductions, steering people to the food and drink. The kitchen is the last thing you should have to worry about on the day of the party. That's why I tried to keep this buffet as simple and self-serve as possible.

For an open house, you really don't need any formal appetizers. Place some bowls of nuts and

137

olives around the room. All the food is chilled or at room temperature, except for the Spaghetti Torta, which can serve as your *pièce de résistance*. To minimize baking time, take it out of the refrigerator when the party starts, so it can return to room temperature. I like to serve it when the house is really packed and the party is in full swing. You may prefer to wait until the rest of the buffet begins to look a little low, but don't wait too long, because it does take up to forty-five minutes to heat through. This is a very substantial dish, so a little will go a very long way, especially with a buffet.

Because there is so much Cobb Salad, I put the chicken and shredded lettuce in a large bowl and arrange all the colorful garnishes on a platter next to it. That way everyone can help themselves easily to what they like, and the dish will stay attractive for a little longer.

Tasty and pâté-like, the meat loaf can be prepared up to three days in advance, and its flavor will actually improve upon sitting. Wait until it's cold to slice it: cut it lengthwise in half and then into ½-inch slices. You should end up with at least forty pieces. Arrange them attractively on a platter and garnish with fresh herbs or olives and cherry tomatoes. Frilly green kale makes a nice plate liner or edging.

Buy a good, large baked ham, preferably presliced. Both the ham and the meat loaf can be eaten with a fork or on bread as a sandwich. Choose an interesting assortment of mustards, pickles and relishes and tempting breads. Either put out a wooden board and bread knife, or have the bread presliced. The less congestion at the buffet table, the better. Be sure the cheeses are at room temperature and consider buying the Swiss sliced.

Though I happen to love my potato salad freshly made, this one stands up nicely for a day or two in the refrigerator. The ratatouille improves if made a day in advance, but let it return to room temperature before serving. The seafood pasta salad can be completely assembled the night before; I prefer to prepare all the components and toss them with the dressing shortly before serving. That way it has a much fresher flavor. If you opt for the second method, you may have a little extra dressing. Set it aside, in case you need it later. Two pastas may seem a little odd in one menu, but these recipes are completely different, and I think you'll find them quite compatible.

Get everything ready for the punch, but mix half of it just before the first guests arrive and refill the bowl later as needed. That way it will stay chilled without getting watered down by melting ice.

As with any buffet, try to set out different dishes in different places, so you don't get any traffic jams in one spot. In planning the space for a party my friends Jean-Michel Savoca and Boyce Brawley of New York Parties always remind me, "Remember the excitement your guests will bring and leave room for them to socialize with one another and to move easily from room to room." The meats, Swiss and Cheddar cheese, bread and condiments in one place and the salads in another would make a lot of sense, with plates, napkins and utensils at a couple of locations.

With a big, all-day affair like this, I never hesitate to use good-quality paper plates and napkins, sturdy plastic utensils and plastic cups. Unless you rent party dishes and hire help, the logistics would be overwhelming otherwise. This way you can enjoy the party as much as your guests, which will guarantee success.

Do-Ahead Planning

Up to 3 days before the party: Make the meat loaf.

Up to 2 days in advance: Poach the chicken for the Cobb Salad. Make the Ratatouille with Goat Cheese.

The day before the party: Prepare the lettuce for the Cobb Salad. Make the Triple-Mustard Potato Salad. Boil the pasta, poach the scallops and make the dressing for the Dilled Pasta Salad with Scallops and Smoked Salmon. Assemble the Spaghetti Torta and make the Parmesan Cheese Sauce.

The morning of the open house: Complete the Cobb Salad. Remove the cheese and the ratatouille from the refrigerator. Complete the Dilled Pasta Salad. Make the Nonalcoholic Party Punch.

About 45 minutes before serving: Bake the Spaghetti Torta and reheat the Parmesan Cheese Sauce.

Spaghetti Torta with Parmesan Cheese Sauce

16 TO 20 SERVINGS AS A SINGLE DISH, 32 TO 40 AS PART OF A BUFFET

Jerrie Strom is a fabulous San Diego–area cook and hostess. She throws extravagant parties for hundreds at the blink of an eye (often for a worthy cause) and attends to every detail with imagination and flair. This is a recipe she served to a large group of food professionals who, I am told, scarfed it down.

2 pounds spaghetti
¼ pound (1 stick) plus 4 tablespoons unsalted butter, melted
3 ounces imported dried mushrooms, preferably porcini
2¼ pounds sweet Italian sausages
2 medium onions, chopped
1 jar (9½ ounces) pimiento-stuffed olives, drained and sliced (2¼ cups)
8 eggs, lightly beaten
¾ cup chopped parsley
3 red bell peppers, roasted (see Note), *diced*
1½ teaspoons salt
¾ teaspoon freshly ground pepper
1 pound whole-milk mozzarella cheese, grated
Parmesan Cheese Sauce (recipe follows)

1. Preheat the oven to 375° F. Drop the spaghetti into a large pot of boiling salted water and cook until tender but still firm to the bite, 10 to 12 minutes; drain. Dump the spaghetti into a very large bowl and toss with the butter.

2. Put the mushrooms in a medium bowl, cover with boiling water, and soak until soft, 20 to 30 minutes. Remove the mushrooms, rinse if gritty and coarsely chop. Strain 1 cup of the mushroom soaking liquid through several layers of damp cheesecloth and reserve for the Parmesan Cheese Sauce.

3. Remove the sausage from its casings and crumble into a large skillet. Fry, stirring to break up any large lumps, until lightly browned, about 10 minutes. With a slotted spoon, transfer the sausage to the bowl with the spaghetti.

4. Pour off all but 2 tablespoons of fat from the skillet. Add the onions and cook until softened and translucent, about 5 minutes. Add to the spaghetti. Add the olives, eggs, chopped mushrooms, parsley, roasted peppers, salt and black pepper. Toss to mix well.

5. Turn half the spaghetti mixture into a very large buttered and floured shallow baking dish. (I use a 15-inch paella pan; you can use 2 baking dishes or springform pans if you don't have one large enough to hold the entire torta.) Sprinkle with the mozzarella cheese to cover evenly and top with the remaining spaghetti mixture. (The recipe can be prepared to this point up to a day ahead. Refrigerate, covered; add 5 to 10 minutes to the baking time if placed in the oven cold.)

6. Cover with foil and bake the torta for 45 to 50 minutes, or until heated through. Serve with Parmesan Cheese Sauce.

Note: You can use roasted red peppers from the jar, but fresh tastes better. To roast bell peppers, cook directly over a gas flame or as close as possible to a hot broiler, turning, until charred all over, about 10 minutes. Transfer to a bag and let steam for 10 minutes. Rub off the peel, rinsing under running water if necessary. Cut out the stem and remove the seeds and ribs.

Parmesan Cheese Sauce

MAKES ABOUT 2½ CUPS

¼ pound (1 stick) plus 4 tablespoons unsalted butter
¾ cup all-purpose flour
4 cups milk
1 cup mushroom soaking liquid (reserved from Step 2 of Spaghetti Torta, above) or 1 more cup of milk
½ cup dry white wine
½ pound Parmesan cheese, freshly grated
¾ teaspoon salt
Several dashes of cayenne pepper, to taste

1. In a heavy, medium saucepan, melt the butter over moderate heat. Add the flour and cook, stirring, for 3 to 5 minutes, without allowing the mixture to color.

2. Whisk in the milk, mushroom liquid and wine. Bring to a boil, whisking until thick and smooth. Reduce the heat and simmer, stirring frequently, for 10 minutes. Stir in the cheese and cook until melted. Season with the salt and cayenne pepper. (The sauce can be made ahead. Dot with butter, cover and refrigerate. Reheat, whisking until smooth. If the sauce is too thick, thin with milk.)

COBB SALAD

40 TO 50 SERVINGS

All the individual ingredients in this California salad are chopped or diced, which makes it easy to eat buffet-style. A food processor saves a lot of effort here.

>	4 pounds skinless, boneless chicken breasts
>	2 heads of iceberg lettuce
>	4 ripe avocados
>	2 large bunches of watercress, tough stems removed, coarsely chopped (about 4 cups)
>	6 hard-cooked eggs, chopped
>	2 bunches of radishes, finely diced (about 1 cup)
>	1½ pounds tomatoes, finely diced
>	2 medium red onions, finely diced
>	½ pound mushrooms, thinly sliced
>	8 ounces Maytag blue or Roquefort cheese, crumbled
>	¾ pound bacon, cooked and crumbled
>	5 tablespoons fresh lemon juice
>	3 tablespoons red wine vinegar
>	¾ teaspoon anchovy paste
>	½ teaspoon powdered mustard
>	½ teaspoon salt
>	½ teaspoon sugar
>	1⅓ cups extra-virgin olive oil

1. Put the chicken in a large saucepan or flame-proof casserole. Add enough water to cover by at least 1 inch. Bring to a simmer over moderate heat and cook until the chicken is opaque throughout with no trace of pink in the center, but still juicy, 15 to 20 minutes. Remove and let cool; then cut into ½-inch cubes. (The chicken can be cooked a day ahead and refrigerated, covered.)

2. Cut out the core of each head of lettuce. Cut the lettuce lengthwise in half. Either shred with a knife or do it the easy way, as I do: Cut each half into 1- to ½-inch wedges and shred in a food processor using the slicing disk. If not serving within the hour, store in the refrigerator in a plastic bag.

3. Peel and pit the avocados. Cut into ½-inch dice. Toss with 2 tablespoons of the lemon juice.

4. To assemble the salad, arrange a bed of the lettuce on each of two large serving platters. Then arrange rows of the other salad ingredients on top— the avocados, watercress, eggs, radishes, tomatoes, red onion, mushrooms, blue cheese and bacon, alternating contrasting colors decoratively. Put the remaining lettuce and the chicken in a large salad bowl.

5. In a jar with a tight-fitting lid, combine the remaining lemon juice, vinegar, anchovy paste, powdered mustard, salt, sugar, olive oil and ⅓ cup of water. Cover and shake vigorously to blend well.

6. Shortly before serving, drizzle a little of the dressing over the Cobb salad and toss the chicken and lettuce with some dressing to coat. Serve the remainder in a small pitcher on the side. (Encourage guests to help themselves to some of the chicken salad from the bowl along with all the goodies on the platter.)

DESSERT AND CHAMPAGNE PARTY
for 36 (clockwise from bottom left):
Cranberry-Raspberry Mousse; Easy
Cream Cheesecake; Chocolate Party
Cake; Butter Pecan Turtle Squares;
Fresh Lemon Roulade.

WEDDING SUPPER for 50 (from left): Gingered Side of Salmon; Fresh Strawberries; Green Bean Salad with Roasted Red Peppers; Fresh Pears and Grapes; Cold Fillet of Beef with Sherry Wine Vinaigrette; Parslied Potato Salad; tomatoes, onions and arugula; Stilton cheese.

COCKTAIL AND HORS D'OEUVRES
PARTY for 15 to 50 (left to right):
Niçoise Swordfish Salad in Endive
Cups; Mushroom-Leek Turnovers;
Coriander Chicken Rolls.

MEAT LOAF FROM THE WALDORF

16 TO 20 SINGLE SERVINGS, 32 TO 48 AS PART OF A BUFFET

Chef John Dougherty made this meat loaf for his visiting aunts because he knew it was the kind of honest home-style food they enjoyed. It turned out so well that he decided to put it on the menu at Oscar's of the Waldorf-Astoria. I like it cold even more than hot, especially in a sandwich with spicy Dijon mustard.

7 slices of firm-textured white bread
¾ cup milk
¾ cup tomato puree
2 medium onions, chopped
1 small red bell pepper, finely diced
1 small green bell pepper, finely diced
2 large garlic cloves, minced
2½ tablespoons vegetable oil
2 pounds lean ground beef
1½ pounds lean ground pork
1½ pounds ground veal
1 cup ketchup
¼ cup Dijon mustard
2 tablespoons Worcestershire sauce
6 dashes of hot pepper sauce
3 eggs
¼ cup chopped fresh basil, or 1 tablespoon dried
1 teaspoon salt
1 teaspoon freshly ground black pepper
½ pound sliced bacon

1. Trim the crusts from the bread and cut the slices into ½-inch dice. Put in a large bowl and add the milk and tomato puree. Let soften while you prepare the vegetables.

2. In a large heavy skillet, heat the oil. Add the onions and sauté over moderately low heat until softened, about 3 minutes. Add the bell peppers and garlic, increase the heat to moderately high and sauté until the peppers are softened but still bright colored and the onions are golden, 3 to 5 minutes longer.

3. Mash the softened bread in the bowl. Add the sautéed vegetables, the beef, pork, veal, ketchup, mustard, Worcestershire sauce, hot sauce, eggs, basil, salt and pepper. Roll up your sleeves and mix very well with your hands. (The recipe can be prepared to this point up to a day ahead. Cover the meat loaf mixture and refrigerate.)

4. Preheat the oven to 375° F. Form the meat mixture into a freeform loaf shape on a large greased baking sheet (with edges to catch the drips). Arrange the bacon slices crosswise over the meat loaf, tucking in the edges underneath. Bake for 70 minutes, or until the internal temperature measures 180° F. Remove from the oven and pour off the fat from the baking sheet. Let stand for at least 10 minutes before slicing. (If you wish to transfer the meat loaf to a platter before slicing, use 2 large wide spatulas.)

TRIPLE-MUSTARD POTATO SALAD

40 TO 50 SERVINGS AS PART OF A BUFFET

There are a million recipes for potato salad, and this one makes it a million and one. My husband's prejudiced, of course, but he thinks it's the best he's ever eaten. Toasted mustard seeds impart a lovely nutty flavor and surprising crunch. If you prefer, you can skip them and call it Double-Mustard Potato Salad. Needless to say, the better the mustard you use, the better this salad will be.

8 pounds red potatoes
2²/3 cups mayonnaise
1/3 cup grainy mustard, such as Pommery
1/3 cup sharp Dijon mustard, preferably imported
1/3 cup fresh lemon juice
1/3 cup mustard seeds
1/3 cup olive oil
Salt and freshly ground pepper to taste

1. Put the potatoes in a large pot of cold salted water to cover. Bring to a boil and cook for 20 to 25 minutes, or until tender; the potato will slip off a knife inserted into the center when it's done. Drain and let stand until cool enough to handle. Peel the potatoes and cut them into 1-inch chunks.

2. In a small bowl, combine the mayonnaise, grainy mustard, Dijon mustard and lemon juice; mix well.

3. In a large serving bowl, combine the potatoes and mustard dressing. Toss to coat.

4. Combine the mustard seeds and olive oil in a medium covered skillet. Cook over moderate heat with the lid on, shaking the pan, until the seeds start to pop in 1 to 2 minutes (you'll hear them). Immediately remove from the heat and keep shaking the pan with the lid on until they stop popping. Scrape the seeds and oil over the potato salad and fold gently to mix them in. Season with salt and pepper to taste. (The potato salad can be made up to 2 days in advance. Cover and refrigerate.)

DILLED PASTA SALAD WITH SCALLOPS AND SMOKED SALMON

24 SINGLE SERVINGS, 36 TO 48 AS PART OF A BUFFET

Everything for this salad can be prepared ahead and refrigerated overnight, but the pasta, seafood and sauce should be tossed together shortly before serving to preserve the creamy consistency.

1¹/3 pounds bay scallops or quartered sea scallops
2 pounds fusilli or shells
2 tablespoons olive oil
2 cups sour cream
1/3 cup Dijon mustard
2¹/2 tablespoons sugar
2/3 cup fresh lemon juice
1¹/4 cups chopped fresh dill (do not substitute dried)
1 cup minced scallion green
1 pound smoked salmon, preferably Norwegian, cut into thin slivers about 1¹/2 inches long

1. Dump the scallops into a large saucepan of boiling salted water and cook for exactly 1¹/2 minutes, or until the scallops are almost opaque throughout; do not overcook or the scallops will be dry. Drain and let cool, then cover and refrigerate until you are ready to toss the salad.

2. In a large stockpot of boiling salted water, cook the fusilli until just tender, 10 to 12 minutes. Drain and rinse under cold running water; drain well. In a large bowl, toss the pasta with the oil. Cover and refrigerate for up to a day.

3. In a small bowl, blend together the sour cream and mustard. Stir in the sugar and lemon juice until well blended. Stir in the dill and scallions. Cover and set aside for up to 1 hour, or refrigerate for up to 24 hours before serving.

4. To assemble the salad, add the sauce to the pasta and toss to coat. Add the scallops and smoked salmon and toss to distribute the seafood throughout. Serve slightly chilled or at room temperature.

LYDIE MARSHALL'S RATATOUILLE WITH GOAT CHEESE

40 TO 50 SERVINGS

Lydie Marshall is a celebrated New York cooking teacher and author of *Cooking with Lydie Marshall.* Her food is even tastier than expected, as you'll find when you try this ratatouille made with sweet red and yellow peppers and goat cheese.

4 pounds eggplant, unpeeled, cut into ½-inch dice
3 tablespoons coarse (kosher) salt
About ⅔ cup extra-virgin olive oil
6 medium onions, sliced
3 pounds red bell peppers, cut into ½-inch squares
3 pounds yellow bell peppers, cut into ½-inch squares
8 medium tomatoes, peeled, seeded and cut into ½-inch dice
4 medium zucchini, cut into ½-inch dice
6 garlic cloves, minced
¼ cup minced fresh tarragon or basil
½ teaspoon freshly ground black pepper
¼ teaspoon cayenne pepper
⅔ pound Bucheron or other soft goat cheese

1. Put the eggplant in a colander and sprinkle with 2 tablespoons salt; toss. Let drain for 30 minutes. Rinse the eggplant under cold running water, drain and pat dry.

2. Heat ⅔ cup oil in a very large (preferably 9-quart) nonaluminum flameproof cassserole. Add the onions and sauté over moderate heat until just beginning to color, 5 to 10 minutes.

3. Add the red and yellow peppers and cook, stirring frequently, until they are slightly softened, 5 to 10 minutes.

4. Add the eggplant and sauté, tossing and adding additional oil if the eggplant begins to stick, until it is translucent on the outside, about 15 minutes.

5. Finally, add the tomatoes, zucchini, garlic and tarragon. Season with the remaining 1 tablespoon salt, the black pepper and the cayenne. Cover and cook for 40 minutes, stirring frequently to prevent sticking.

6. Uncover the pan and cook until the liquid is reduced to a syrupy consistency, about 15 minutes. Remove the pan from the heat. (The recipe can be prepared ahead to this point. Refrigerate, covered. Reheat before proceeding.)

7. Crumble half the goat cheese into the vegetables and stir to mix. Crumble the remaining cheese over the top of the ratatouille, cover the pan and let stand for 5 minutes to let the cheese melt.

NONALCOHOLIC PARTY PUNCH

MAKES ABOUT 3 GALLONS

So many different flavors blend together in this delightful tropical mix that the resulting drink is sophisticated and refreshing, and the lack of alcohol is not apparent.

2 bottles (1½ quarts each) Mauna L'ai guava/
*   passion-fruit drink*
2 bottles (1½ quarts each) Cranberry Juice
*   Cocktail*
2 quarts grapefruit juice, preferably from the
*   refrigerated section of the supermarket*
3 bottles (1 liter each) ginger ale
2 trays of ice cubes plus a big bag of cubes for
*   individual drinks*
4 or 5 limes, halved lengthwise and cut into thin
*   slices*

1. In a large punch bowl or in several large pitchers, blend together the Mauna L'ai, cranberry juice, grapefruit juice and ginger ale. Add the 2 trays of ice cubes and the lime slices. Put the remaining ice in an ice bucket.

2. To serve, put 2 or 3 ice cubes in an old fashioned glass or punch cup and ladle on the punch, making sure everyone gets a slice of lime.

PARTY PUNCH WITH A WALLOP: Make the punch as above, but omit the ginger ale. Instead add 1 bottle (750 ml) vodka and 1 bottle (750 ml) golden rum, such as Mount Gay or Bacardi Gold Reserve. Serve smaller portions.

HELP

I wrote this book to guide you through a big party or dinner for a large crowd without any additional help. However, there's no question your job will be easier if you have an extra pair of hands. Straightening the kitchen in between courses makes a large sit-down dinner much more manageable. Getting rid of dirty dishes and glasses at a buffet or open house keeps the room attractive and the party fresh. And there are special occasions, such as a wedding or graduation in the home, when you really want to be a guest at your own party. Remember that help doesn't always wear a uniform. If you have a child or close relative of appropriate age, try recruiting him or her for a favor or nominal fee. Teenagers and older people are often happy to work for a reasonable hourly rate. Some high schools and colleges have programs that train young people for exactly this kind of work—serving and cleaning up, though, of course, not bartending. Someone—friend or spouse—should be assigned to tend bar, whether that means mixing drinks or just making sure bottles are opened, there's enough ice and the punch bowl is full.

If you decide to hire help for a special occasion, be sure to check references. Unless you know of someone through a personal recommendation, go through an agency that specializes in household personnel. Be sure the duties of any outside help are clearly defined beforehand and check if fees include a tip or not. They usually don't, and a cash tip at your discretion is expected; 15 percent is the norm. Don't be shy about setting up your own rules—such as no smoking—to anyone who works for you for the evening. And make it clear to anyone hired to serve that he or she will be expected to double—taking coats, bussing dirty ashtrays and dishes and helping to clean up in the kitchen, as well as passing food. Try to allow time for a dry run, or at least a few moments to show them where everything is. If you're having a stranger into your kitchen, it's best to have all serving pieces out and marked with what they're to be used for.

A professional caterer will tell you that you need one server for every ten guests at a buffet, or three waiters for every twenty guests at a sit-down dinner, plus kitchen help and a bartender. Since most of us cannot afford that kind of help, I'd say that at a big open house or buffet, a bartender is nice to have, but one person to clean up in the kitchen, keep the room in order and help serve can make all the difference in the world.

Wedding Supper

FOR 50

Smoked Salmon Rillettes

Niçoise Swordfish Salad in Endive Cups

Crudités with Provençal Basil Dip

Rich Liver Mousse with Toasted Hazelnuts
(page 65)

Mushroom-Leek Turnovers

∎

Cold Fillet of Beef with Sherry Wine
Vinaigrette

Parslied Potato Salad

Green Bean Salad with Roasted Red
Peppers

Karen Lee's Gingered Side of Salmon (page
112)

∎

Stilton and Brie

Baskets of Pears, Grapes and Strawberries

∎

Wedding Cake

This is not just a hypothetical party; it is the menu I created for my own wedding, several years ago. We decided to get married at home—it was a second marriage for both of us and we wanted the affair to be small, intimate and very special. To make life easy, I hired an excellent caterer to supply all the hors d'oeuvres as well as the plates, silverware, glasses, napkins, trays, coffee urns, etc., and the waiters and bartender. All these things can be rented separately, but having the caterer act as general contractor made life very easy.

Since the caterer has many hands, there were six or seven canapés as well as crudités with two dips. I prepared the main-course Fillet of Beef, the Parslied Potato Salad and Green Bean Salad with Roasted Red Peppers the day before; the caterers arranged it on platters for me. A neighborhood baker duplicated one of Rose Levy Beranbaum's chocolate wedding cakes and decorated it like dotted Swiss to match my dress.

If you want to stage your own wedding, I cannot recommend this strategy highly enough. The caterers thought of all sorts of tiny details that might not have occurred to me; for example, tea and brewed decaf as well as low-calorie sweetener next to the regular coffee urn, lots of extra champagne glasses, tiny blush rosebuds for the top of the cake. Everyone had a wonderful time, and I felt like a pampered guest in my own home. The day turned out exactly as I had hoped it would—perfect. If you do want to produce the entire event yourself, you can do it with enough time, planning and advance preparation.

Do-Ahead Planning

Up to 2 months before the wedding: Make a double recipe of the Mushroom-Leek Turnovers and freeze them unbaked.

3 days before the wedding: Make a double recipe of the Rich Liver Mousse with Toasted Hazelnuts. Roast the peppers for the green bean salad, doubling the amount. Buy a wheel of ripe brie and an impressive wedge of Stilton cheese.

2 days in advance: Make the Smoked Salmon Rillettes and the Provençal Basil Dip.

The day before the wedding: Prepare the vegetables for the crudités and refrigerate them in plastic bags. Make the swordfish salad and prepare the endive. Roast the fillets, let cool and refrigerate, well wrapped. Make the Parslied Potato Salad. Blanch 8 pounds of green beans and make the Sherry Wine Vinaigrette with Shallots and Capers. Wash the fruit.

The day of the wedding: Don't underestimate how nervous you will be, no matter how much you're in love. Do everything as far ahead as possible, and get as much help from family and friends as you're willing to accept.

Up to 3 hours in advance: Assemble the Niçoise Swordfish Salad in Endive Cups. Slice the beef and arrange the platters. Cover with plastic wrap. Complete a double recipe of the Green Bean Salad with Roasted Red Peppers. Remove the cheese from the refrigerator. Marinate two salmons for Karen Lee's Gingered Side of Salmon.

Up to 2 hours in advance: Grill or broil the salmon.

Slice the bread early in the day and set aside in plastic bags, so the slices can be thrown into baskets when it's time. All the dips and spreads should be in serving dishes ready to be put out. The turnovers are popped frozen into the oven just before serving. If possible, set out the wedding cake a good hour or two before the ceremony.

SMOKED SALMON RILLETTES
MAKES ABOUT 4 CUPS

A rich hors d'oeuvre spread like this, served with toasted croutons of French bread, can be put to good use on any number of occasions. For a smaller group, this recipe can be cut in half easily.

> 1 pound smoked salmon, such as Norwegian or Scottish
> ⅓ cup finely diced red onion
> 3 tablespoons vodka
> 1½ tablespoons fresh lemon juice
> ¼ teaspoon freshly ground black pepper
> 3 or 4 dashes of cayenne pepper, to taste
> ¾ cup heavy cream
> ¼ pound (1 stick) unsalted butter, melted and cooled to tepid
> 2 tablespoons rinsed and drained tiny (nonpareil) capers

1. In a food processor, combine ¾ pound of the salmon with the red onion, vodka, lemon juice, black pepper and cayenne. Puree, scraping down the sides of the bowl once or twice, until the salmon and onion are minced.

2. With the machine on, slowly add the cream through the feed tube; scrape down the bowl. Gradually add the melted butter. Turn the mixture into a medium bowl.

3. Finely dice the remaining ¼ pound salmon. Fold the diced salmon and the capers into the puree. Pack into crocks or a serving bowl, cover and refrigerate for at least 3 hours and up to 2 days before serving.

Niçoise Swordfish Salad in Endive Cups

MAKES 5 DOZEN

This wonderful hors d'oeuvre, from caterer Rick Rodgers of New York City, combines the lush flavors of the Mediterranean in a light package that's easy to pick up. It utilizes the natural shape of Belgian endive leaves, so there are no fussy containers to prepare. Best of all, the components can be made ahead and assembled several hours before serving. For a smaller group, halve the recipe exactly.

6 to 8 heads of Belgian endive
2 pounds swordfish steak, cut 1 inch thick
1 cup plus 2 tablespoons extra-virgin olive oil
1 cup (8 ounces) Kalamata or Mediterranean
   olives, pitted and coarsely chopped
6 tablespoons chopped fresh basil
6 tablespoons fresh lemon juice
Salt and freshly ground pepper
6 ounces sun-dried tomatoes in olive oil, drained
   and cut into thin strips, about 1 ½ inches
   long and ¼ inch wide

1. Wipe the outside of the endives with a damp paper towel. Cut off about ¼ inch of the base and separate the head into leaves. Reserve 60 of the largest; discard the small inner leaves or reserve for salad. (The endive can be prepared a day ahead and stored in the refrigerator wrapped in moist paper towels inside a plastic bag.)

2. Preheat the broiler with the rack set about 3 inches from the heat. Pat the swordfish dry and brush both sides of the fish with 2 tablespoons of the olive oil. Broil the swordfish, turning once, for about 4 minutes on each side, or until just barely opaque throughout. It will feel slightly firm to the touch; do not overcook, or the fish will be dry. Let cool slightly, then remove and discard the skin and cut the fish into ⅜- to ½-inch cubes.

3. In a medium bowl, combine the swordfish, olives and basil. In a small bowl, whisk together the remaining 1 cup olive oil and the lemon juice. Pour over the swordfish salad and toss to coat. Season with salt and pepper to taste. Cover and refrigerate until ready to assemble. (The swordfish salad can be prepared up to a day ahead.)

4. To assemble the hors d'oeuvres, scoop 1 heaping teaspoon of the swordfish salad into each endive cup, letting excess dressing drain off as you spoon it up. Garnish each piece by laying a strip of sun-dried tomato diagonally across the salad. (The recipe can be completely assembled up to 4 hours before serving, covered with plastic wrap and refrigerated.) Serve slightly chilled.

Provençal Basil Dip

MAKES ABOUT 3 ½ CUPS

1 log (9 ounces) mild goat cheese, such as
   Montrachet
1 package (8 ounces) cream cheese
1 ½ cups fresh basil leaves, lightly packed
8 sun-dried tomato halves, optional
1 large garlic clove, crushed
1 cup heavy cream
⅓ to ½ cup extra-virgin olive oil
Salt and freshly ground pepper

1. In a food processor, combine the goat cheese, cream cheese, half the basil, the sun-dried tomatoes and the garlic. Puree until smooth.

2. Add the remaining basil. With the machine on, add the cream and ⅓ cup olive oil through the feed tube. If necessary, thin with a little more olive oil, 1 tablespoon at a time. Season with salt and pepper to taste. Cover and refrigerate for up to a day, but be sure to let soften before serving.

MUSHROOM-LEEK TURNOVERS

MAKES ABOUT 6 DOZEN

2 medium leeks (white and tender green), well
    rinsed, drained and chopped
3 tablespoons unsalted butter
¾ pound mushrooms, minced
¾ teaspoon dried tarragon, crumbled
¾ teaspoon salt
½ teaspoon freshly ground black pepper
3 or 4 dashes of cayenne pepper
2 tablespoons all-purpose flour
¾ cup heavy cream
1 tablespoon fresh lemon juice
1½ ounces mild goat cheese, such as Montrachet
Flaky Cream Cheese Pastry (recipe follows)
1 egg, beaten with 2 teaspoons water to make a
    glaze

1. In a large skillet or flameproof casserole, cook the leeks in the butter over moderate heat, stirring occasionally, until they are tender but not brown, 5 to 10 minutes.

2. Increase the heat to moderately high and add the mushrooms. Cook, stirring frequently, until the juices they give up evaporate and the mushroom pieces separate and begin to brown, about 10 minutes. Season with the tarragon, salt, black pepper and cayenne.

3. Sprinkle on the flour and cook, stirring, for 1 to 2 minutes. Add the cream and cook, stirring, until the filling thickens to a mass. Stir in the lemon juice and goat cheese and cook, stirring, until the cheese melts and blends evenly. (The filling can be made a day ahead. Let cool, then cover and refrigerate.)

4. Roll out half the cream cheese pastry about ⅛ inch thick. Using a 2½-inch round cutter, preferably with a crinkled edge, cut out as many circles as possible. Scoop up ½ teaspoon of the mushroom-leek filling, squeeze it into a lozenge shape and set in the middle of each circle. Fold over the dough to make a semicircle and press the edges, beginning in the middle, to seal. Crimp the edges of the pastry with the tines of a fork. Prick each turnover once or twice with the fork to allow the steam to escape. Gather together the scraps of dough and set aside. Repeat with the second half of the dough. Combine all the scraps of dough, roll out and use for more turnovers. (The recipe can be prepared to this point up to 3 months ahead. Put the turnovers on ungreased baking sheets, brush with the egg glaze and

freeze until they are hard. Then transfer to plastic bags or a covered container and freeze until you are ready to serve them.)

5. To cook, preheat the oven to 350° F. Arrange the frozen turnovers on ungreased baking sheets. Bake for 12 to 15 minutes, until golden, crisp and hot.

FLAKY CREAM CHEESE PASTRY

1½ packages (12 ounces) cream cheese, at room
    temperature
½ pound (2 sticks) unsalted butter, at room
    temperature
¾ teaspoon salt
3 cups all-purpose unbleached flour

1. In a food processor, combine the cream cheese with the butter. Process until blended and smooth. Add the salt. Gradually add the flour, processing until well blended.

2. Divide the pastry in half and form each piece into a ball; then flatten into a ½-inch-thick disk. Wrap both pieces of pastry separately in plastic bags and refrigerate for at least 30 minutes before rolling out.

COLD FILLET OF BEEF WITH SHERRY WINE VINAIGRETTE

ABOUT 50 SERVINGS

4 whole fillets of beef (about 5 pounds each),
    trimmed and tied
½ cup Cognac
½ cup minced shallots (about 6 large)
2 teaspoons salt
4 teaspoons coarsely cracked pepper, preferably
    Tellicherry (I crush mine in a mortar)
½ cup fruity extra-virgin olive oil
Sherry Wine Vinaigrette with Shallots and
    Capers (recipe follows)
6 large bunches of arugula, tough stems removed
Parslied Potato Salad (page 154)
8 large ripe tomatoes, sliced
6 medium red onions, thinly sliced

1. Trim any excess external fat from the beef and place the fillets in a large roasting pan or shallow baking dishes. Rub each fillet with about 2 tablespoons of the Cognac. Sprinkle the minced shallots over the meat. Season each fillet with ½ teaspoon of the salt and 1 teaspoon of the pepper. Rub 2 tablespoons of the olive oil all over the meat. Set aside at room temperature for 30 minutes, turning once or twice.

2. Preheat the oven to 450° F. Place a large ovenproof skillet or flameproof gratin dish over high heat. Add 2 of the fillets and cook, turning, until browned all over, about 5 minutes. Transfer to the roasting pan and repeat with the other 2 fillets.

3. Put the roasting pan in the oven and roast the fillets for 15 to 20 minutes, until the internal temperature reaches 125° to 130° F. for rare. Let stand for at least 15 minutes. (The recipe can be prepared ahead to this point.) Let stand at room temperature for several hours or wrap the meat and beans separately and refrigerate overnight. Let return to room temperature before serving.)

4. Carve the fillets into slices about ½ inch thick. Arrange the arugula around the edge of 2 large platters. Mound half the potato salad in the center of each platter. Decoratively arrange rows or circles of the beef, tomatoes and onions. Drizzle about ¼ cup of the dressing over the meat on each platter. Pass the remaining dressing separately.

SHERRY WINE VINAIGRETTE

MAKES ABOUT 4 CUPS

¾ cup sherry wine vinegar
¼ cup Dijon mustard
1½ teaspoons salt
1½ teaspoons coarsely cracked pepper
3 cups extra-virgin olive oil
¾ cup minced shallots (about 8 large)
¾ cup minced fresh parsley
⅓ cup tiny (nonpareil) capers, rinsed and drained
½ cup minced fresh tarragon, or 4 teaspoons dried

In a medium bowl, whisk together the vinegar, mustard, salt and pepper. Gradually whisk in the olive oil until well blended. Add the shallots, parsley, capers and tarragon. Mix well.

Parslied Potato Salad

ABOUT 50 SERVINGS

Because there's no mayonnaise in this light, flavorful potato salad, it can be set out at room temperature for hours.

12 pounds large waxy potatoes
1¼ cups dry white wine
8 large shallots, minced
1 cup red wine vinegar
2 tablespoons Dijon mustard
1 tablespoon plus 1 teaspoon salt
2 teaspoons freshly ground pepper
2 cups extra-virgin olive oil
1 cup chopped fresh parsley

1. Put the potatoes in a large stockpot of salted water, bring to a boil and cook until the potatoes are tender, about 25 minutes from the time the water boils; drain.

2. As soon as the potatoes are cool enough to handle, peel off the skins and slice the potatoes. Put them in a large bowl and toss with the wine while they are still warm. Add the shallots and toss to mix.

3. In a medium bowl, whisk together the vinegar, mustard, salt and pepper until blended. Gradually whisk in the olive oil.

4. Pour the vinaigrette over the potatoes and toss to coat. (The recipe can be prepared ahead to this point and set aside at room temperature for several hours or refrigerated overnight.) Toss with the parsley shortly before serving.

Green Bean Salad with Roasted Red Peppers

24 SERVINGS

4 pounds green beans, trimmed and broken in half
2 medium red onions, thinly sliced
2 large red bell peppers, roasted, peeled, seeded and cut into very thin strips about 1½ inches long
3 tablespoons sherry wine vinegar
⅔ cup extra-virgin olive oil
Salt and freshly ground pepper

1. In a large stockpot of boiling salted water, cook the beans until they are tender but still slightly resistant to the bite, 3 to 5 minutes. Drain into a colander and rinse with cold running water; drain well.

2. In a large salad bowl, combine the green beans, red onions and roasted red peppers. Drizzle on the vinegar and oil. Toss well. Season with salt and pepper to taste and toss again. Serve at room temperature.

Cocktail and Hors d'Oeuvres Party

FOR 15 TO 50

It's impossible to talk about a cocktail party in the usual ways, because it is so versatile, and the number of people invited can vary so much. That's why I've chosen the "one from column A, one from column B" approach. Given your guest list and the tone you wish to set, you can design your own menu from the choices listed below. Begin with at least five items: for example, purchased assorted cheeses and olives, a spread, a dip with crudités and one piecemeal hors d'oeuvre—hot or cold. Add another item for every five more guests up to thirty-two; then add another dish for every eight guests.

Depending on which foods you choose, you may have to double recipes. Allow one ounce of cheese, smoked salmon or cured or smoked meat per person. There should be at least two, and preferably three, of any one hors d'oeuvre and about one-quarter cup of a spread for each guest. This varies, of course, depending on the number of choices and total amount of food available. Whenever you are in doubt, remember that cheese, nuts and chips can take up the slack. An invitation to a cocktail party implies drinks and nibbles, not a filling supper.

Don't try to do too much. Only a few hot hors d'oeuvres are given in this book because without help I think it is very difficult even just to reheat and pass around a tray. There's nothing wrong with having all the food chilled or at room temperature. Set out anything you can ahead. Get platters prepared and spreads and dips put in bowls. Prepare crudités a day ahead and refrigerate them in a bowl of cold water or in plastic bags with a damp paper towel. If you have the time to cook, prepare the bulk of the food yourself. If you don't, buy plenty of cheese and cured meats, smoked salmon, olives and nuts. The few dishes you do pass around will stand out as stars.

When choosing the menu for a cocktail party, keep in mind that spicy, salty foods are pleasant with drinks, but offer a nice mix of flavors and textures. Balance creamy and spicy, smooth and crunchy, seafood, vegetables and meats. An eclectic blend of tastes is highly desirable with this kind of piecemeal sampling of foods and makes for a great party.

BUY

Nuts
Olives
Cheese
Smoked salmon
Prosciutto or speck, thinly sliced
Pepperoni
Caviar
Crudités
Tortilla chips
Crackers, Melba toast, cocktail rye and
    pumpernickel bread and/or baguettes of French
    bread

DIPS AND SPREADS

Provençal Basil Dip (page 151)
Rich Liver Mousse with Toasted Hazelnuts
    (page 65)
Smoked Salmon Rillettes (page 150)
Gingered Eggplant Spread (page 134)
Sour Cream and Two-Caviar Dip (page 133)
Chipotle Chile Mayonnaise (page 49)
Fresh Tomato Salsa (page 89)

COLD OR ROOM-TEMPERATURE CANAPÉS AND HORS D'OEUVRES

Cheese Straws (page 104)
Louisiana Shrimp (page 133)
Niçoise Swordfish Salad in Endive Cups (page 151)
Pesto Deviled Eggs (page 103)
Pepper-Pecan Cornbread (page 121)
Caviar Nachos (page 88)
Marinated Black Olives (page 63)
Gougères (page 67)
Spiced Nuts (page 88)

HOT HORS D'OEUVRES

Grilled Stuffed Grape Leaves (page 48)
Coriander Chicken Rolls (page 110)
Mushroom-Leek Turnovers (page 152)
Grilled Clams (page 50)
Barbecued Carnitas with Chipotle Chile
    Mayonnaise (page 49)

BAR

Bloody Marys
Golden Margaritas by the Batch (page 88)
Chilled white wine
Red wine
Assortment of hard liquor, if you wish: gin, vodka,
    Scotch, bourbon, rum, sweet and dry vermouth
Plenty of mixers and nonalcoholic beverages: club
    soda, cola (regular and diet), orange juice, tonic

Index

Appetizers
  barbecued carnitas, 49
  caviar nachos, 88
  grilled clams, 50
  grilled stuffed grape leaves, 48
  mushroom-leek turnovers, 152
  pesto deviled eggs, 103
  rich liver mousse with toasted
    hazelnuts, 65
  see also hors d'oeuvres
apricot(s)
  apple crisp, 31
  chocolate pecan fruit tart, 128
asparagus and mushrooms with
    sesame-orange dressing, 112
avocado
  shrimp and papaya salad with
    coconut-lime dressing, 41
  strawberry and orange salad, 67

Barbecue(d)
  brisket of beef, mesquite-smoked,
    123
  carnitas, 49
  sauce, Texas-style, 123
bean(s)
  bacon and brandy baked, 136
  black, salad with toasted cumin and
    jalapeño peppers, 52
  corn and rice salad with chile
    vinaigrette, 92
  green, salad with roasted red
    peppers, 154
  green, with lemon butter, 58
beef
  cold fillet of, with sherry wine
    vinaigrette, 153
  grilled marinated flank steak, 117
  mesquite-smoked barbecued brisket
    of, 123
  roast fillet of, 36
beverages
  golden margaritas by the batch, 88
  nonalcoholic party punch, 148
  passion fruit mimosas, 65
bread
  French walnut, 38
  pudding, strawberry-chocolate chip,
    53
  zucchini, from the Inn at Thorn Hill,
    83
  see also cornbread
brie, truffled, 113
brussels sprouts, creamed chestnuts
    and, 26

Carrot(s)
  composed salad of beets, cucumber,
    watercress and, 15
  ginger soup, curried, 96
  and jicama salad, 92
  and snow peas, glazed, 84
caviar
  nachos, 88
  two, dip, sour cream and, 133
cheese straws, 104
cherries and pineapple jubilee, 85
chestnuts, creamed brussels sprouts
    and, 26

chicken
  cheese tortilla casserole, 90
  coriander rolls, 110
  couscous with lamb, sweet potatoes
    and, 61
  cutlets, mustard-pecan, 45
  grilled pepper-lime, 50
  mesquite-grilled sausages and, 41
  oven-baked deviled, 31
  pasta salad with lemon-sesame
    dressing, 116–117
  smoked, torte, 111
condiments
  chipotle chile mayonnaise, 49
  cranberry chutney, 27
  fresh tomato salsa, 89
  herbed lemon-walnut mayonnaise, 36
corn
  grilled, San Miguel style, 51
  rice and bean salad with chile
    vinaigrette, 92
cornbread
  pecan stuffing, 96
  pepper-pecan, 121
  sage, 81
couscous, 62
  with lamb, chicken and sweet
    potatoes, 60
cranberry
  chutney, 27
  raspberry mousse, 127

Desserts
  almond custard torte with peaches
    and raspberriers, 39
  apricot-apple crisp, 31
  bittersweet chocolate truffle torte,
    101
  bourbon-peach trifle, 114
  brownie sundaes, 107
  butter pecan turtle squares, 131
  chocolate cream frosting, 129
  chocolate pecan fruit tart, 128
  cranberry-raspberry mousse, 127
  easy cream cheesecake, 100
  fresh lemon cream, 130
  fresh lemon roulade, 130
  fresh strawberry sundaes with
    strawberry sauce, 107
  hazelnut dacquoise with chocolate
    cream, 16
  hazelnut roulade with banana cream
    and hot fudge sauce, 59
  honey-pecan cake, 119
  hot fudge sauce, 46
  individual meringue shells, 28
  lemon mousse meringues with
    raspberry sauce, 27
  marbled sour cream coffee cake, 77
  Margaret Hess's best fudge brownies,
    107
  pastry cream, 39
  pecan pastry, 128
  pineapple and cherries jubilee, 85
  profiteroles, 46
  raspberry sauce, 28
  Rose Levy Beranbaum's chocolate
    party cake, 129

strawberry-chocolate chip bread
  pudding, 53
strawberry corn shortcakes, 125
thumbprints, 84
toasted coconut flan, 93

Egg(s)
  baked with mushrooms and browned
    onions, 66
  pesto deviled, 103
  and potato salad with roasted red
    peppers, 124
eggplant
  Lydie Marshall's ratatouille with goat
    cheese, 147
  spread, gingered, 134

Fennel
  braised, au gratin, 100
  romaine and radicchio salad, 113
fish
  dilled pasta salad with scallops and
    smoked salmon, 146
  Karen Lee's gingered side of salmon,
    112
  Mediterranean seafood casserole, 14
  seafood medallions, 35
  smoked salmon rillettes, 150
  swordfish, Niçoise salad in endive
    cups, 151
  see also shellfish

Goose, 25
  roast stuffed, with port sauce, 24
gougères, 67
grape leaves, grilled stuffed, 48
green bean(s)
  with lemon butter, 58
  salad with roasted red peppers, 154

Ham, 135
  braised in port, 82
hors d'oeuvres
  cheese straws, 104
  coriander chicken rolls, 110
  gingered eggplant spread, 134
  Louisiana shrimp, 133
  Niçoise swordfish salad in endive
    cups, 151
  Provençal basil dip, 151
  smoked salmon rillettes, 150
  sour cream and two-caviar dip, 133
  spiced nuts, 88
  see also appetizers

Jicama and carrot salad, 92

Lamb
  barbacoa of, 89
  couscous with chicken, sweet
    potatoes and, 61
lasagna
  noodles, homemade, 12
  three-mushroom, with Gorgonzola
    sauce, 13
leek
  mushroom turnovers, 152
  and potato soup with port and
    Gorgonzola, 44

lemon
  cream, fresh, 130
  mousse meringues with raspberry
    sauce, 27
  roulade, fresh, 130

Main courses
  baked eggs with mushrooms and
    browned onions, 66
  barbacoa of lamb, 89
  chicken cheese tortilla casserole, 90
  cold fillet of beef with sherry wine
    vinaigrette, 153
  couscous with lamb, chicken and
    sweet potatoes, 61
  dilled pasta salad with scallops and
    smoked salmon, 146
  grilled marinated flank steak, 117
  grilled pepper-lime chicken, 50
  ham braised in port, 82
  herbed roast pork loin, 56
  Karen Lee's gingered side of salmon,
    112
  Lydie Marshall's ratatouille with goat
    cheese, 147
  meat loaf from the Waldorf, 145
  Mediterranean seafood casserole, 14
  mesquite-grilled chicken and
    sausages, 41
  mesquite-smoked barbecued brisket
    of beef, 123
  mustard-pecan chicken cutlets, 45
  oven-baked deviled chicken, 31
  roast fillet of beef, 36
  roast stuffed goose with port sauce,
    24
  roast turkey with pecan-cornbread
    stuffing, 97
  Roquefort Caesar salad, 55
  shrimp boil, 105
  smoked chicken torte, 111
  spaghetti torta with parmesan cheese
    sauce, 139
  three-mushroom lasagna with
    Gorgonzola sauce, 13
mayonnaise
  chipotle chile, 49
  herbed lemon-walnut, 36
meat
  loaf from the Waldorf, 145
  see also specific meat
mushroom(s)
  and asparagus with sesame-orange
    dressing, 112
  baked eggs with browned onions
    and, 66
  leek turnovers, 152
  potato salad with sweet sausages and,
    118
  three, lasagna, with Gorgonzola
    sauce, 13

Nonalcoholic party punch, 148
noodles, homemade lasagna, 12
nuts, spiced, 88

Olives, marinated black, 63

onion(s)
  browned, baked eggs with
    mushrooms and, 66
  grilled sweet, salad, 52
orange
  avocado and strawberry salad, 67
  radish salad, 63

Pastry
  cream, 39
  flaky cream cheese, 152
  gougères, 67
  pecan, 128
peach(es)
  almond custard torte with
    raspberries and, 39
  bourbon trifle, 114
peas
  puree of watercress and, 37
  snow, glazed carrots and, 84
pecan
  butter, turtle squares, 131
  chocolate fruit tart, 128
  cornbread stuffing, 96
  honey cake, 119
  mustard chicken cutlets, 45
  pastry, 128
  pepper cornbread, 121
pepper(s)
  jalapeño, black bean salad with
    toasted cumin and, 52
  pecan cornbread, 121
  roasted red, egg and potato salad
    with, 124
  roasted red, green bean salad with,
    154
pesto deviled eggs, 103
pineapple and cherries jubilee, 85
pork
  barbecued carnitas, 49
  loin, herbed roast, 56
  and prune dressing, 24–25
potato(es)
  creamed, with garlic and thyme, 37
  and egg salad with roasted red
    peppers, 124
  au gratin, 83
  and leek soup with port and
    Gorgonzola, 44
  oven-roasted garlic, 57
  and rutabaga puree, 26
  salad, parslied, 154
  salad, triple-mustard, 146
  salad with sweet sausages and
    mushrooms, 118

Quail, grilled marinated, 68

Radish-orange salad, 63
raspberry(ies)
  almond custard torte with peaches
    and, 39
  cranberry mousse, 127
  sauce, 28
  sauce, lemon mousse meringues
    with, 27
ratatouille with goat cheese, Lydie
    Marshall's, 147

rice
  corn and bean salad with chile
    vinaigrette, 92
  Ruth's Spanish, 42
  salad, Giovanna's shocking pink, 119
  wild, risotto, 99
  wild, salad, Ila's, 113
rutabaga and potato puree, 26

Salad
  avocado, strawberry and orange, 67
  black bean, with toasted cumin and
    jalapeño peppers, 52
  carrot and jicama, 92
  chicken pasta, with lemon-sesame
    dressing, 116–117
  Cobb, 140
  composed, of carrots, beets,
    cucumber and watercress, 15
  corn, rice and bean, with chile
    vinaigrette, 92
  Creole coleslaw, 124
  dilled pasta, with scallops and
    smoked salmon, 146
  egg and potato, with roasted red
    peppers, 124
  Grandma Grandbouche's curly
    endive, 30
  green bean, with roasted red
    peppers, 154
  grilled sweet onion, 52
  Ila's wild rice, 113
  lentil, with goat cheese and sun-dried
    tomatoes, 118
  minted yogurt, 42
  Niçoise swordfish, in endive cups,
    151
  orange-radish, 63

parslied potato, 154
potato, with sweet sausages and
  mushrooms, 118
red and green coleslaw with blue
  cheese dressing, 135
rice, Giovanna's shocking pink, 119
romaine, radicchio and fennel, 113
Roquefort Caesar, 55
triple-mustard potato, 146
24-hour, 106
sauce
  Creole butter dipping, 105
  hot fudge, 46
  mustard, 56
  Parmesan cheese, 139
  raspberry, 28
  Texas-style BBQ, 123
  see also condiments
sausages
  mesquite-grilled chicken and, 41
  potato salad with mushrooms and,
    118
shellfish
  clam pie with sage-corn crust, 80
  dilled pasta salad with scallops and
    smoked salmon, 146
  grilled clams, 50
  Louisiana shrimp, 113
  Mediterranean seafood casserole, 14
  oysters with ginger beurre blanc, 23
  seafood medallions, 35
  shrimp, avocado and papaya salad
    with coconut-lime dressing, 41
  shrimp boil, 105
soup
  curried carrot-ginger, 96
  leek and potato, with port and
    Gorgonzola, 44

maple-butternut bisque, 81
turkey stock, 98
spaghetti torta with Parmesan cheese
  sauce, 139
spice blend, basic, 122
spiced nuts, 88
spinach, microwave emerald, 45
strawberry(ies)
  avocado and orange salad, 67
  chocolate chip bread pudding, 53
  chocolate pecan fruit tart, 128
  corn shortcakes, 125
  sundaes, fresh, with strawberry
    sauce, 107
sweet potatoes
  couscous with lamb, chicken and, 61
  gratin of, flambéed with bourbon, 99

Tomato(es)
  salsa, fresh, 89
  sun-dried, lentil salad with goat
    cheese and, 118
truffled brie, 113
turkey
  giblet pan gravy, 98
  roast, with pecan-cornbread stuffing,
    97
  stock, 98
turnips, pickled, 63

Vegetables, oven-roasting, 57
vinaigrette
  chile, corn, rice and bean salad with,
    92
  sherry wine, 153

Zucchini bread from the Inn at Thorn
  Hill, 83

CREDITS

An Elegant Dinner with Fine Wines (page 18): Antique French buffet, Pierre Deux, 369 Bleecker St., N.Y.; St. Remy and Brummel wineglasses, Baccarat, 55 E. 57 St., N.Y.; flowers, Very Special Flowers, 215 W. 10 St., N.Y.

Backyard Barbecue (page 20): hand-thrown ceramic plates, Claudia Reiss for Sweet Nellie, 1062 Madison Ave., N.Y.; Grill by Weber; hand-blown glasses, Simon Pearce, 385 Bleecker St., N.Y.

Noonday Brunch (page 69): Faience dinnerware, tablecloth and napkins, Pierre Deux, 870 Madison Ave., N.Y.; flowers, Very Special Flowers; "Mermaid" flatware, Georg Jensen from Royal Copenhagen, 683 Madison Ave., N.Y.

Christmas Dinner (pages 70–71): "Hawthorne" porcelain dinnerware, Cerelene at Baccarat; flowers, Very Special Flowers; "Mermaid" flatware and "Acorn" carving set, Georg Jensen from Royal Copenhagen.

Southwestern Buffet (pages 72–73): hand-thrown terra-cotta dinnerware, Barbara Eigen for Lee Bailey at Saks Fifth Avenue; hand-blown glasses, Simon Pearce; flowers, Very Special Flowers.

Easy Southern Shrimp Boil (pages 74–75): Hand-blown crystal glasses and carafe, Simon Pearce; flowers, Very Special Flowers; tablecloth, Trouvaise Francais, 552 W. 87 St., N.Y.; "Mermaid" flatware, Georg Jensen from Royal Copenhagen.

Dessert and Champagne Party (page 141): flowers, Very Special Flowers; sterling silver coffee service, Georg Jensen from Royal Copenhagen; crystal bowl, Baccarat.

Wedding Supper (pages 142–143): "Paris" champagne flutes and champagne bucket, Baccarat; "Marly" flatware from Christofle; "Dans du Printemps" Limoges porcelain, Cerelene at Baccarat; flowers, Very Special Flowers; pedestal, fruit dish and strawberry basket, Classical Creamware.

Cocktail and Hors d'Oeuvres Party (page 144): martini glasses, Royal Copenhagen; tray and napkin, Frank McIntosh at Henri Bendel, 10 W. 57 St., N.Y.